Pulp Surrealism

Pulp Surrealism

INSOLENT POPULAR CULTURE IN
EARLY TWENTIETH-CENTURY PARIS

ROBIN WALZ

UNIVERSITY OF CALIFORNIA PRESS
Berkeley   Los Angeles   London

University of California Press
Berkeley and Los Angeles, California

University of California Press, Ltd.
London, England

© 2000 by the Regents of the University of California

Library of Congress Cataloging-in-Publication Data

Walz, Robin, 1957–.
    Pulp surrealism : insolent popular culture in early twentieth-
century Paris / Robin Walz.
        p.   cm.
    Includes bibliographical references and index.
    ISBN 0-520-21619-9 (alk. paper).
    1. Paris (France)—Intellectual life—20th century.   2. Popular
culture—France—Paris—History—20th century.   3. Surrealism
(Literature).   4. French literature—20th century—History and
criticism.   5. Social change.   I. Title.
DC715.W26   2000
306'.0944'361904—dc21   99-34874

Manufactured in the United States of America

This book is a print-on-demand volume. It is
manufactured using toner in place of ink. Type and
images may be less sharp than the same material seen in
traditionally printed University of California Press editions.

The paper used in this publication meets the minimum requirements
of ANSI/NISO Z39.48-1992 (R 1997) (*Permanence of Paper*).

For Carol Prentice

Contents

Illustrations and Tables

Acknowledgments

While writing this book has involved much individual labor, many people have helped me along the way. This project began as a doctoral dissertation directed by Ted Margadant, Susanna Barrows, and Cathy Kudlick, and I thank them for planting the seed of an idea that this should be a book rather than just a project to satisfy a degree requirement. Research support for came from a University of California Regents' Fellowship and a University of California at Davis Humanities Grant. I received much support and useful criticism from members of the Berkeley French History salon, especially Marjorie Beale, Vanessa Schwartz, and Tyler Stovall. Among many colleagues at the University of California at Davis, Karen Halttunen, Liz Constable, Mike Saler, Anne Scott, and the "Dissertations Anonymous" cohort read and critiqued the early manuscript. Presenting portions of various chapters at meetings of the Western Society for French History, the Society for French Historical Studies, and the American Historical Association, the Feuillade Centennial Conference at the University of Wisconsin at Madison, and the Cross-Cultural Women's History Program at the University of California at Davis, assisted me in thinking through the interdisciplinary aspects of this book and gave me confidence that it could be pitched to a wide readership. Numerous individuals from these forums gave me useful criticism and encouragement, including Richard Abel, Don Crafton, Tom Gunning, Vicki Callahan, Rudolf Kuenzli, Tip Ragan, Rachel Fuchs, Vinni Datta, Paul Mazgaj, Bud Burkhardt, Rosemary Wakeman, and Michael Wilson. Dominique Kalifa has enthusiastically embraced my work from the French side of the Atlantic and persuaded me to join *La Société des Amis de Fantômas* and *L'Association des Amis du Roman Populaire*. Sheila Levine, Dore Brown, Juliane Brand, and Hillary Hansen from the University of California Press have been wonderfully supportive and patient through the various stages of the book production process, Charles Dibble was a superb copyeditor, and the press readers of earlier drafts of this manuscript have made it clear to me that I am a cultural historian rather than a literary theorist.

Then there are those sources of individual support and inspiration. From the beginning, Elliott Smith, my best friend and coeditor of the Fantômas Web site, thought this book better than a lot of the stuff he culls from the shelves at Moe's Books. My pal Deb Akers thinks so, too. I thank Peter Blomquist for instilling in me a love for all things French. But foremost and above all, Carol Prentice has loved and supported me throughout my life transition from dreamer to scholar. Together with our children, Heather and Shane, my family has kept me whole. To one and all, a heartfelt thank you.

Introduction

In February 1924, surrealist Louis Aragon read the following in the daily Parisian newspaper *L'Intransigeant:* "Anniversary of the fall of the pick-axe. Boulevard Haussmann has reached rue Laffitte."[1] The "huge rodent" of the boulevard's expansion, as Aragon later described it in *Le Paysan de Paris,* was about to devour the "pâté of shops" in one of his favorite urban hideaways, the double-galleried Passages de l'Opéra. For more than half a century, the modest shopping, business, and residential arcade had been fortuitously spared Baron Georges Haussmann's design for the completion of his namesake boulevard. In the years immediately following the Great War, the marginal establishments of the passageway had delighted members of the Paris dadaist and surrealist movements, who enjoyed a Dada cocktail at the Certa café, the outmoded melodramatic performances staged in the Théâtre Moderne, and the sensual pleasures of the arcade's baths and Madame Jehan's massage parlor. As the "Great Opening of Haussmann Boulevard" progressed and the inevitable demolition of the arcade drew near, Aragon ruminated, "No one can anticipate the consequences or repercussions of that kiss upon the vast body of Paris."[2]

Of course, Aragon knew the principal result, as did every other newspaper reader: the triumph of *la circulation* across the city. It marked an end to the first quarter of the twentieth century, when pedestrians, carts, horses, bicycles, and automobiles shared the boulevards. Henceforth, automobiles would dominate the hierarchy of transportation on the streets, relegating pedestrians to the sidewalks, leaving cyclists at their peril, and banning carts and horses altogether. But beyond these surface effects, Aragon wondered about the as-yet indeterminate cultural and intellectual forms that would emerge out of this latest wave of urban modernization. Old habits of *la flânerie*, Aragon predicted, would be transformed by new and unknown modes of strolling, radically changing not just a city neighborhood, but an entire mentality. One of these perceptual reorientations was provided by surrealism, the science of the ephemeral.

Personally, Aragon experienced surrealism in a double sense—as the surrealist literary and artistic movement organized by André Breton and as a cultural passage of time. For a few decades, beginning about 1890 and ending somewhere around 1930, cultural and technological modernities of the nineteenth and twentieth centuries overlapped, and their ruptures were evident everywhere: International expositions and commercial mass marketing signaled a growing shift in economic orientation from industrial production to consumer capitalism. Paris had been electrified, but the amalgamation of the gas industry since the mid-nineteenth century guaranteed that gas lighting held a secure position in Paris until the 1920s. An array of public transportation vehicles were variously powered by steam, gasoline, or electricity, while the automobile was rapidly replacing horse-drawn carriages and bicycles for personal transportation. The development of the subway—the Métropolitain—and overland suburban rail systems displaced social identities, allowing for swift passage between Parisian localities, as well as making possible the separation of residence, work, and entertainment between Paris and the suburbs. And while the telephone provided instantaneous personal communication within Paris and between the metropolis and the city's periphery, the relatively underdeveloped telephone system constrained the use of that technology in creating a transgeographic sense of personal identity.[3]

Surrealism exploited this transitory moment for its own avant-garde artistic and political purposes. The juxtapositions of everyday life in the rapidly transforming Parisian landscape inspired the movement's members. In his surrealist novel of Paris, Aragon committed himself to inhabiting old cultural spaces, open to the chance sensations they offered, trying to capture something of their fleeting nature. "Each day alters the sense of modern existence," he wrote. "A mythology comes together, and comes apart. It's a knowledge of life only for those with no experience. It's a gay science that begets itself and then commits suicide."[4] The goal of surrealism was not simply to create an artistic movement but to reconfigure human consciousness in objective accordance with this new and constantly changing reality. By formulating new associations out of the incoherences of everyday life, the entourage proclaimed surrealism an objective reality infused throughout contemporary culture.

This book provides an interpretive history of the cultural intersection between mass print culture and surrealism in France during the early twentieth century. At the founding of their movement, the surrealists drew inspiration from currents of psychological anxiety and social rebellion that ran through certain expressions of mass culture, such as fantastic popular fiction and sensationalist journalism. The provocative nature of such insolent mass culture, displaying a flagrant disregard for cultural conventions and social proprieties, resonated with the intellectual and political preoccupations of the surrealists. Sometimes the connections were pronounced, as these sources of mass culture produced surreal visions in advance of the surrealist movement itself. In other instances, mass-produced commodities served as points of departure for surrealist inquiries. Yet these artifacts of mass culture and surrealism were neither subsumed by nor reducible to each other; what they shared was an overlapping and intersecting cultural terrain.

The following chapters explore this cultural intersection between mass print culture and surrealism. This project implicitly calls into question assumptions about the avant-garde origins of modernism by looking for surreal perspectives at the level of mass culture itself. Here, I follow the lead of intellectual historians Stephen Kern and Donald Lowe, who have argued that a "perceptual revolution," emphasizing modernist synchronies of time and space, occurred in the realms of physics, philosophy, psychology, mathematics, literature and the arts at the turn of the century.[5] My focus on mass print culture broadens the social and cultural base of this perceptual revolution by demonstrating that such modernist sensibilities were not only generated from the "high" cultural realms of experimental art, literature, music, philosophy, and physics but were woven into the cultural fabric more generally, in such "low" sources as pulp novels and newspaper sensationalism. This book also supplements, and to some extent displaces, the place of the Great War as the harbinger of twentieth-century modernity, a standard historical thesis that, in my view, overemphasizes the destructive and negative aspects of modernity.[6] While the Great War was the most cataclysmic and traumatic event of the early twentieth century, it should not overshadow the multitude of less dramatic cultural connections that bridge the historical break between the nineteenth and twentieth centuries.

Toward this end, this book explores mass print culture as one of the cultural milieux from which surrealism emerged.[7] The surrealists did not so much create as discover the surreality of their epoch. I am less concerned in the chapters that follow with the activities or opinions of the surrealists themselves than in enlisting their service in directing me, as a cultural historian, toward caches of mass culture that display affinities with surrealism. It is precisely this connection that wrests a popular dynamism out of what is otherwise merely commercial mass culture. It is my hope that this book will provide historians and cultural-studies critics, as well as general readers interested in French popular culture, with a fresh basis for reevaluating both the popular aspects of mass culture and the revolutionary aims of the surrealist movement.

WHAT IS SURREALISM?

Like so many titles in the *Que sais-je?* (What do I know?) series of pocketbooks, "What is surrealism?" is a larger and more complex question than one of those slim volumes, or this one, can adequately address in a condensed manner. André Breton, founder and magus of surrealism, himself was continually asking the question, and he answered it in various formulations throughout his life.[8] The present work is neither a general introduction to surrealism nor to its basic corpus; those tasks have been more than amply covered.[9] Neither is this book a substitute for reading the great surrealist novels of Paris, Aragon's *Le Paysan de Paris*, Breton's *Nadja*, and Philippe Soupault's *Les Dernières nuits de Paris*.[10] Yet a brief overview of surrealism may be useful in understanding the designs of this book. In this endeavor, I apologize in advance both to aficionados, who may find my characterizations of surrealism crude, and to the uninitiated, who may find them esoteric.

The surrealist movement was founded in 1924, an outgrowth of the Paris dada movement of 1919. In the first "Manifesto of Surrealism," founder André Breton proclaimed, "Surrealism is based on the belief in the superior reality of certain forms of associations hitherto neglected, in the omnipotence of dream, in the disinterested play of thought. It tends to ruin, once and for all, all other psychic mechanisms and to substitute itself for them in solving all the principal problems of life."[11] The goal of surrealism was to objectively reconfigure consciousness according to the double processes of "ideological unchaining" (*désenchaînement*, a radical critique of status quo values and common sense), and the reformulation of thought according to previously unknown associations.[12] These new, surreal visions were expressed principally through poetry and prose, collages and paintings, exhibitions and manifestoes. The revolutionary nature of surrealism as an intellectual project lay in the degree to which its adherents pushed their peculiar blend of skepticism and self-authority. All forms of received knowledge were rejected out of hand and were replaced by new associations: "The more the relationship between the two juxtaposed realities is distant and true, the stronger the image will be— the greater its emotional power and poetic reality. . . ."[13] This higher reality, a *sur*-reality, dismantled, reformulated, and expanded one's perceptions of common reality.

It is important to note that the surrealists did not regard the individual psyche as the source of surreal associations. Rather, the goal was to expand an individual's consciousness to incorporate previously unknown realities into a richer and more complex image of modern life. The reconfiguration of consciousness was objective in the sense that vast and obscure realms, not only the Freudian biological unconscious but the entirety of material and cultural worlds, actually existed independently of an individual's consciousness (*ego, le moi*). To characterize the often shocking and overpowering experience of this greater reality, the surrealists invoked such categories as the marvelous (*la merveille*), convulsive beauty (*la beauté convulsive*), and mad love (*l'amour fou*). They also developed a wide range of techniques, from automatic writing and dream recollections to "exquisite corpse" word-and-image games, to provoke their own powers of perception in order to comprehend this greater surreality. In their cultural and political radicalism, the surrealists regarded themselves as revolutionary prophets of the modern epoch.

To date, most critical discussions of the origins of surrealism have focused upon the high-brow cultural realms of literature and art criticism. In *L'Histoire du Surréalisme* (1944), Maurice Nadeau, the first chronicler of the surrealist movement, established an elaborate literary and artistic genealogy of surrealism.[14] Guillaume Apollinaire, Max Jacob, and Jacques Vaché provided the poetic impulses toward surrealism; Charles Baudelaire, Alfred Jarry, Lautréamont (Isidor Ducasse), and Arthur Rimbaud were its "literary stimulators"; Giorgio de Chirico, Marcel Duchamp, and Francis Picabia were its inspirational artists. As an avant-garde movement, surrealism was the heir of cubism and Zurich dadaism. In the main, Nadeau provides a good point of departure.

But it is a limited slice of cultural life. Such a list of origins cannot explain why, for example, Fantômas, the ambiguous anti-hero of a series of sensationalist pulp novels, occupied a place on the genealogical tree of "Erutaréttil" (*Littérature* spelled backwards). Or why serial murderer Henri Désiré Landru, the "Bluebeard of Gambais," was favorably ranked on a dada literary value chart. Or why the surrealist inquiry "Is Suicide a Solution?" was accompanied with dozens of suicide *faits divers* (sensationalist news blurbs) in the premier issues of *La Révolution Surréaliste*. With the exception of film, the popular origins of surrealism have been neglected.[15] In this book, popular culture takes center stage.

WHAT IS POPULAR CULTURE?

Popular culture, like surrealism, is difficult to define precisely. Yet here too an overview may assist readers unfamiliar with the issues, as well as clarify my own use of the term. Traditionally, a distinction is drawn between mass and popular culture. The opposition is based largely upon the differing social bases of cultural production; mass culture is produced by an entrepreneurial elite and marketed to the general population, while popular culture is generated by the people (*populo, menu peuple*, the folk) themselves. In France, and in Europe generally, the ascendancy of mass culture began in the sixteenth century with the advent of the printing press, the Protestant and Catholic Reformations, and the social rise of European commercial and professional elites.[16] As the forces of Atlantic commercial capitalism and early industrialization began to transform traditional social relations at the end of the eighteenth century, a revival of elite interest in popular culture occurred among national folktale collectors and the Romantics.[17] The full flowering of mass culture commenced during the late nineteenth-century Belle Époque, with the transition from industrial to consumer capitalism, the implementation of compulsory national education programs, and the advent of communications technologies such as the mass-circulation daily newspaper, the telegraph and telephone, the cinema, and soon thereafter wireless radio.[18] In the twentieth century, numerous European intellectuals generated critiques of mass culture, among which perhaps the most widely known are Henri Lefebvre's critique of the society of consumption, the culture-industry thesis of Max Horkheimer and Theodor Adorno, and the concept of cultural hegemony extrapolated from the writings of Antonio Gramsci.[19]

In recent decades however, some historians and intellectuals have questioned whether a sharp distinction between mass and popular culture can be maintained. Presumed processes of social homogenization and ideological domination associated with mass culture have been challenged by both social historians and critical theorists.[20] In this book, I also question the usefulness of maintaining a strict distinction between mass culture and popular culture, particularly in twentieth-century Western

Europe and North America, where the popularity of mass culture vastly overreaches the influence of folk cultures. Instead, I employ the surrealists to help me sift through the morass of mass culture to recover a "secret history" of popular culture in early twentieth-century France.[21] That is, the surrealists guide me, as a cultural historian, to specific expressions of mass culture whose cultural meanings remain partially detached from the ideological interests or social values of their commercial production.

I consider mass culture "popular" when it satisfies two requirements:[22] First, the source of mass culture must be socially widespread in its consumption, in aggregate numbers, across social classes, and at differing cultural levels. That is, the popularity of mass culture should not be dismissed as a false consciousness imposed by elites upon the people, but regarded as culture whose popular reception is socially widespread. Second, the specific expressions of mass culture considered must lend themselves to diverse interpretations. That is, mass culture should not be reduced to genre formulas or socially normative ideological messages, but should be actively interpreted in its cultural and historical specificity for a diversity of meanings. In this sense, teasing a surrealist perspective out of specific examples of mass culture becomes a popular practice of interpreting cultural materials that would otherwise remain banal and quotidian.

In the following chapters, popular culture is kept in the foreground and the opinions of the surrealists to the back. In this regard, my approach differs from other recent works that have sought to establish a common modernist aesthetic running between mass culture and early twentieth-century avant-garde movements.[23] The products of art museum exhibitions and academic art history, these works employ an influence and diffusion model in which mass culture provokes artistic inspiration, is transformed into art, and then is accepted or rejected by a wider audience. Sidra Stich's *Anxious Visions: Surrealist Art* exhibition, for example, underscored the destructive and traumatic effect of the Great War in establishing the historical context within which psychological anxiety and fragmentation of the human body become key formal elements in surrealist art. In *High & Low: Modern Art and Popular Culture*, an exhibition organized by Kirk Varnedoe and Adam Gopnik, newspapers, graffiti, caricature, comic books, and advertising images become the raw materials that inspire twentieth-century artists. In Jeffrey Weiss's *The Popular Culture of Modern Art*, an aesthetic of incomprehension and uncertainty is seen as characteristic of modern culture generally and is expressed most dynamically in Picasso's cubist art and Duchamp's ready-mades. In each of these cases, mass culture is interpreted from a high artistic perspective: History assumes the status of context, mass culture becomes fodder for avant-garde artistic inspiration, and the artists retain their position as cultural innovators.

The interpretive approach used in this book, by contrast, seeks an innovative dynamism at the level of mass culture itself. The surrealists become less important as an experimental avant-garde than as guides to culturally dynamic sources of mass culture. No doubt the rapidly modernizing urban landscape of turn-of-the-century Paris provided the city's inhabitants and visitors with an abundance of new and unusual juxtapositions. But within the routine of daily life, it is less than certain that those novel vistas automatically produced a modernist or surreal consciousness. It is equally, and perhaps more, likely that the incoherences of daily life were subsumed under what André Breton called "the paucity of reality" (*le peu de réalité*), classified and circumscribed by received patterns of thought. The surrealists were well aware that on an everyday basis commercial mass culture was not experienced as incomprehensible but as ordinary and banal.

Yet at the beginning of their movement, the surrealists saw a revolutionary potential in mass culture to produce a new consciousness. In many works of surrealism, there are multiple references to the artifacts of everyday life. The cultural terrain of Breton's *Nadja*, for example, includes flea markets, newspaper clippings, *faits divers*, bookstores, theater melodramas, movie houses, the Opera Passageway, the Hôtel Henri IV, the Nouvelle France bar, signs for *bois-charbons* and for Mazda lightbulbs. While these and other novel juxtapositions afforded by modernizing Paris and its signs of mass culture may not have automatically invoked surreal visions, the terrain of everyday life fed surreal perceptions. Whatever the place of these objects and signs at the level of common reality, they became talismans of surreality as well. As literary and artistic provocateurs, part of the surrealist project was to illuminate the extraordinary in a mass culture that might otherwise pass as quotidian.

In some instances, though, there was a close proximity between mass culture and surrealism. Francis Lacassin, a leading French critic of popular novels and other forms of *paralittérature*, has commented upon the intersections between the enormously popular turn-of-the-century *Fantômas* crime novels and surrealism: "In *Fantômas*, there was an overflowing of the fantastic into daily life that appeared to have an affinity with surrealist preoccupations—an insolent challenge of aesthetic and social taboos, a relentless demystification, an historical continuity with what André Breton called dark humor. And above all, objective chance."[24] Two attributes from Lacassin's comment resonate in the present study. The first, concerning the fantastic in daily life, recalls the observation of J. H. Matthews, in his groundbreaking study *Surrealism and Film*, that an ordinary commercial film which "overspills the mold in which it has been cast" lends itself to surrealist appropriation.[25] Amid the commercial excesses of production and consumption in highly developed consumer societies, social convention and genre formulas do not completely bind the diversity of messages circulated in mass culture. The sources of pulp fiction and sensationalist journalism explored in this book share this tendency to "overspill the mold." The second characteristic is that such mass culture may be explicitly insolent. Cultural effrontery, social contempt, and political provocation were central agendas of the surrealist movement, and its members felt affinities with impudent currents running through mass culture. The early surrealists mined mass culture for gems that were both *insolite* and insolent.

The chapters that follow are organized as a series of microhistories, each exploring those out-of-the-ordinary and impertinent elements which establish critical intersections between mass culture and surrealism. The first chapter explores Aragon's political choice to locate the first portion of *Le Paysan de Paris* in the Opera Passageway arcade. In distinction to critical theorists who have interpreted Aragon's book in relation to philosopher Walter Benjamin's unfinished arcades project, I have examined the disreputable history of the passageway itself. The accursed status of the Opera Passageway inspired Aragon, although he cared more for his own surreal visions than for the actual fate of the arcade. By extension, I argue that Aragon's choice to organize this section of *Le Paysan de Paris* as a guidebook served as a technique to force his readers' imaginations out of common reality and into surreality. Chapter two examines the enormously popular series of *Fantômas* crime novels by Pierre Souvestre and Marcel Allain, written between 1911 and 1913. In thirty-two consecutive novels produced in as many months, *Fantômas* was an impossible serial tale of displaced identities, ephemeral realities, objective chance, and unmotivated criminality. Surreal before the letter, the popularity of the novel series surpassed its later avant-garde appropriation. Chapter three recounts the fantastic story of Henri Désiré Landru, who was executed in 1922 for the murder of ten women. The Parisian press ran wild with the criminal possibilities of the Landru Affair, and in the process it elevated a small-time swindler to a mythic status as the "Bluebeard of Gambais." A surreal, dark humor was key to both the fashioning and the dissolution of the image of Landru as a sadistic murderer of women. The fourth chapter reconceptualizes the surrealist inquiry, "Is Suicide a Solution?" In the premier issue of *La Révolution Surréaliste*, the surrealists juxtaposed this question with reprints of actual suicide *faits divers*. These *faits divers* detached the issue of suicide from a particular kind of late-nineteenth-century social morality and instead appealed to an unconscious human resonance in newspaper readers with those desperate individuals who, like the surrealists, fundamentally rebelled against the meaninglessness of contemporary life.

These are not the only examples of turn-of-the-century French mass culture that display close affinities to surrealism, but they show them spectacularly well. In each instance, print mass culture established the possibility of the existence of a popular imagination that exceeded the ideological limitations of commercial or social class interests. In addition, I have striven to show that, through mass consumption, the social basis of reception for such a surrealist mentality was widespread. Guidebooks to Paris, the *Fantômas* series, and Parisian daily newspapers were consumed in the millions of issues. These forms of mass culture cut across social classes, found adherents at multiple intellectual levels, and, in translation, crossed language and national barriers as well. These issues were important to the surrealists, who believed that the future success of the surrealist revolution in consciousness depended upon such an expanded social base.

This book, then, explores the historical intersection between the popularity of particular examples of mass print culture and relates them to the emergence of surrealist sensibilities in early twentieth-century France. In the division between history as knowledge and as interpretation, this book contributes primarily to the latter, although I trust readers will learn something of the former as well. It does not establish an exhaustive genealogy of the mass cultural origins of surrealism. Rather, it dusts off a few choice skeletons from the closet and tries to discover what might have drawn surrealists to them. At the very least, I hope that I have delighted and provoked you, *cher lecteur.*

/ The Baedeker of Hives

paysan, anne (de pays), n. Homme, femme de compagne.—
Par extens. Rustre, personne grossière: *Un franc* paysan.—
Œnol. Se dit, dans la classification des vins de Bordeaux,
de ceux qui occupent le dernier rang.

peasant (from *pays*, country), n. Countryman or country-
woman.—*By extension*, Unsophisticated, uncouth character:
A simple peasant.—Œnology. Name commonly given to the
lowest order of Bordeaux wine classifications.

Larousse du XXe siècle (1932)

Toward the end of the first half of *Le Paysan de Paris*—that portion dedicated to the Opera Passageway—some of the owners of the arcade's
shops got a peek at what surrealist Louis Aragon had been writing about
them since the summer of 1924. The commercial proprietors, Aragon recounted, were shocked by a series of articles in the literary review in
which installments of his novel first appeared.[1] "The other day, there was
a meeting of the arcade big shots. One of them brought along Numbers
16 and 17 of the *Revue Européenne*. They discussed it bitterly. Who provided this information? . . . They would like to meet him, this obstinate
enemy, this Machiavellian character. And what would they say to him?
What would bees say to the Baedeker of hives?"[2]

   At first the shopkeepers failed to connect the author of the articles with
the dadaist habitué of the arcade's Certa café. Instead, they suspected a

completely innocent commercial agent, who up to that point had faith-
fully represented the passage's interests, of having betrayed them. Shortly
thereafter, Aragon's articles were attacked in the *Chaussée d'Antin*, a local activist newsletter that defended the interests of the neighborhood's
shopowners against the Haussmann Boulevard Realty Company. The
arcade's proprietors found the financial disclosures in Aragon's articles,
as well as his surreal embellishments, frightening: "Where did he get
those figures? *Is it possible?*"[3]

A few pages further into his novel, Aragon confessed that he had a
propensity toward effusive descriptions. He did not like the idea of a
world determined by facts; he preferred the powers of chance to those of
observation. The arcade's commercial terrain provided Aragon with a
rich source for surrealist musings, continually turning its images and objects into something else. Walking-canes in an illuminated display first
became luminous fish in the darkened ocean of the passageway, then
swaying kelp, then prostitute-sirens from the Rhineland. The true name
of this arcade, Aragon proclaimed, was the *Passage de L'Opéra Onirique*:
the Arcade of Dream Divinations. Everything base was transformed into
the marvelous: "The foreigner reading my little guide lifts his head, and
says to himself, 'It's here.'"[4]

The task of this opening chapter is to explore the intersection of the
history of the Opera Passageway and Aragon's *Le Paysan de Paris*. Insofar
as Aragon included descriptive details about the Opera Passageway in
his book, it has sometimes been used as a guide to the arcade itself.[5] But
Aragon's choice of the Opera Passageway as a central location in the
novel was more strategic than documentary. Generally, the arcade's historical reputation was one of marginal commercial success and social dis-
repute. By the 1920s, the passageway had become an impediment to the
completion of boulevard Haussmann, an urban renovation that would
facilitate the flow of automobile traffic in the metropolis at the expense of
the neighborhood's residents and the arcade's proprietors. In addition to
being an "ur-form" of modernity and an "outmoded space," in 1925 the
Opera Passageway was a socially contested urban space. Aragon used
the contemporary controversy of its imminent destruction to draw attention to his own book, a "Baedeker of hives," designed to capsize and

capture the reader's imagination with its instantaneous and continually metamorphosing visions.

THE PASSAGES DE L'OPÉRA

Since 1919, the Certa café within the Opera Passageway had served as the favorite bar and unofficial office of the Paris dada movement's entourage. Located in lower Montmartre, the commercial arcade was tucked away within a building block whose double-entranced facade opened onto the northern side of the boulevard des Italiens. The labyrinthine location of the Certa kept the activities of the dada group out of view of both the bustling activity of the boulevard and the Left Bank literati. A forgotten location amid the urban landscape of early twentieth-century Paris, it was the perfect spot to feed the conspiratorial imaginations of those writers and artists who would soon proclaim the surrealist revolution.

The first half of the nineteenth century had been the heyday of covered passageways in Paris. According to the *Guides Joanne* (predecessor to the *Guides Bleus*), in the mid-nineteenth century there were more than 150 *passages* and *galeries* in Paris. The most elegant were covered passageways which served as commercial arcades, characteristically "lined with luxurious stores and splendidly illuminated by gaslight, providing a place for an evening promenade or rendezvous when it rains."[6] Of sixty-three covered passageways built in Paris, from the Galerie de Bois in 1786 to the Palacio de la Madeleine in 1935, two-thirds were constructed under the Restoration and the July Monarchy, including the Passages de l'Opéra in 1822.[7] Establishments in these covered passageways included restaurants, cafés, clothing boutiques, and bookstores, such entertainments as theaters, ballrooms, and panoramas, and the purchased services of reading libraries, bathhouses, and toilets. As a social space, the arcades were renowned for a characteristic trilogy of loafers (*flâneurs*), pickpockets, and prostitutes. According to one guide of the era, the arcades were an "Eldorado of nonchalance."[8] By the time the dada group had discovered the Certa café in the early twentieth century, many passageway arcades suffered from decades of relative neglect.

In recent years, philosopher Walter Benjamin's *Passagen-Werk* has re-awakened a critical interest in the arcades and their relation to surrealism.[9] Rather than blaze a theoretical path along the lines of Benjamin-inspired studies, I have pursued a more modest historical inquiry that provides a supplemental perspective to those accounts. Among Parisian arcades, the Opera Passageway had a particular and checkered history. The arcade served as the location for Aragon's surreal musings for first half of *Le Paysan de Paris*, and he well may have drawn inspiration from its long-standing insolent reputation. Yet Aragon's scathing comments about the arcade's businessmen suggests that he may have cared less about the passageway itself than in exploiting its ill repute for his own purposes. A brief recapitulation of Benjamin's interest in the arcades, in relation to surrealism, will help draw out this distinction.

As presented in his well-known essay, "Paris, Capital of the Nineteenth Century," the arcades were a crucial architectural form for Benjamin for a number of reasons.[10] First, the arcades shared an affinity with Charles Fourier's utopian socialist vision of social harmony through architecture during an era of early industrial capitalism. Second, the concentration of consumer goods within the arcades was culturally dynamic and innovative, creating aesthetic affinities in this new era of industrial art, connecting mass merchandise displays and Grandville's fantastic caricatures, dioramas and photography. Third, the arcades, and later the boulevards during the Haussmannization of Paris, created a new social space, successively inhabited by a vacuous bourgeoisie driven by commodity fetishism (criticized by the likes of Honoré de Balzac and Gustave Flaubert), a modern urban crowd of dandies, *flâneurs*, and prostitutes (celebrated by Charles Baudelaire), and historically visionary Communards (championed by realist painter Gustave Courbet, revolutionary politician Auguste Blanqui, socialist theoretician Karl Marx, and iconoclastic poet Arthur Rimbaud).

To give his research into these historical realms of nineteenth-century Parisian urban culture contemporary significance in the interwar years of the twentieth century when he wrote the essay, Benjamin drew inspiration from Michelet's dictum that "Each age dreams its successor."[11] According to critical theorist Susan Buck-Morss, Benjamin saw in the arcades "ur-form" ruins that anticipated the rise of spectacular commercial capitalism. Benjamin believed that a dialectical reading of a wide range of such nineteenth-century culture, discerning "modern" from "ruin," could help to establish a critical philosophy of history for the twentieth century.[12] The significance of such an analysis lay in the ability to engage simultaneously in ideological critique and social description. This approach to cultural analysis, sorting through historical ruins to separate out capitalist contradictions from utopian socialist possibilities, is referred to as the "redemption of physical reality."[13]

In "Surrealism, the Last Snapshot of the European Intelligentsia," Benjamin identified surrealism as the only intellectual movement of his contemporary era to dream the future out of the ruins of outmoded, nineteenth-century cultural modernity.[14] Given the surrealists' complete rejection of bourgeois ethics and values and their pursuit of new forms of consciousness, Benjamin found a "profane illumination" in surrealism. The shocking and mysterious effects provoked by surrealist experiments with chance encounters, states of intoxication, and the atmosphere of places, Benjamin emphasized, had their source in the concrete, material basis of everyday life. Benjamin hoped that such a surreal illumination could emerge directly from materialist culture itself, through a historically critical analysis of "dialectical images,"[15] and he criticized the surrealists for their self-assigned role as magicians of the world.

Looked at another way, though, the crucial distinction is between common reality and surreality, not between materialism and alchemy. For the surrealists, the everyday world was already classified and ordered according to previous patterns of thought, circumscribed by what Breton called the "paucity of reality" (le peu de réalité), the "least common denominator of mortals."[16] While modern Paris provided a cultural terrain for surrealist inspiration, Breton knew that the commercial and political interests transforming the urban landscape resisted and thwarted surrealism. "I know that in Paris, on the boulevards, the beautiful luminous signs are making their appearance. Those signs mean a great deal to me as I walk, but actually they represent only that which annoys me."[17] While the technological wonders of contemporary life suggested new possibilities of consciousness for Breton—"wireless telegraphy, wireless telephony, wireless imagination"—poetic reconfiguration was required to achieve the transformation to surreality.

Moreover, surrealism could not be achieved solely through ironic negation; positive revaluation was required as well. In the classic debate over the distinctions between dada and surrealism, dadaist Tristan Tzara insisted upon the continual negation of all artistic values, while surrealist Breton modified his anti-art stance toward the rehabilitation of such values as beauty and love.[18] In this surrealist transposition of aesthetics, the imaginative powers of the interpreter were indispensable. Surrealism, while formed out of everyday culture, was not directly expressed by it (as Breton would later argue against Georges Bataille in the "Second Manifesto of Surrealism"). Even in its psychic automatism, surrealism required the participation of the alchemist to achieve the metamorphosis to the marvelous. As quintessentially represented by Robert Desnos semiconsciously dictating prose from trance states, the production of surrealist texts necessarily entailed a performative dimension.[19]

The Opera Passageway, with its mishmash of shops and their curiously populated window displays, was not intrinsically surreal. Neither did the arcade inspire surrealists simply because it was an "outmoded space."[20] The marginality of the Opera Passageway to the city's commercial and urban landscape was not a by-product of the twentieth century; its fringe status had been intrinsic to the structure since its opening a century earlier. While some sources claim that the Opera Passageway had been one of the fashionable arcades of the Restoration and the July Monarchy, other sources suggest that it suffered from commercial failure and had always been a location of social vice.[21] Reviewing the checkered past of the arcade assists in discriminating between its inherited characteristics and those surreal manifestations conjured up by Aragon in the *Passage de l'Opéra Onirique*.

In 1821, Viscount Morel-Vindé was granted permission to build a double-barreled commercial arcade on family-owned property in the Chaussée d'Antin district of the second *arrondissement* (today the ninth). Less than twelve feet wide, the arcade's three-story galleries ran north and south, the Clock Gallery (*galerie de l'Horloge*) to the east and the Barometer Gallery (*galerie du Baromètre*) to the west (pl. 1). Constructed

Plate 1. Galerie de l'Horloge, Passages de l'Opéra, Ninth Arrondissement, 4 October 1919. (Photo: Charles Lansiaux. Collection: Bibliothèque Historique de la Ville de Paris)

in 1822 and expanded in 1823, the sixty-one ground-floor spaces in the
Opera Passageway were originally designed to take advantage of the
flow of foot-traffic to the Opera, which had been relocated to the adjoining Royal Academy of Music following the assassination of the duc de
Berry on the steps of the rue Richelieu Opera House on 13 September,
1820. It is doubtful, however, that the passageway ever gained much of a
clientele in this regard; the Opera's main entrance was on rue Le Peletier,
whereas the two galleries of the arcade opened onto the boulevard des
Italiens. The only access to the Opera was at the very back of the arcade,
where an extremely narrow alleyway (periodically closed by the police)
connected rues Grange-Batélière and Le Peletier. Unlike many other
Paris passageways, which provided connecting routes between main
thoroughfares, the Opera Passageway was something of an urban backwater from the beginning. Its design was less a channel than an eddy. In
contrast to the bustling activity of the boulevard des Italiens, for the En-
glishwoman of letters Frances Trollope in 1835, as for Aragon and Breton
in 1919, the arcade primarily provided shelter from the rain.[22]

The commercial enterprises of the Opera arcade were never all that
impressive. Comprising second-rate boutiques, its allure was more
chintz than satin. Although the 1826 *Guide des Acheteurs, ou Almanach des
passages de l'Opéra* boasted a kind of modern glamour, most of the shops
sold a mélange of odd merchandise (*bimbeloterie*).[23] The largest concerns
of the passageway were jewelry and porcelain shops which, despite elaborate descriptions in the *Guide des Acheteurs* concerning the noble history
of these craft professions, sold factory-manufactured ornaments, metal-
plated accessories, and artificial pearls.[24] On the whole, the Opera Passageway may have confirmed the suspicions of those contemporaries
who claimed the arcades were lackluster commercial ventures.[25] Indeed,
great commercial success seems to have eluded the arcade's merchants.
Throughout the nineteenth century, its establishments frequently closed
or changed ownership.[26] The touted attraction of the "Europorama,"
offering dioramic views of European cities and an exhibition map of Jeru-
salem, was replaced by a children's theater in 1834, an "automatic museum" in 1845, and was followed by a series of ball, dance, and dramatic
theaters, until its final incarnation as the Théâtre Moderne in 1904.[27]

After a fire destroyed the Royal Academy of Music in 1873, the Passages de l'Opéra lost even the marginal connection to its namesake.[28]

As a social institution, however, the reputation of the arcade was famous, if not infamous, as a key gathering-site of the Parisian *demi-monde*. According to Musée Carnavalet director Georges Cain, this "foul *passage noir*, illuminated by hazy lamps, emitting nasty smells from neighboring ovens, and equally distressing odors," was the low-life rendezvous of Opera sycophants, bit actors, and stagehands, as well as dandies, evening adventurers, and casual prostitutes of all regimes, 1821 to 1873.[29] While the reputable society of king, emperor, and *tout Paris* attended masked balls at the opera house of the Royal Academy of Music, the expansive basement underneath the Opera Passageway served as the location of the somewhat more disreputable, licentious, and lascivious *bal d'Italie* (although there was significant crossover in clientele from the former to the latter). The Opera Passageway was also known as the *petite bourse du soir*, where financiers and politicians could conduct their unofficial business transactions without attracting the watchful eye of the police. Criminal loitering and prostitution were common features of many of the arcades, and under the July Monarchy police prefect Mangin regulated the business hours of certain arcades and cracked down on street prostitutes (*filles publiques*).[30] Among arcades, the Opera Passageway enjoyed the dubious distinction of being the only one under surveillance by direct royal ordinance, and it was noted in guidebooks for having its "indecent and ignoble alleyways" closed at night for public benefit.[31]

The story of the covered passageways during the Second Empire and Third Republic, with the Haussmannization of Parisian boulevards and the appearance of department stores such as La Samaritaine and Le Bon Marché, is usually recounted as one of decline.[32] What is certain is the arcades received diminished attention in guidebooks to Paris. In *Calignani's New Paris Guide* for 1844, for example, the arcades were praised as convenient and successful commercial ventures: "All the taste and elegance of the Parisian shopkeepers are here displayed, and they are the grand resort of all the loungers of the town."[33] By 1873, however, Calignani's *Guide* merely stated that "These are a grand resort of all the loungers of the town."[34] Without the accompanying taste and elegance, presumably the status of the "loungers" diminished as well. By the late nineteenth and early twentieth centuries, passageways received scant mention in Paris guidebooks, and those few mentioned were noted only by address.[35]

What is less clear is whether this decreased vogue for the arcades actually meant, as Edmond Beaurepaire claimed in *La Chronique des rues* (1900), that as commercial and urban centers the arcades were "languishing, abandoned, and left in the dust."[36] As late as 1916, for example, the Commission Municipale du Vieux Paris noted that although business in the passageways had slowed considerably, nonetheless they were concentrated in some of the most vibrant neighborhoods in Paris. Foot-traffic in the nearly three kilometers of combined passageways, the commission concluded, continued to be active.[37] Thus, while situated in the shadow of the boulevard and department store, in many neighborhoods the arcades remained active commercial and social spaces.

The Opera Passageway displayed these ambiguities well. While the Eugène Rey bookstore was the only establishment with a commercial profile worthy of inclusion in the 1920 *Bottin-Mondain*, a number of the arcade's establishments had remained in business for several decades. Of the shops mentioned by Aragon in *Le Paysan de Paris* in 1925, the medical supply and gun shops had opened in 1877, the cane and pipe shop in 1882, the Flammarion bookstore in 1888, Vodable's tailor shop in 1891, the Eugène Rey bookstore and Vincent's barbershop in 1898, the print shop and the bathhouse in 1899, Arrigoni's restaurant and *L'Événement* printshop since 1905, and the Biard café and Saulnier's restaurant since 1910.[38] Other enterprises, such as shoe-shine stalls and *prix-fixe* restaurants, occupied the same spaces, although their owners changed. Some businesses, such as Arrigoni's restaurant and the Certa café, were prosperous enough that when the passageway was destroyed in 1925, they successfully moved to other locations.[39] While not as glamorous as Le Bon Marché or La Samaritaine, the relative longevity and modest prosperity of some of the Opera arcade's shops suggest that their characterization as "outmoded" and "ruins" requires further consideration.

Aragon's *Paysan de Paris* recapitulates many of the commonly known features of the Opera Passageway, and in some ways, his documentary observations are unexceptional; it is the anomalies in his descriptions that provoke greater interest. Why, for example, does Aragon rename the *galerie de l'Horloge* the "Thermometer," instead of leaving it the "Clock"? Is it merely to make the names of the two galleries rhyme? Or are Barometer and Thermometer a better pair for determining the "weather" of the arcade? Or do the allusions to pressure and temperature assist the reader in making an imaginary transformation of the arcade from an inanimate structure into a living one, pulsating with blood and libido? Aragon's lacunae are equally provocative. What is the Dada cocktail, priced at four francs, that appears on the menu from the Certa café reprinted in *Le Paysan de Paris*? And why does that woman from the handkerchief shop keep getting locked into her own boutique, having to be rescued by her customers?[40] Whatever documentary evidence about the Opera passageway might be contained in *Le Paysan de Paris*, suggestive details woven into the printed pages remind the reader that the meaning of Aragon's prose lies elsewhere.

THE ODOR OF *VIEUX PARIS*

As art historian Molly Nesbit has stated, *Le Paysan de Paris* "gave off the odor of a guide to *Vieux Paris*" while remaining essentially a literary work of surrealism.[41] At times in the book Aragon evokes a near-nostalgia for the old places of the arcade, now finally being destroyed by the last vestiges of Second Empire Haussmannization (itself something of an urban anachronism by the 1920s). But the odor of *Vieux Paris* was more the novel's by-product than its essence. Aragon felt little attachment for the passageway itself. He was put off by the shopkeepers' petty responses to his articles in the *Revue Européenne.* And despite his affectionate remarks for the owner of the Certa café, he did not frequent the establishment after it moved to the rue d'Isly. It seems unlikely that nostalgia was Aragon's primary motivation.

Insolence seems a better choice. The Opera Passageway was generally despised by preservationists and modernizers alike. In 1916 the Commission Municipale du Vieux Paris had agreed, in principle, that the

arcades were worthy of historical preservation.[42] The destruction of the
Opera Passageway, however, passed unregistered in their *procès-verbaux*.
Among urban modernizers, most would agree with Edmond Beaurepaire's turn-of-the-century assessment of the arcades that "Progress has
condemned them, and frankly, it's not worth getting upset about."[43] Neglected by those who ostensibly cared about such matters, and scorned
by champions of urbanization, the Passages de l'Opéra fell to the pick-
axe in February 1925. Within this historical context, Aragon's choice to
situate his ruminations within the Opera Passageway assumes political
significance. Against a naive faith in historical progress, conservative or
modern, Aragon's writings about the passageway exuded an "organization of pessimism."[44] Whatever odor *Le Paysan de Paris* gave off, it was designed to offend the tastes of established society.

In the last quarter of the nineteenth century, *Vieux Paris* had ceased to
describe a premodern social order, and had come to express a conservative sense of nostalgia evoked directly from the urban landscape itself. In
the early nineteenth century, *ancien* Paris, Paris *d'autrefois*, or *Vieux* Paris
referred to former social classes and professions, and to traditional entertainments, festivals, and parades.[45] After midcentury, however, the urban landscape of Paris was becoming increasingly detached from this social conception. "Nearly every day, the Paris prefecture gives its blessing
to the renaming of streets with complete indifference to the activities of
the neighborhood," P. L. Jacob complained in *Curiosités de l'histoire du
vieux Paris* (1858). "This practice, which shows no sign of slowing down,
occurs without any respect for the people who live there."[46] Jacob ob-
jected to the renaming of streets, precisely because it entailed a loss of
memory of Paris as a lived social space.

With the Haussmannization of Paris during the Second Empire, *con-
servateurs* of "Old Paris" turned archaeological ruins into direct expressions of various golden ages, from Lutèce to the Ancien Régime, detached from either social origins or the contemporary context. This shift
in the meaning of the Parisian landscape, whereby city fragments constituted a kind of nostalgic imagination, was formalized in the creation of
the Commission Municipale du Vieux Paris in 1897.[47] With the founding
of this commission, the modernization of Paris—entailing widespread

urban transformations in the construction and distribution of water supply, electrification, and transportation—now assisted an immense preservation effort.

In preparation for the Universal Exhibition of 1900, the Commission
Municipale du Vieux Paris produced a small tourist pamphlet to promote
its own conservation efforts.[48] In the past, the commission lamented, the
architectural and archaeological preservation of Paris had been largely a
piecemeal affair. The commission boasted that, thanks to its efforts, the
march of progress would actually go hand-in-hand with preserving the
appearance and memory of the old city (the archaeological opportunities created by the construction of the metropolitan subway system in
1898 providing the most illustrative example). Conserving these bits and
pieces of the city, the commission assured the readers of its pamphlet,
amounted to no less than the spiritual glory of Paris itself:

> Its museums . . . its monuments . . . its panoramic views . . . its incompa-
> rable river . . . the fantastic profiles of medieval fortresses . . . the palaces
> of the monarchy . . . the multiple clocks, domes, and campaniles that
> silhouette the horizon. Its flower gardens, and finally, the luxurious
> Parisian forest, so dear to the population. . . .
> Isn't Paris the real birthplace (*patrie*) of these enumerated wonders,
> the sacred source from which the arts, sciences, and letters spring
> forth?[49]

Since 1897, the commission bragged, it had preserved the Hôtel de
Toulouse, the Palais Royal, the Arc de Triomphe, and many churches,
plaques, and street names. Where demolitions were unavoidable, architectural wonders and old neighborhoods could be preserved in paintings,
drawings, and photographs, and conserved in the Musée Carnavalet.

This impulse to conserve, and to create, nostalgic feelings about the
Parisian landscape through buildings, material fragments, and images,
goes a long way toward understanding the cultural shift in *Vieux Paris*
from a social to an imagined urban space. A nostalgic Parisian *pittoresque*
was overlaying and dissolving—and would eventually replace—an
earlier sense of the Parisian *vie populaire*.[50] This nostalgia for images of
nineteenth-century Parisian popular life, which no longer had actual ties

to the modern city, increased as the twentieth century developed. André Warnod, prolific popular author and member of *Vieux Montmartre*, waxed nostalgic about bals, cafés and cabarets, the lives of popular artists and entertainers of Old Paris, and he lamented the lost art of *flânerie* in contemporary Paris.[51] Eugène Atget's photographs of forgotten shop signs and traditional street trades (*pétits métiers*) were purchased by, and safely tucked away within, the Musée Carnavalet. Many guidebooks to Paris were abundantly illustrated with sketches of picturesque Parisian *types.* Photo-illustrated books such as *Les Cent Vues de Paris,* and tourist guidebooks such as Baedeker's handbook and Hachette's *Guides Bleus,* equated the glory of the contemporary urban landscape with sites and images of monumental Paris.[52] Nostalgia for *Vieux Paris* was not necessarily opposed to modern urbanization. On the contrary, the contemporary transformation of the urban landscape made an antiquarian, imaginary past possible, preserved in museum artifacts, documents, and photographs.

But the odor of *Vieux Paris* that Aragon evoked in his surrealist novel was neither picturesque nor practical; it offended both antiquarians and moderns. By locating the first part of his surrealist novel in the Opera Passageway, Aragon let the imagination of his double, a crude and uncouth "peasant," loose within a forgotten urban terrain (pl. 2). His peasant was not simply a naïf, he was the descendent of Restif de La Bretonne's *paysan perverti,* who reveled in his self-corruption.[53] The peasant was singular, like the heady glass of red wine he enjoyed—*un sens unique.* The peasant was not drawn to the commercial spectacle of Paris: He preferred the sensual favors sold by the women of Madame Jehan's massage, or the anonymous intercourse permitted through bath chamber vents, to the commercially packaged sexual fantasies advertised in the pages of *La Vie Parisienne.* Aragon appropriated, from the previous century, the attributes of Balzac's *Les Paysans*—drunken, debauched, envious, insolent, cynical, and deviously clever—and he enlisted that scorned identity in a surrealist revolution of peasant versus bourgeois. The fantasies embedded in *Le Paysan de Paris* were less an expression of *Vieux Paris* than its subversion.

In the early twentieth century, the contested urban space of the Opera Passageway made the location a political springboard for Aragon's literary diatribe. Yet he was not the only person to comment on the passing of

Plate 2. A provincial prepared for a trip to the City, c. 1900.
(Postcard from author's collection)

the arcade. While neglected in official treatments of Paris, in antiquarian
histories, or commercial guides, the destruction of the Opera Passageway
was amply covered by Parisian newspapers. Many Parisian dailies carried articles about the destruction of the Opera Passageway in the months
before the completion of boulevard Haussmann in February 1925. For
the duration of the previous year, the arcade had been the only obstacle

preventing the joining of boulevards Haussmann, Italiens, and Poisson-nières. By writing about the arcade at the moment of its disappearance, Aragon participated in a contemporary political debate about the meaning of modern life and urbanization.

Early into *Le Paysan de Paris,* Aragon reproduces a number of placards posted by the arcade's disgruntled business owners as their storefronts were being demolished.[54] In the face of certain expropriation, some of the arcade's businesses held out as long as possible. Excerpts from these handbills, highlighting the fundamental injustice of being driven out of business in the name of progress, were reproduced in the newspapers as well. *Le Temps* quoted a bill posted on the shoe-shine's windows, "My lease runs eleven more years! I cry out, Thief! Everything must be liqui-dated."[55] *Le Matin* quoted the same cynical placard as Aragon, from the wine merchant who ended his complaint, "Long live Justice!"[56] But mostly, the proprietors were trying to salvage what they could from their doomed businesses, "Final day! Sale on everything in stock! Unbeliev-ably low discounts!"[57] The arcade's proprietors remained businessmen to the end (hence Aragon's chastising of their small-mindedness when they discovered his articles in *La Revue Européenne*).

Some journalists expressed their sympathies for the fate of the arcade's merchants in commentary articles. In his "Mon Film" column for *Le Jour-nal,* popular novelist and journalist Clément Vautel lamented the loss of the arcade to urban development.[58] With the vestiges of Haussmanniza-tion finally and irreversibly set into motion, a boulevard of Second Em-pire design was sluggishly being realized fifty-five years into the Third Republic, Vautel sarcastically remarked. In his view, commercial specu-lators profited the most from the boulevard's expansion, and their gains were insufficient to compensate for the losses incurred by the evicted. Vautel was particularly sad about the closing of the Rey and Flammarion bookstores. Undoubtedly, he concluded ironically, some new establish-ments will profit from the bookstores' displacement, "The buck will chase away the book!"[59] Other articles expressed a restrained sense of community loss in the face of inevitable urban modernization. In *Le Fi-garo,* Emile Darsy wrote nostalgically about the closing of *Le Pousset* bar —the last refuge of *boulevardiers,* veterans of European and colonial wars, and tourists from the provinces—located along the facade of the Passageway.[60] *Le Temps* journalist Georges Montorgeuil paid tribute to Vincent's barbershop, which he claimed (exaggeratedly) had passed from father to son for a hundred years.[61]

Yet even for these journalists, the forward historical march of urbanization seemed inevitable. "Everything passes, even passages," noted *Le Journal*.[62] More thoroughly than other reporters, this anonymous journalist articulated the absurd place of the Passages de l'Opéra amid the contemporary Parisian landscape.

> Along the boulevard, the brilliant facade [of the Opera Passageway] joined in the movement and splendor of Parisian life; so many vibrant, charming, and well-patronized boutiques—Roddy, Pousset, the Khédive, the Flammarion and Rey bookstores. Inside, it was something else entirely: shoe-shine stalls, dismal herb-shops, empty and half-closed-up bazaars. The composition of assembled shops—some stores with display cases filled with indiscernible objects, poorly illuminated and never sold, other shops of extremely fine quality, including some astounding lingerie, and a few popular hideaways—was simultaneously quite modern and extremely old.[63]

The Opera Passageway clung to a tenuous existence during a period of rapid urbanization. It did not require an aesthete like Aragon to see fantastic juxtapositions inherent in the continued existence of the Opera Passageway. No one doubted the arcade's inevitable passing; the question was what its disappearance portended.

In this brief moment of contested meaning over the fate of the Opera Passageway, Aragon's explicit nemesis in *Le Paysan de Paris* was the daily, *L'Intransigeant*. Among Parisian newspapers, *L'Intransigeant* was the most enthusiastic in its support of the destruction of the Opera Passageway in order to complete boulevard Haussmann, for that would open up the flow of automobile traffic in the center of the city. In the mid-1920s, front-page newspaper coverage of *la circulation*, the traffic circulation problem across Paris, was second only to *la vie chère* of postwar inflation. In this discussion, *L'Intransigeant* came down fully on the side of the automobile: "The street is not a garage. It exists for the swift flow of traffic. Those who cannot follow at this speed obstruct traffic. Even if the street belongs to everyone, it is not for those who obstruct it."[64] To facilitate the flow of automobile traffic, the newspaper suggested banning horse-drawn carts in the city altogether, moving bus stops to the sides of the street (rather than the center), consolidating bus lines, and terminating overland rail systems on the periphery of the city. Further, it advocated posting traffic signals on street corners, widening commercial streets for truck transportation, and combining electric, gas, compressed air, and water lines in common underground canals. Finally, the newspaper praised the city's *Comité de la circulation* for having recently adopted many of these suggestions. *L'Intransigeant* fully ascribed to an ethos of modern and rational urban development.

Since February 1924, when Aragon first read in the pages of *L'Intransigeant* that boulevard Haussmann had reached rue Laffitte, until the arcade's destruction a year later, the daily proclaimed its open hostility to the continued existence of the Opera Passageway as an obstruction to rational urban design. The newspaper charted the advancement of boulevard Haussmann from rue Tailbout to rue Laffitte, to rue Drouot, and finally to the boulevard des Italiens.[65] Over the course of that year, the Opera Passageway was frequently discussed in *L'Intransigeant* and always in derisive terms. In the summer of 1924, the newspaper printed a photograph of the facade of the *"Passages de l'Opéra, Galerie Baromètre"* and noted with disappointment that the inhabitants were refusing to leave their shops, despite the fact that this was the final building standing in the way of the completion of boulevard Haussmann.[66] In January of 1925, the newspaper carried a photograph of Vincent's barbershop, depicting two middle-aged barbers attending to customers seated along the mirror-lined walls. After the fifteenth of January, the newspaper gloated, the passageway's barber would be forced to abandon his "salon."[67] At the end of February, *L'Intransigeant* published a photograph of old shopsigns being removed from the passageway's facade in order to make room for the new, glamorous signs that would soon illuminate the future boulevard Haussmann.[68] The newspaper expressed no sympathy for the residents of two hundred apartments destroyed in the course of the arcade's demolition. Instead, it complained that promised new apartment buildings had not yet been constructed and that the Chaussée d'Antin subway station had not been completed.

The newspaper's position against the Passages de l'Opéra had been made clear by Lucien Descaves early in the fall of 1924.[69] After Aragon's articles had already begun appearing in the *Revue Européenne* that summer, Descaves posed the question: Why all this fuss about the destruction of the Opera Passageway? The Salmon and Pont-Neuf arcades had disappeared without any great commotion, he noted. The latter had been discredited by no less than Emile Zola (in *Thérèse Raquin*). Besides, Descaves claimed, there were still the Panoramas and other passageways—the Passages Jouffroy, Verdeau, Vivienne, Colbert, Choiseuil, and Madeleine. "If that doesn't suffice," he concluded, "then you're being difficult."

Descaves's own journalism career had begun in the Opera Passageway, working for the weekly magazine *L'Événement*, which had published out of the arcade for two decades. The magazine's owner, Edmond Magnier, was nice enough, Descaves opined, but he was without financial resources, poorly managed a fledgling magazine, and lacked commercial ambition. (Descaves found the same faults in the passageway's aging barbers.) Ultimately, it boiled down to the fact that the Opera Passageway had always been a commercial and urban backwater. Quoting from Alfred Delvau's 1867 *Les Lions du jour*, Descaves reiterated: "A passageway is a sort of jetty going through freestone, which assists pedestrians in cutting from one street to another, rather than being swept along by the flow of traffic. But what distance does the Opera Passageway diminish? What kind of shortcut is it?. . . . " The principal defect of the Opera Passageway was that it had no rational function within the overall design of the city. Providing shelter from the rain no longer sufficed.

It is within the context of *L'Intransigeant*'s heralding of a narrowly commercial conception of urban modernization, and the venom it displayed for the continued existence of the Opera Passageway as an impediment, that Aragon's choice to locate his surrealist musings within the arcade assumes an immediate and localized political meaning. As a direct rebuke to the newspaper, Aragon championed all the attributes of the arcade that were despised by the modernizers. Like his fellow surrealists

Francis Picabia and Marcel Noll, he had rented hotel rooms let by the week or month and he frequented the arcade's brothels and public baths.[70] Like Philippe Soupault and André Breton, Aragon delighted in the campy melodramas staged in the Théâtre Moderne.[71] The principal activity of the Opera Passageway was *flânerie*. The slothful pleasures of daydreaming, intoxication, idle conversation, and illicit sexual contact determined its entertainment value. But beyond these immediate sensual satisfactions, the Passages de l'Opéra provided a shortcut to the surrealist imagination.

THE IMAGINARY CITY

> You see, dear reader, living in Paris costs less than at home.
> Paris is Paradise for travelers of limited means.
> All pleasures, all comforts, are possible for a modest sum.
> Here, no one cares how you support your lifestyle.
> In a word, it's anonymity.
> You are free to do whatever you like.
> *Guide de Poche 1900*

Aragon cared about the decrepit Opera Passageway insofar as it inspired him to surrealist visions. Aragon's concrete experiences of wandering about the arcade were poetically transposed into writing. The meandering design of *Le Paysan de Paris* was designed to reproduce a corollary surreal effect upon the reader's imagination, forcing out familiar reading habits through a continually shifting textual terrain of random juxtapositions and metamorphosing visions.[72] To accomplish this, Aragon wrote a guide to the surrealist imagination in the style of a guidebook to Paris.

To understand this design, it helps to compare *Le Paysan de Paris* with actual guidebooks to Paris. In the opening portion of the novel, Aragon systematically takes the reader through the Opera Passageway, noting location numbers and giving a brief characterization of each shop. He enters the "Gallery of the Thermometer" at the Eugène Rey bookstore (where one could read magazines without having to buy them), pauses briefly at no. 2 (the concierge's lodging), continues on to the cane shop (of prostitute-sirens), and so on to *Le Petit Grillon* café, the ladies' and men's hairdressers, and to the shop of Vodable, "The Gentleman's Tailor." After moving down and back up that gallery, Aragon then crosses over to the Gallery of the Barometer, where his wandering leads to his two favorite spots in the arcade, the Théâtre Moderne and the Certa café. Throughout, Aragon describes his field of vision, notes unusual juxtapositions of objects filling the arcade's shops, comments upon the activities of its inhabitants, and lets his mind wander into philosophical speculations and flights of fancy. The book's documentary style is punctuated with surreal visions. It is a guidebook to surrealism.

Yet by employing this design, Aragon implicitly reminds the reader that actual guidebooks also rely upon imaginary visions, albeit in a greatly weakened form. Contemporary walking guides to Paris, such as the *Guide pratique à travers le Vieux Paris,* employed strolling techniques similar to Aragon's.[73] Readers were invited down orderly, textual promenades of Parisian neighborhoods and boulevards; the contemporary location of businesses and buildings were identified, as were the historical associations such places should evoke. A typical promenade was "Number 15, Neighborhoods of The Trinity and Our Lady of Lorette," a tour of the ninth *arrondissement* that included the Opera Passageway.[74] The guide led the reader down rue Caumartin (nos. 65 to 1) and then turned right up the boulevard de la Madeleine ("the even-numbered buildings are built on the site of the former rue Basse-du-Rempart, which extended down to the city wall built by Louis xiii"). The guide next led the reader down the boulevard des Capucines, which featured the place de l'Opéra ("built between 1858 and 1864, where Charles Garnier's opera house was constructed from 1861 to 1875"). After a brief detour down the rue de la Chaussée-d'Antin ("it was called rue Mirabeau in 1791") and rue Meyerbeer ("[Léon] Gambetta resided at number 55"), the guide arrived at the boulevard des Italiens: "Number 12. Opera Passageway (1823), opens to the Morel-Vindé Hotel, previously known as the Gramont Hotel; it led to the Opera on rue Le Peletier."[75] The walking itinerary continued for another dozen pages, among which the Opera passageway was one of the least remarkable notations.

But by now, this guide to *Vieux Paris* had established an imaginary affinity with surrealism; through the written text, the reader was required to imagine himself immersed in impossible simultaneities of time and space—a watered-down version of Benjamin's adage about the surreal power of words to supersede material reality: "Language takes precedence."[76] Overly pedantic, banal, and narrowly limited in its vision, the guide nevertheless asked the reader to imagine that the sites existed in spaces simultaneously occupied by Roman Lutèce, medieval, aristocratic, revolutionary, and contemporary Paris. It invited the reader to envision features no longer there—a road now filled by rows of buildings, streets and buildings with alternate names, the Le Peletier opera house (which had burned down in 1873). As such, this guide to *Vieux Paris* was a catalog of impossible classifications, a morass of details about which cardinal lived here or which duchess lived there, a literary reference from the nineteenth century, the name of a café from two hundred years earlier. In its textual excess, the reality of the lived-city was displaced by the presence of words.

Some guidebooks also played to the sensual desires of their readers. The illicit pleasures Aragon enjoyed in the Opera Passageway were the subject of another genre of commercial guides. The *Guide des Plaisirs à Paris*, for example, instructed the French-speaking tourist in Paris on "How to have a good time, Where to have a good time, What you have to see, What you have to know, How you have to do it."[77] In this guide to "Paris Pleasures," tourists were given a textual promenade through the low-life entertainments of Montmartre cabarets, public balls, after-hours restaurants, and the underground dens of criminals, prostitutes, and transients (pl. 3).

Vastly outstripping the repertoire of the Opera Passageway, the *Guide des Plaisirs à Paris* provided readers with countless opportunities to purchase pleasure. If one went to *L'Abbaye de Thélème* after hours, this otherwise respectable restaurant was transformed into a "Rabelaisian Love Mass" from ten o'clock at night until sunrise. One could frequent *Le cabaret de l'Enfer* ("Hell Cabaret"), which required purchasing a ticket "Good for entry into the Hot Pot" (*à la chaudière*), or the macabre *Le cabaret du Néant* ("Obliteration Cabaret"), where the customers were called *asticots de cercueil* ("coffin worms"). For voyeurs, the lesbian bar

Plate 3. Cover of *Guide des Plaisirs à Paris,* c. 1900. (Special Collections: California State University, Hayward Library)

Le Hanneton ("The Beetle") was characterized by the guide as a "must-see pathological curiosity." The guide also provided information about the dangerous and sordid realms of Paris (*les dessous*), low-life bars such as *Le Chien-qui-fume* ("The Smoking Dog") and underground restaurants such as *Le Père Coupe-Toujours* ("Father Always-Cuts-the-Drinks"). Readers also learned about the nocturnal byways of Les Halles and the open-air dances located on the netherworlds of the Paris periphery (*bals de barrières*), but they were advised that none but the courageous should frequent them. The guidebook even had a dictionary of French slang at the back, so that the tourist could feign familiarity with local speech.

This genre of guidebook was available to the English-speaking tourist of Paris as well. Prohibition-fleeing tourists from America may have delighted in Basil Woon's *The Paris That's Not in the Guidebooks*, and Bruce Reynolds's *Paris With the Lid Lifted* and *A Cocktail Continentale* ("Concocted in 24 Countries, Served in 38 Sips, and a Kick Guaranteed").[78] On a certain level, the textual appeals to unbridled sensuality found in these "pleasure guides" were no less imaginary than Aragon's book, and they certainly offered a more abundant selection. But a crucial distinction separated this genre from his "Baedeker of Hives," articulated in a phrase found on the cover of the *Guide des Plaisirs à Paris*: "With this guide, one can set a budget for one's pleasures in advance." *Renseignements*—information and instructions—was the overriding principle in all such "practical" guides: which attractions and monuments to see, which restaurants to frequent (and how much it would cost), prices for ground transportation, and tables of monetary exchange rates. Above all, commercial guides protected readers against the dangers of being disoriented and lost in Paris. But such a loss of bearings was precisely what the surrealists wanted their readers to experience.

Therein lay the critical difference in imaginary trajectory. Commercial guidebooks organized tourists' expectations of the city, whereas the surrealist authors of Paris sought to destabilize their readers' imaginations. In the novels of Aragon, Breton, and Soupault, the experiences of wandering through Paris were given form as surrealist literature. Various explanations have been offered for how their experiences were transposed into writing. In *Le Paysan de Paris*, Aragon identified the libido as the unconscious force attached to his field of vision.[79] Some years later in *Les Vases communicants*, Breton claimed that material things themselves exercise a powerful influence upon the mind as an invitation to "come to the other side" (*passer le pont*), in the same way that the elements of a dream control the dreamer.[80]

Contemporary critics have developed these ideas further. Literary critic Rose M. Avila has located the origin of Aragon's surrealist visions in a sublime bodily frisson, in which external reality and the poet's pleasure principle paradoxically merged into each other.[81] Art critic Hal Foster claims that Aragon and Breton used the technique of the *dérive*, aimless wandering through the outmoded quarters of the city without forethought or plan, as a method for provoking uncanny experiences that were then recorded as surrealist texts.[82] Literary theorist Margaret Cohen has sought an Althusserian structural corollary to the libido in the Parisian landscape itself, whereby the intersection of the totality of economic, social, political, and ideological discourses creates "the collective equivalent to the individual unconscious."[83] Yet by whatever method those surrealist authors fused material reality with their imaginations, the pleasures discovered by readers of their novels were provoked by the printed word. As literary critic Peter Collier has emphasized, while strolling and the free play of desire were experiential motors for Aragon and Breton, ultimately their fantastic and impossible writings were what mattered most, "a collage of rival texts, creating a new reality transgressing the framework both of traditional text and conventional reality."[84] Paris was an ideal setting for *Le Paysan de Paris*, *Nadja*, and *Les Dernières Nuits de Paris*, for the city landscape leant itself to surreal juxtapositions whose corollary written texts forced readers' minds out of everyday concerns and mental habits.

A dim awareness of the city's capacity to overwhelm the tourist was a latent dimension even in "practical guides" to Paris. In addition to organizing a vast amount of information about the city, these guidebooks provided instructions on how to safely traverse this potentially threatening environment. One such guide, *Guide de Poche 1900*, was written for budget-conscious French provincials ("How to get by in Paris on 4 or 5 francs a day") coming to Paris to visit the Universal Exhibition. The first chapter of the guidebook was devoted to forewarning the reader of the certain dangers befalling the provincial tourist.[85] When arriving in the station, the guide warned, wait until the train completely stops before disembarking, for disoriented movements may result in physical injury. Once inside the station, beware of station porters who may steal your bags or demand exorbitant tips, or of seemingly friendly con-men who smile as they fleece you of wallet, purse, or suitcase (*vol à l'américaine*). Once outside the station, be on guard for thieving taxi drivers (*maraudeurs de nuit*). But above all, the guide emphasized, know where you are going in advance. The best housing arrangements are those made by parents or family acquaintances, but if you have neither, write to us at the guide and we will send you a complimentary list of recommended hotels. After a brief account of how to plan one's budget wisely, the remainder of the guidebook described famous locations and monuments of Paris and was illustrated with sketches of *pittoresque* Parisian street types.

With the guidance of the *Guide de Poche*, even provincials of limited means could avoid the certain but unknown dangers of the city. Other and more familiarly known commercial guides, like Baedeker's *Guides* and Hachette's *Guides Bleus*, were pitched to a middle-class clientele. Since the urban dangers associated with traveling on a shoestring budget were not as great a concern for the bourgeois traveler, these guidebooks focused their efforts upon "reliable information." The guides contained everything the traveler could possibly want to know, "to employ his time, his money, and his energy so that he may derive the greatest possible amount of pleasure and instruction from his visit."[86]

Both Baedeker's and the *Guides Bleus* (previously *Guides Joanne*) had been published in multiple editions since the mid-nineteenth century.[87] Each volume opened with practical information about how to get around the city and where to find essential services such as hotels, restaurants, the post office, monetary exchange offices, theaters, music halls, concerts, sporting clubs, and foreign embassies. An historical essay on French history and art followed. The guides established itineraries for touring the city based upon the divisions of Right Bank, the Cité, and Left Bank. All of the museums in Paris were listed, with a complete inventory of all of the collections in the Louvre (which constituted a substantial portion of each guide). Typically, the guides ended with brief descriptions of Versailles, Fontainebleau, Château-Thierry, Chantilly, and St. Denis (more fully detailed in an additional *Environs de Paris* volume). Throughout each guidebook, multiple maps were inserted in the text, together with a detachable map book located at the end of the volume, so the reader could always cross-reference his location.

While the *Guide de Poche* explicitly warned its readers about an urban terrain fraught with danger, Baedeker's handbooks and the *Guides Bleus* implicitly guarded their patrons against direct contact with the actual city. Under the guise of being authoritatively informative, the instructions provided guidance to make it possible for the tourist to traverse Paris without anxiety. Moreover, the various editions of Baedeker's and the *Guides Bleus* maintained a standard format that played down actual urban transformations and helped the reader familiar with the format feel at home. A stable text stood in for a constantly changing city. As such, commercial guidebooks to Paris constituted an extremely narrow kind of modern imagination for its readers, a monumental ideology devoid of historical processes and social references.[88]

The surrealist impulses in *Le Paysan de Paris*, *Nadja*, and *Les Dernières Nuits de Paris*, by contrast, ran in the opposite direction. The "anxious visions," as Sidra Stich has characterized the psychological effect of surrealist art,[89] of those books challenged their readers' imaginations to achieve a level of mental complexity equal to the unconstrained urban landscape. In those surrealist novels, there was nothing precious about the city itself. If Paris had been the capital of Europe in the nineteenth century, for the surrealists it was the *capitale de la douleur*, painfully giving birth to the twentieth century.[90] Whether the newborn would develop a surreal consciousness was uncertain. As Philippe Soupault commented about Georgette and her brother Octave in *Les Dernières Nuits de Paris*, two ordinary Parisians with whom the novel's narrator earlier had been fascinated, but was now just bored:

> One day, in a café—one of those cafés they love so much—I saw them listening with particular attention to a refrain spit out by a gramophone: it was the hackneyed of the hackneyed:
>
> *Paris, c'est une blonde.*
> *Paris unique au monde.*
>
> The imbecilic words spilled themselves before them and they listened with open mouths, ravished, convinced.[91]

Soupault's recasting of Mistinguett's popular song, *Ça, c'est Paris!* ("Paris is a blonde/Paris, unique in the world") expressed the denouement of consciousness, not its liberation. As it was commercially configured, nothing about the city automatically invoked surrealism.

At the same time, Paris was at the center of the surrealist revolution in consciousness. As a continually transforming urban landscape, the city overflowed with a concentration of ready-made materials that the surrealists hoped they could poetically reconfigure for a revolutionary audience.[92] Mass culture was the common denominator of consumer capitalism, but its meaning was not restricted to a bourgeois conception of social order or its entrepreneurial values. A prescient surrealist forebear, Baudelaire had recognized half a century earlier in "The Painter of Modern Life" that the spectacle of modern life could be detached from inherited aesthetic traditions and reformulated into instantaneous images which captured the ephemeral beauty of the present moment.[93] In many ways, *Le Paysan de Paris* was Aragon's extensive soliloquy to the same. Neither logic, philosophy, nor religion could guide an individual reliably through modern life in any meaningful way, Aragon concluded in "The Peasant's Dream" at the end of his novel. Rather, he appealed to individuals to give poetic form to their own, concrete experiences of the contemporary world.[94]

Such poetic reconfigurations could be cached nearly anywhere, even in the pages of Aragon's nemesis, *L'Intransigeant*. During the summer of 1924, the same time that the newspaper was gloating about the imminent demolition of the Opera Passageway, *L'Intransigeant* carried a series of front-page commentary articles by eminent artists and authors on the imaginary dimensions of life in contemporary Paris. In a characterization more modernist than surreal, Fernand Léger compared Paris to a gigantic movie. The spectacle of modern life, Léger suggested, is a vast electric and mechanical spectacle of rapidly multiplying images, conducted by an accelerating current, a expansive network within which humans move in rhythm.[95] In an intermittent column titled "Petits Films de Paris," novelist Pierre Mac Orlan discovered a "new romanticism" in the shadows of Parisian nightlife. The lures of old criminal underworld haunts of the Belle Époque, Mac Orlan noted, were being superseded by the charms of modern fox-trot bars.[96] According to poet André Salmon, the city produced "unconscious poets" across the social spectrum; bank tellers who dream they are in nightclubs while on the job, chauffeurs who create collages out of magazine advertisements, and little boys who mistake the métro kiosk for a movie-ticket counter ("Excuse me please, but when does the next Charlot [Charlie Chaplin] movie begin?").[97]

Even surrealist Philippe Soupault took his turn writing for *L'Intransigeant*.[98] In "Our Other Daily Bread, 'My Newspaper,'" Soupault wrote about the inestimable influence of the daily paper upon the contemporary mentality. Thanks to a single, folded piece of newsprint, produced in concert with the telegraph, the telephone, and the typewriter, time and space had ceased to be meaningful as categories. "Our newspaper" not only tells us about "our neighborhood," he noted, but about what is happening in San Francisco and in Timbuktu as well. In the cold light of rationality, he emphasized, there is no reason that we have to know about some man who has just won the lottery, the sudden death of some forty-eight-year-old millionaire, or the automobile accident of Baroness X. These *things* interest us, Soupault asserted, simply because we have developed a taste for reading them, on a daily basis. And we have come to believe that we *must* read about them, on a daily basis.

Thanks to the international daily newspaper, Soupault believed his consciousness was simultaneously connected with thousands, or even millions, of other readers: "Faithful readers, we are not isolated, and we hear the heartbeat of the world itself." The details in the press that fascinated Soupault, and that he assumed also seized the minds of sympathetic readers, fed the eccentric and insolent spirit of surrealism itself. In this way, mass culture contained both the raw materials and poetic visions ready to assist the surrealist revolution in consciousness. The urban landscape of Paris inspired poetry. Surreal gems could be unearthed from the most banal sources of print mass culture. The 1920s seemed primed for the surrealist revolution.

2 The Lament of Fantômas

THE POPULAR NOVEL AS MODERN MYTHOLOGY

Listen up all! . . . Silence please.
To these acts lamentable.
Of crimes unmentionable.
Tortures and brutalities
Ever unpunished, alas!
By the criminal, Fantômas.

Robert Desnos, *La Complainte de Fantômas*

On the third of November 1933, radio audiences throughout France and Belgium listened to a reading by poet Robert Desnos of his *Complainte de Fantômas*, set to music by Kurt Weill.[1] In twenty-five cantos, Desnos had created an epic poem out of the thirty-two *Fantômas* detective novels by Pierre Souvestre and Marcel Allain, published two decades earlier as part of Arthème Fayard's "Popular Book" series. The radio audience awaited the instantaneous shivers guaranteed in the recounting of the exploits of the villainous Fantômas, his mistress Lady Beltham, his nemeses Inspector Juve and the journalist Fandor, and Hélène, the tormented daughter of Fantômas.

Desnos's "Lament" was the swan song of a surrealist fascination with *Fantômas*. Anyone who stumbles across secondary references to *Fantômas* discovers the litany of surrealists and avant-garde aesthetes who celebrated the series—Guillaume Apollinaire, Louis Aragon, André Breton, Colette, Blaise Cendrars, Jean Cocteau, Juan Gris, Max Jacob (who, together with Apollinaire, founded a *Société des Amis de Fantômas*), René Magritte, André Malraux, Ernest Moerman, and Philippe Soupault, among others.[2] The implication is nearly always that the success of the series benefited enormously from the support of the surrealists and the literary avant-garde. *Fantômas* has gained thereby a sort of "high culture" status by association, a popular corollary to Lautréamont's *Chants de Maldoror*. Some critics claim that without the support of surrealists there would have been no myth of *Fantômas*. Others consider *Fantômas* neither mythic nor popular, despite its reputation, and the sooner forgotten the better.[3]

But much of the commentary on *Fantômas* has gotten the set of historical and cultural influences backward. Viewed chronologically, it becomes clear that the cultural dynamism of the series came first. *Fantômas* was pure pulp carnival, a mishmash of flat characters, stilted dialog and cheap thrills, the popular-novel equivalent of the melodramas staged in the Théâtre Moderne so affectionately described by Aragon in *Le Paysan de Paris* and Breton in *Nadja*. The narrative trappings of *Fantômas* were arcane, melodramatic, Belle Époque schlock—the "family circle" of principal players, the Manichaean opposition of good versus evil, the sublimity of overstated rhetoric, and the spectator's total pleasure in riding along for the performance. Yet *Fantômas* exceeded the boundaries of its melodramatic trappings. Moral restitution was fundamentally denied through the motif of the escape of Fantômas at the end of each episode. All the reader was left with was an endless, yet predictable, string of murders, thefts, disguises, pursuits, traps, confrontations, arrests, and escape—and not a bit of it plausible.

Desnos captured a sense of the cultural dynamism of *Fantômas* in the "Lament." The poem overflows with horrific images, poetic equivalents to the original lurid, full-color book covers illustrated by Gino Starace. In a large bell, a mustachioed artisan hangs upside down as a human clapper, swinging from side to side, raining blood, sapphires and diamonds onto the street below. A low-life tavern proprietress, La Toulouche, recovers a treasure box from the entrails of a cadaver, surrounded by a gang of Parisian underworld *apaches* with monikers like "Pretty Boy" (*Beaumôme*), "Bull's Eye" (*Oeil-de-Boeuf*) and "Gas Pipe" (*Bec-de-Gaz*). Masked bandits brandishing revolvers drive a city bus into a bank, bursting through walls, crashing into counters, strewing money all about. Under gray Parisian skies, a horse-drawn taxi aimlessly clops down the road, with a wide-eyed corpse as its coachman.

And who—or what—creates these horrific scenes? Fantômas! Fantômas strips the gilding from the dome of the Invalides each night. Fantômas poisons a baroness with opium-laced bouquets of black roses. Fantômas releases plague-infested rats upon ocean liners and crashes passenger trains. Yet the ever-vigilant Inspector Juve of the Sûreté is always close behind. Assisted by Jérôme Fandor, young and energetic journalist for the Parisian daily *La Capitale*, the heroic duo are determined to pursue the "Genius of Crime" until they catch him at last. But Fantômas *always* escapes.

This "song of Fantômas," Desnos concluded, this image of evil whose very name evokes involuntary shudders, is dedicated to all the people of France and throughout the world—from Montmartre, to the Eiffel Tower and Montparnasse, and far beyond, to England, Holland, Monte Carlo, Rome, Moscow, South Africa, and Mexico. After wishing his listening audience a long life, Desnos left this final, parting image:

> His boundless shadow extends
> Over Paris and all coasts.
> What then is this gray-eyed ghost
> Whose silence surges within?
> Might it be you, Fantômas,
> Lurking upon the rooftops?

The geographical point of origin was Paris, but the cultural topography was imaginary and international. The immense shadow of Fantômas, for Desnos and the surrealists, was a metaphor for a surreal epoch. *Fantômas* was not an image created by the surrealists, but rather a dark spectacle viewed by them, part of an emergent modern mythology in the early decades of the twentieth century.

This chapter examines *Fantômas* within a wider cultural realm of popular crime fiction in early twentieth-century France. My argument is that *Fantômas* was surreal before the letter, and the surrealists later recognized the "Lord of Terror" as their confrère. In the twilight of the Belle Époque, *Fantômas* was a crime-fiction sensation, creating popular entertainment out of indeterminate identities, incoherences of time and space, technological gadgetry, and unmotivated violence. During the interwar period, the surrealists and other avant-garde aesthetes incorporated Fantômas imagery and iconography into their own works. What the surrealists added to *Fantômas* was a critical perspective, an ambivalent relationship with popular crime fiction that attempted to release the more fantastical elements of detective stories from their bourgeois social moorings.

The popular effect of *Fantômas* was carnivalesque but in a peculiarly twentieth-century fashion. *Fantômas* operated outside logic and deduction, and it offered no moral or social restitution. Instead, it was a *récit impossible*, an impossible story of displaced identities, detours, paradoxes, and violence. The crime serial was a mass-culture compendium of a surreal, modern mythology in the process of formation. A carnival open to all, at sixty-five centimes per novel, *Fantômas* was practically free.

LE LIVRE POPULAIRE

The story of *Fantômas* begins before the appearance of the first novel, with the *Livre Populaire* series of inexpensive novels published by the Parisian firm Fayard in the opening decade of the twentieth century. In 1894, Arthème Fayard II inherited the publishing house after the death of his father, who founded the business nearly forty years earlier. The younger Fayard brought an expansive entrepreneurial spirit into his father's company. In a bold marketing move, Fayard founded the "Modern Library" (*Modern Bibliothèque*) of complete and illustrated literary volumes at 95 centimes each. Priced at substantially less than the standard book price of 3 francs 50, Fayard astutely reasoned that volume — in the range of hundreds of thousands of imprints—would create the margin of profit.

The "Modern Library" series was so successful that, in 1905, Fayard introduced *Le Livre Populaire,* or "Popular Book" series. Similarly minded publishers had also begun to produce cheap series of popular adventure and detective novels, such as *Le petit livre* ("The Little Book") by J. Férenczi, *Le livre national* ("The National Book") by Jules Tallandier, and pocketbook-format novels by Pierre Lafitte. When Fayard developed the *Livre Populaire* series, he responded to this competition by lowering the cost per volume to sixty-five centimes (the cost of a week's worth of a daily newspaper) and increasing the number of pages. Displaying full-color illustrated paper jacketcovers, Fayard's advertising promised, "The Popular Book series is the only collection that offers the reader, for a mere 65 centimes, in volumes of 400 to 800 pages, complete works by our most famous and popular novelists. Beware of Imitations!"[4] Never mind that the print was minuscule and often smeared or illegible (which later led surrealist poet and detective novelist Léo Malet to comment, "I always suspected that by economizing on ink, Fayard hoped to render the working class blind as well!"), the point was that virtually anyone could afford to buy one of these books.[5]

Most of the books in the original *Livre Populaire* series of 112 novels, published from 1905 to 1914, were reprints of nineteenth-century popular novels that had originally appeared as *feuilletons*—novels serialized in newspaper daily installments. Illustrator Gino Starace designed the covers of the original series.[6] A wide range of genres was represented within *Le Livre Populaire,* from such "social" novels as *Les Mystères de Paris* by Eugène Sue, *Les Mystères de Londres* by Paul Féval, *Les Ouvrières de Paris* by Pierre Decourcelle, and *La Porteuse de pain* by Xavier de Montépin, to the "sword-and-cape" adventures of *Carot Coupe-Tête* by Maurice Landay and *Les Pardaillan* by Michel Zévaco.

The "Popular Book" series also reprinted works by Emile Gaboriau (1832–73), the father of the French detective novel, including *La Corde au Cou, Le Dossier No. 113, L'Affair Lerouge,* and *M. Lecoq.* Unlike the nineteenth-century detectives of America and England, such as Edgar Allan Poe's chevalier C. Auguste Dupin or Arthur Conan Doyle's Sherlock Holmes, Gaboriau's detective, Monsieur Lecoq, was not an amateur sleuth but an inspector of the Sûreté, the investigative branch of the

French police system. The French detective story based upon the exploits of police inspectors extended back to the highly embellished *Mémoires* of Sûreté chief detective François Vidocq (1775–1857). Nineteenth-century French literature developed a popular tradition of Sûreté inspectors as detectives in adventure novels. Within this tradition, the principal detective in *Fantômas* is Inspector Juve of the Sûreté.

Among the nineteenth-century series of novels reprinted in *Le Livre Populaire*, undoubtedly *Rocambole* by Ponson du Terrail (1829–71) had the closest affinities to *Fantômas*.[7] The novels glorified a *justicier* avenger named Rocambole, whose adventures were entirely implausible and wholly imaginary. In them, Paris was populated by false princes and stranglers from Bombay. Since police and the institutions of the law were completely unable to stop these exotic and nefarious bandits, the series relied upon Rocambole as the pivotal action character. The adoption of the adjective *rocambolesque*, "resembling by its astonishing improbabilities (*invraisemblances*) the adventures of Rocambole," speaks to the lasting impact of the series upon French cultural memory.[8]

Popularity based upon a broad readership, rather than the supposed values of "the people," is the key ingredient toward understanding what was "popular" in these nineteenth-century novels. Generally, these authors presented "the people" as a degraded class of sordid habits and displaying a propensity toward criminality.[9] The morally virtuous working-class characters in these novels bore unmistakable affinities to their bourgeois authors. Despite social criticisms of squalid urban environments contributing to human degradation, these popular-novel authors seemed committed to the bourgeois correction of their lower-class subjects. Such nineteenth-century novels were not popular because of these bourgeois virtues, however, but because they constituted a nineteenth-century version of the carnivalesque.

According to Jean-Claude Vareille, a leading French critic of *para-littérature*, the carnivalesque features of a nineteenth-century popular novel are not the same as those identified by the well-known literary formalist, Mikhail Bakhtin. In contrast to Bakhtin's method of dialogic "heteroglossia," which teases a contested ideological terrain out of sophisticated literary texts, Vareille finds a carnivalesque quality in the excesses and inversions of the "monologic" characteristics that overdetermine the meaning of nineteenth-century popular novels.[10] That is, the structure of popular novels is built upon strict oppositions of interdiction versus transgression, the law versus crime, the quotidian versus the exceptional, the categorical versus the ludic. The polyphonic effect in these popular novels, Vareille asserts, was created by repetitious, melodramatic interplays between flat characters and Manichean oppositions. Peter Brooks has argued along similar lines that metaphoric gesture in melodramatic texts "evokes meanings beyond its literal configuration."[11] The ability of these novels to exceed their genre form opened them to popular interpretations beyond the values of their bourgeois authors.

This interaction between the stilted dialogue of flat character types, and the nearly endless repetition of limited story plots, invited a certain kind of popular imaginary reading. The reader derived pleasure not from a sophisticated literary construction but from the exploits and details that filled a highly melodramatic form. The reader of *Fantômas* already knew, for example, that Fantômas "did it" (every time) and that he would escape (every time). But it was exactly *how* he did it, and how he would escape, that one had to read for in each episode. Such a combination of structural constraints and rhetorical excesses was not accidental; indeed, it was intrinsic to the "melodrama of psychology" in such popular novels.[12] These melodramatic constraints were modern in the sense that they provided a new yet familiar set of cultural expectations during a century in which socioeconomic modernization was rapidly eroding traditional social values.[13] These features were precisely what made these nineteenth-century novels popular.

In this tradition, *Fantômas* has been identified as the final and supreme example of the *roman populaire*. One notable popular-novel feature in *Fantômas* is its "pastiche of orality," or a predominance of dialog over description.[14] The conversations in *Fantômas* are highly theatrical, continually stating and restating the obvious in stilted and overdrawn terms. When Fantômas asks Juve's assistance in escaping from prison in return for revealing Fandor's whereabouts, the detective responds, "Help you, Fantômas? No! You are the Genius of Evil. Everything you do yields terrifying results. Never, not for any price, not even the life of Fandor, would I become an instrument of your nefarious work. . . . "[15] Such dialog creates its own sense of enjoyment, beyond the literal meaning of the words themselves.

Another popular-novel feature in *Fantômas* is the meandering storyline, which continually branches off in various directions and decenters the action through innumerable loose ends. Many nineteenth-century popular novels were originally written as *feuilletons*, serialized in newspapers. The fragmented and wandering plots of these novels may be partially accounted for by the time constraints these authors worked under to produce daily installments, as well as the fact that they were paid for their efforts by the line. This episodic construction of the nineteenth-century popular novel often resulted in less-than-meticulously developed characters and plots. In *Fantômas*, the meandering effect resulted from the pressure placed upon Souvestre and Allain to produce a four-hundred page novel every month for thirty-two consecutive months. *Fantômas* marked an increased intensity in cultural production even beyond that of the conventional newspaper *feuilleton*.

This demanding production schedule, however, contributed to *Fantômas* becoming one of the twentieth century's first success stories in pulp fiction. *Fantômas* was one of the few examples within Fayard's "Popular Book" series that was, from its inception, conceived of both as an entirely new series of previously unpublished novels and located within an entirely contemporary era.[16] In April 1910, Fayard approached Souvestre and Allain to discuss launching a new series of detective novels. Pierre Souvestre, Parisian *mondain* and political Bonapartist, was a journalist for *L'Auto* (the sports newspaper ancestor to *L'Équipe*) and an occasional contributor to *Comœdia*. When he met Souvestre in 1906, the younger Marcel Allain was a journalist for a monthly racing magazine, *Le Poids lourd*. Souvestre and Allain's working relationship has often compared to that of their heroes, Juve and Fandor, with Souvestre serving as Allain's mentor. They began collaborating on magazine articles in 1907, and their first fictive work, *Le Rour*, "a great adventure and detective novel," appeared both as a *feuilleton* in *L'Auto* and in a complete volume in 1909.

Fayard was impressed by Souvestre and Allain's second "theatrical and detective" novel, the photograph-illustrated *La Royalda*, published in

Comœdia as a *feuilleton* in 1910. After meeting with Souvestre and Allain that April to discuss launching a detective series for his publishing firm, Fayard presented Souvestre with a contract to produce twenty-four novels over as many months. The series was called "Fantômas," because Fayard had misread Souvestre's suggested title, "Fantômus" (a sort of Latinization of the French *fantôme* which, as Allain later remembered it, they had made up on the subway ride to see Fayard). Inspired by an advertisement (for *Pilules Pink*) of an elegantly dressed, masked man looming over the Parisian landscape and spreading little pink pills everywhere, Fayard replaced the pills with a dagger held behind the masked gentleman's back for the original *Fantômas* book cover and promotional poster (pl. 4).[17] After a few months of haggling over the terms, on 14 January 1911, Souvestre signed the contract with Fayard. The first installment of *Fantômas* appeared the following month. Thus, out of misrecognition (from "Fantômus" to "Fantômas") and excess (thirty-two novels in as many months rather than the originally contracted twenty-four), *Fantômas* became a pulp fiction reality.[18]

A high consumer demand in France for crime and detective stories was already in the making half a decade before *Fantômas*. The "gentleman-burglar" Arsène Lupin short stories by Maurice Leblanc began to appear in the weekly magazine *Je sais tout* in 1905, and were first collected and was released in book form by publisher Pierre Laffitte in 1907. That same year, Gaston Leroux's *Le Mystère de la chambre jaune*, featuring the "extraordinary adventures of Joseph Rouletabille, reporter," appeared in the literary supplement of the weekly *L'Illustration*, and was published as a book by Laffitte in 1908. A master-criminal precursor of Fantômas, *Zigomar* by Léon Sazie, appeared as a *feuilleton* in the daily *Le Journal* in 1909. The popularity of Zigomar, a hooded criminal and murderer who continually evaded the police, was so great that the Pathé film studio commissioned director Victorien Jasset to make Zigomar movies in 1910. Fayard sought to ride the crest of this wave of popularity in France, and *Fantômas* surpassed his expectations.

In addition to a general popular interest in crime and detective stories, French consumers were also growing accustomed to reading about the exploits of their favorite heroes and villains on a regular basis. In the

Plate 4. Cover of the first edition of *Fantômas*, c. 1911. (Collection: Société des Amis de Fantômas, Paris)

opening decade of the twentieth century, independent weekly magazines featuring American detectives became enormously popular in France. For twenty-five centimes an issue, French readers could enjoy thirty-two-page weekly installments of *Nick Carter, le grand détective américain* or, for the even lower price of ten centimes, the adventures of *Nat Pinkerton, le plus illustre détective de nos jours* (loosely inspired by the adventures of American detective Allan Pinkerton).[19] Although the setting was in America, *Nick Carter* and *Nat Pinkerton* were translated into several European languages and were published internationally by Éditions A. Eichler, in Dresden, London, and Paris. In France, both series featured full-color covers and ran continuously from 1907 until the Great War, *Nick Carter* appearing in 273 installments in two series and *Nat Pinkerton* in 322 episodes. Each series was revived in the 1920s, in 169 and 175 issues, respectively.[20]

The *Nick Carter* detective magazines were more stories of criminal and police exploits than puzzles of detection. The titles of the episodes point toward many themes later found in *Fantômas*—murder (*La Pointe du poignard, Un Quadruple assassinat*), horror (*Un Maître du crime, Le Diable dans une maison de fous*), action (*L'Homme aux nerfs d'acier, Une Périlleuse aventure*), mystery (*Dans le Brouillard, Le Singulier nœud coulant*), ruse (*Les Aventures d'un pendu, Le Voleur volé*), movement (*Sur le Chemin des coyotes, La Locomotive no. 13*), and technological wizardry (*Le Mystère du téléphone de l'Hudson, Le Choc électrique*). The adventures were recounted in the active first-person voices of Nick Carter, and his partners Chick and Patsy. Over the course of the series, there were multiple Nick Carters, the creation of various "anonymous" authors, including John Russell Coryell, Thomas Harbough, and Frederick Van Rensselaer Dey. In the 1920s, in separate episodes, each of those three "anonymous" authors killed off the American detective, by suicide, natural causes, and terminal illness. *Fantômas* also shared this tendency to make principal characters appear and disappear, killing them off or resuscitating them, as any particular episode demanded.

In *Fantômas*, the monthly production of complete novels over a period of three years signaled both a quantitative and qualitative augmentation over the weekly detective magazines. To meet the terms of their contract and churn out complete novels of more than 380 pages each month, Souvestre and Allain developed the following writing strategy: During the first week, they outlined the novel, chose chapter titles, and sketched a basic plot outline. Allain conveyed the story line to Gino Starace, who illustrated the cover. For the next two weeks, Souvestre and Allain alternated dictating the stories to secretaries—sometimes onto wax rolls, which were transcribed and submitted for editing. For plot ideas, Souvestre and Allain plagiarized shamelessly—from their own previous works of fiction, as well as from the adventures of Arsène Lupin, Joseph Rouletabille, and Zigomar.[21] During the final week, Souvestre and Allain exchanged copies, wrote transitional paragraphs to get in and out of each other's sections, and submitted the manuscript to Fayard. If the surrealists dreamed of "automatic writing" and "exquisite corpses," Souvestre and Allain cranked out well over 12,000 pages of them in just under three years (a decade later, surrealist Philippe Soupault defied anyone to match such a prodigious output as the coauthors of *Fantômas* without strict obedience to an "absolute psychic automatism").[22]

Fantômas's innovations in mass cultural production were matched by its mass consumption. Fayard published over five million copies of thirty-two *Fantômas* novels, which made it by far the best-selling single series within *Le Livre Populaire*.[23] On the heels of the completion of the novel series, Louis Feuillade directed five *Fantômas* films for Gaumont studios.[24] In July 1914, Guillaume Apollinaire reviewed *Fantômas* in the literary journal *Mercure de France*.[25] The current rage for *Fantômas*, Apollinaire observed, was due to the reciprocal influences of cinema and novel. Although *Fantômas* had attracted a reading audience on all social levels, reaching even into the high literary and artistic world, Apollinaire asserted that there were only a few *bon esprits* who appreciated the series with the same good taste as himself.

Apollinaire's review raises the issue of the attraction of the literary avant-garde, and later the surrealists, to *Fantômas*. How was it that the surrealists, dedicated to the destruction of bourgeois art and society, whose political affinities were with the radical political left, included Fantômas in their pantheon? *Fantômas* was, after all, invented by two very bourgeois journalists, Pierre Souvestre and Marcel Allain, who displayed no great appreciation for the sophisticated literary currents of the era. The series was published by Arthème Fayard, a member of the Action Française (and briefly future editor of *Je suis partout*, the French fascist journal of the 1930s). The five *Fantômas* movies were directed by Louis Feuillade, an ultra-Catholic and political monarchist. It is difficult

to imagine any of these parties lending their signatures to the manifestoes of surrealism—or the surrealists wishing them to do so.

Nonetheless, the surrealists had nothing but praise for the *Fantômas*
novels and movies. Given the chasm between the commercial interests of
its production and the goals of surrealism, the surrealist connection to
Fantômas must be sought at the level of the series itself. Beyond sales figures, *Fantômas* was a highly imaginative genre of popular literature whose
poetics exceeded the social and political conservatism of its production. It
was the surrealist project to liberate such imaginary elements from their
bourgeois constrictions and toward a revolution in consciousness.

> *Fantômas*
> "Fantômas."
> "What did you say?"
> "I said . . . Fantômas."
> "What does that mean?"
> "Nothing . . . and everything."
> "Still, what is it?"
> "Nobody . . . yet nevertheless somebody!"
> "For the last time, what does this somebody do?"
> "Spreads terror!!!"

The opening lines from an after-dinner conversation at the chateau of
the marquise de Langrune are perhaps the most widely quoted passage
of the entire *Fantômas* series. The first of thirty-two novels, *Fantômas* has
been reprinted more than nine times in France and translated into numerous European languages. This initial installment introduced the principal characters and set much of the tone for what would follow. Yet the
epic nature of *Fantômas* emerged only after numerous novels. The most
notable feature of both the title character and the series was that Fantômas was *L'Insaisissable*, "The Unseizable," a never-ending story of elusive
criminals and unstoppable crimes.

The wildly fantastic excesses of *Fantômas* are most obvious from the
grand roman perspective of all thirty-two adventures. Yet the first novel
provides a representative microcosm of the whole. The murder of the
marquise de Langrune in the bedroom of her Dordogne chateau—corpse

sprawled on the floor, a gash in the throat nearly severing the head from the body—provides a horrific opening to *Fantômas*. Etienne Rambert, an elderly businessman and longtime friend of the marquise, arrives at the chateau the next morning. Rambert accuses his son, Charles, of having committed the act, perhaps in a fit of insanity. Soon thereafter, Inspector Juve of the Paris Sûreté, disguised as a vagrant, arrives to investigate the murder. He is about to arrest Charles Rambert for the murder, when both son and father disappear.

Inspector Juve then receives a cable from the Criminal Investigation Department in Paris: "Return immediately to Paris. We are convinced that an extraordinary crime lies behind the disappearance of Lord Beltham. Confidentially, we suspect the hand of Fantômas in it." In Paris, Juve discovers the corpse of Lord Beltham in a trunk in the apartment of a certain Gurn, an English soldier formerly under Lord Beltham's command during the Boer War. Coincidentally, Etienne Rambert reappears and confesses his participation in the accidental drowning of his son to the police. The jury, sympathetic to the grief-stricken and emotionally overwrought father, acquits Rambert of the charge of manslaughter.

Across Paris, Russian princess Sonia Danidoff is robbed at the fashionable Hôtel Palais Royal, located on the Place de l'Étoile at the end of the Champs Élysées: While in her bath, the princess is threatened by a masked man in formal attire, who makes off with 120,000 francs and her diamond necklace. Investigating the case in disguise as businessman Henri Verbier, Juve follows a suspicious hotel cashier, Mademoiselle Jeanne, to her room. When Verbier makes a pass at the young woman, Mademoiselle Jeanne delivers him a knock-out blow. Elsewhere in the hotel, Etienne Rambert receives Mademoiselle Jeanne, who is actually the young Charles Rambert in disguise. Rambert gives his son men's clothing and a wallet full of money, and sends him off.

Later, at a disreputable Montmartre tavern, *Au Cochon de Saint-Antoine* ("St-Anthony's Pig"), Inspector Juve captures the young Rambert. After submitting Charles to a test of physical strength on a "dynamometer" developed by French forensics innovator Alphonse Bertillon, Juve declares the young man physically incapable of having killed the marquise. To protect Charles's identity, Juve renames him "Fandor" ("Fan-" being the prefix to both Fantômas and Fandor, but the name could also mean Juve's "golden boy," *fan-d'or*). Henceforth in the series, Jérôme Fandor is a journalist for the famous Parisian daily, *La Capitale*, and Juve's Fantômas-pursuing companion.

A seemingly unconnected series of events draws the first of the *Fantômas* novels to a close: Gurn is apprehended at the villa of his mistress, Lady Beltham, and taken to the Santé prison to await trial for the murder of Lord Beltham. Fandor brings Juve news concerning the sinking of the passenger steamship *Lancaster*, which listed Etienne Rambert among its victims. Meanwhile, Juve finds a torn map of the Dordogne region in Gurn's apartment that corresponds to a map fragment found earlier near the marquise's chateau. At Juve's request, the marquise's former servant, Dollon, sets off for Paris with the missing fragment. But en route, Dollon is thrown to his death from the train.

Finally, Gurn's trial commences. At the height of the trial, Juve presents a fantastical case of ratiocination against Gurn. The various crimes, Juve claims—the murder of Lord Beltham, the robbery of Sonia Danidoff, the murder of the marquise Langrune, as well as of her servant Dollon—were all committed by the same person. Etienne Rambert, the masked gentleman, and Gurn, are all . . . Fantômas! When the presiding judge questions Juve's story on a number of counts—the unrelated nature of the crimes, the differences in age and constitution between Rambert and Gurn, the death of Rambert aboard the *Lancaster*, Gurn's imprisonment during Dollon's death—Juve simply asserts that Gurn is Fantômas. And for Fantômas, nothing is impossible.

While the court does not accept Juve's Fantômas obsessions as evidence, Gurn is nonetheless sentenced to death for the murder of Lord Beltham. But in a brilliant switch on the morning of the execution, an actor named Valgrand (who has been playing Gurn in a theatrical dramatization of the Lord Beltham affair) is mistakenly guillotined in Gurn's place. In a shock of realization, Juve rushes forward and retrieves the severed head from its basket, covered with actor's make-up and blood. "Curses!" Juve shouts. "Fantômas has escaped! Fantômas is free! He had an innocent man executed in his place! Fantômas! I tell you, Fantômas is alive! . . ."

The subsequent novels establish the recurring features of the series. Any pretense of detection gives way to a succession of exploits, either the elaborate traps and horrific crimes of Fantômas or the obsessive pursuits and daredevil antics of Juve and Fandor. As the emphasis upon activity increased, however, the characters and their relationships to each other ossified. Fantômas reveals himself as one person of countless plastic identities rather than many persons with the same identity. He increasingly appears *en cagoule,* in black tights beneath a cape and cowl. Fandor becomes Juve's inseparable hot-headed young assistant, and the two of them form a kind of father-son relationship. Lady Beltham, the emotionally tormented lover of Fantômas, vacillates between assisting the Lord of Terror and seeking her personal revenge against him. The lowest social echelon of *la pègre,* the "lazy criminal classes" composed of the brutally violent Parisian *apaches* and their *casque d'or* women, constitutes the underworld criminal arm of Fantômas's machinations. Bouzille, a humorous alcoholic tramp who lives on the margins of society and collaborates equally with, Fantômas, Juve and Fandor, becomes the most frequently recurring minor figure.

The most important new character in the series appears in the eighth novel, *La Fille de Fantômas.* Hélène, the daughter of Fantômas, is a modern heroine, an action character who embodies the demonic union of the series. She hates her father, the evil Fantômas, but as a dutiful daughter she is obliged to honor him. She harbors unrequited love for Fandor, but as a skull-tattoo-bearing, occasionally opium-smoking, and often assumed-identity child of the Genius of Evil, Hélène's distrust of Juve keeps her love for Fandor largely unrequited. The only other Fantômas family member, Vladimir, the son of Fantômas, makes a brief appearance late in the series, in *Le Train perdu,* but he is shot and killed in Mexico by Juve eight episodes later in *La Série rouge.* With the inclusion of Hélène, the melodramatic family saga of *Fantômas* is more or less complete.

As a series, *Fantômas* occupies a cultural position at an historical crossroads of popular fiction. In sharp contrast to nineteenth-century sword-and-cape, social, and detective adventure stories, there is little or no concern in *Fantômas* for moral resolution, social progress, or law and order. Action, crime, and horror provide the impetus for telling a story. While the conflict between criminal and detective anticipates the twentieth-century *roman policier,* the narrative structure falls significantly short of the classic murder mystery developed in the 1920s: Those genre narrative devices in murder mysteries generally characterized as the "movement from concealment to disclosure," such as logic-and-detection, the dénouement of the culprit, backward linear construction, or mystery as puzzle, are either missing or flagrantly abused in the *Fantômas* series.[26] There is really never any question of "whodunit": Fantômas, with or without his associates, did it. Every time.

Yet by expanding the notion of what constitutes the enigma at the heart of the mystery, *Fantômas* is closely related to the detective genre: *Fantômas* is a mystery in the sense of being a *récit impossible,* an impossible story of factual indecision, paradoxes, detours, and displaced identities.[27] It was precisely these impossible elements that attracted the surrealists to *Fantômas.* Aesthetes, such as Apollinaire, read *Fantômas* on the surreal level of its imaginary poetics. Surrealist artists and writers incorporated enigmatic *Fantômas* imagery into their own projects. But before examining such surreal appropriations, the impossible *Fantômas* must be examined independently.

MODERN MASKS

To play out their roles, the principal characters in *Fantômas* are often someone else; sometimes they are several characters in the same novel. The art of disguise, including transvestitism, was typical of *justicier,* or avenger, and detective novels in the Belle Époque.[28] But the characters in *Fantômas* are not merely "disguised" as someone else. For the practical purposes of the novel, they actually have to *be* someone else. In *Le Pendu de Londres,* for example, Fantômas not only pretends to be the London dentist Dr. Garrick and the American detective Tom Bob; the story requires that the reader accept him as a known resident of the Putney district and one of Scotland Yard's top Council of Five detectives. Within the first nine *Fantômas* novels, Lady Beltham is the widow of Lord Beltham, the Mother Superior of the Sainte Clotilde convent in Nogent, the grand duchess Alexandra of Hesse-Weimar, Madame Garrick (wife of Dr. Garrick) of London, and secretary Mathilde de Brémonval of the Paris Galleries department store in Paris. In the closing pages of *La Fille de Fantômas*, Teddy, an energetic and athletic male companion to Fandor, is revealed as Hélène, the daughter of Fantômas (in the following episode, *Le Fiacre de nuit*, Fandor occasionally slips into referring to Hélène as "Teddy"). Juve and Fandor, especially the former, frequently disguise themselves as Parisian *apaches* and pass unnoticed among their number not only in dress but in their command of *argot* (street slang) as well.

The characters do not simply "pass for" someone else when they assume these identities: The novel settings and interpersonal relations require that the characters *be* someone else. If merely disguised, how could Dr. Chaleck (Fantômas) practice at the Lariboisière Hospital without being accepted as a surgeon? Or Alexandra (Lady Beltham) be accepted into the Royal Court of Hesse-Weimar? Or Juve pose as Cranajour, when the latter is already a well-known thug among the Parisian *apaches?* The ephemeral qualities of the story turn on these phantasmic identities. In return, countless personalities are infused into a limited cast of characters.

In contrast to the nineteenth-century popular novel, there is no real "unmasking" in *Fantômas*, because there is no real "someone else" behind the mask. The character of Fantômas is the supreme illustration of this, for he only assumes an identity when he is someone else.[29] When he does not assume an identity, he is merely a figure *en cagoule*, a shadow. Over the course of the first twelve novels, Fantômas is businessman Etienne Rambert, an English soldier named Gurn, surgeon Dr. Chaleck, underworld gang-leader Loupart, an esteemed banker named Nanteuil, German ambassador Baron de Naarboveck, the marquis de Sérac of the Court of Hesse-Weimar, concierge Madame Cerion, a tramp called Ouaouaoua, con-man Père Moche, the renowned American detective Tom Bob, London dentist Dr. Garrick, the owner of the Paris Galeries department store Monsieur Chapelard, Russian naval officer Ivan Ivanovitch, Tsar Nicholas II, and an interrogating magistrate from Calais named Pradier. As the series continues, Fantômas's number of aliases diminishes and increasingly he assumes his role *en cagoule*, in black tights, cape and cowl. Under this appearance, however, he loses virtually all physically distinctive features, other than being characterized as having a physically developed, though supple, body. Rather, he directly assumes his archetypal personality as the "Lord of Terror." The "man of a thousand faces" and the "man without a face" are one and the same.

The other master of disguise is Inspector Juve. It is usually made clear to the reader that Juve is "under cover" when he is someone else—most often a vagabond or Parisian *apache* (knowledge of Fantômas's identities, by contrast, is more often withheld). But for Juve as well, the success and identity of his character depends upon the ability to be someone else. In *Le Pendu de Londres*, Juve chooses "Disguise no. 6" for a particularly demanding transformation into "Policeman 416" in London. None of the other characters in the story seem to notice that this British inspector does not speak English, or, if he does, that he has a French accent (it was only in the eleventh novel in the series, *L'Arrestation de Fantômas*, that Souvestre and Allain recognized that the international exploits of Fantômas might entail language difficulties). In *L'Agent secret*, both Fantômas and Juve assume the identity of Valgaulame, an accordion-playing murderer and blackmailer. Not only do the other characters in the novel not realize that Valgaulame is a false identity; they seem unable to tell the difference between the way Fantômas and Juve each have assumed the role.

The significance of Juve's disguises comes out most forcefully in those moments when he and Fantômas are mistaken for each other. The inability to tell the difference between Fantômas and Juve on the basis of appearances emerges with full force at the end of *Un Roi prisonnier de Fantômas*, when Juve is imprisoned by his Sûreté commander, Monsieur Harvard, for actually being Fantômas. Juve's obsessions with Fantômas, and his fantastically elaborated ratiocinations of the criminal's activities, may well have raised suspicions among readers early in the series about the possibility of Juve being Fantômas. Harvard's arrest of Juve cements those suspicions by making clear that all identities revolve around Fantômas. Yet it dispels them as well, for Juve is released at the end of the subsequent episode. In two other instances, Juve willingly assumes the persona of Fantômas—in *Le Magistrat cambrioleur* (resulting once again in Juve's temporary incarceration) and *Le Train perdu* (in which even Fantômas's minions and mistresses mistake the detective for the Lord of Terror). Conversely, Fantômas successfully assumes the identity of Juve in *L'Évadée de Saint-Lazare* and *La Série rouge*. Beyond Edgar Allan Poe's chevalier C. Auguste Dupin, whose exploits required the detective to think like the criminal, the repetitious system of semblances in *Fantômas* blurs all distinctions between the two.

One peculiarly modern aspect of *Fantômas*, then, is that masks and identities are interchangeable, continually changing, and essentially equal. As elaborated by film critic Linda Williams, Fantômas surrealistically functions as a "figure of desire."[30] The character oscillates between being a figure of condensation, in which all crimes and murders are committed by the same Fantômas, and a figure of displacement, whose assumed identities are constantly changing. The point is made explicitly by Juve during a heart-to-heart conversation with Fandor:

> "Who is Fantômas, other than Fantômas? Do you understand me well, Fandor?" Juve continued, becoming increasingly excitable. "Admittedly, we have seen in the course of our checkered existence a distinguished gentleman like Etienne Rambert, a strapping Englishman like Gurn, a vigorous character like Loupart, and a tottering and frail old man like Chaleck. Gradually, we have come to know that each was Fantômas. But that's all we know.
>
> "When Fantômas is seen as he really is, without artifice, undisguised, no paste-on beard or wig, the true visage of Fantômas is under his black cowl. . . . That's what we have never been able to see, and what makes our endless pursuit of the bandit so difficult . . . Fantômas is always someone, sometimes two persons, but never himself."
>
> Once Juve got going on this subject, there was no stopping him, and Fandor did not dare to interrupt. For whenever the conversation turned to Fantômas, the two men were hypnotized by this mysterious being, so well named, for he truly was a phantasm. . . .[31]

At bottom, all masks and disguises are signs of Fantômas, but Fantômas is simultaneously anyone and no one. André Breton opens *Nadja* with the question, "Who am I?" and replies, "I haunt." So does Fantômas.

The clearest expression of the ephemeral Fantômas's ability to "possess" identity comes in the sixth novel in the series, *Le Policier apache.* At the center of the story, the grand duchess Alexandra (Lady Beltham) hosts a masked ball for *Tout Paris* high society. A guest dressed as Fantômas enters the party and takes off his cowl to reveal that he is the American detective Tom Bob (beneath the Tom Bob appearance, the reader later learns, he is Fantômas again). Jérôme Fandor comes dressed as a second Fantômas, but cannot reveal himself to anyone other than the grand duchess Alexandra, for the police are after him as an accomplice of Juve (who has been imprisoned for being Fantômas since the previous episode). A third Fantômas, who later turns out to be a Sûreté police officer, is found dead in the winter garden, stabbed through the heart. But the dying "Fantômas" has managed to stab the arm of his "Fantômas" assassin, whom the cloak room attendant recognizes as Tom Bob. When the police examine Tom Bob's arms, they display no injury. It is *Juve's* arm that bears the mark of the knife slash—even though he has been imprisoned (as Fantômas) in the Santé the entire time. Everyone appears to be Fantômas, but Fantômas cannot reveal himself as Fantômas.

THE SWERVE

One of the fundamental characteristics of the *Fantômas* series is the ability to swerve the story through space and time.[32] Narrative coherence depends upon the title character's capability to be anyone and anywhere, at any time, in order to sustain the action. It is a further condition that the reader set aside the question of what happens to one or another of his identities when Fantômas is yet someone else. Finally, the serial construction of the story required that Fantômas always escape. To enjoy the story, the reader has to accept these fundamental incoherences of time, space, and character. Above all, Fantômas is *l'Insaisissable*, the "Unseizable."

While Paris is the geographic setting for the first six novels, Fantômas often appears in a variety of locations under his various guises, more or less at the same time. In *Un Roi prisonnier de Fantômas,* for example, Fantômas is both the marquis de Sérac and his own concierge, Madame Cerion. Although the reader might accept that Fantômas was Madame

Cerion when he wanted the marquis to be absent, this does not account for what became of *her* while Fantômas was the marquis (or the German ambassador Baron de Naarboveck, or the tramp Ouaouaoua, all of whom appear during the course of the same novel). This ability of characters to continually appear and fade out of existence without anyone noticing was one of the things Breton loved about the melodramas staged in the Théâtre Moderne.[33] Fantômas appears and disappears when the story, not reality, requires.

Hélène, the daughter of Fantômas, is the other main swerve character. Unlike Juve, Fandor, or Lady Beltham, whose identities are more or less stable beneath their disguise aliases, Hélène seeks to abandon her identity as the daughter of Fantômas by becoming someone else. In *La Fille de Fantômas,* her introductory episode, she assumes the identity of a young man named Teddy in order to avoid recognition by her father. When Juve and Fandor discover that Teddy is Hélène, she flees South Africa. In *Le Fiacre de nuit,* when her alias as saleswoman Mademoiselle Raymonde is revealed, she responds by becoming a ship's assistant, a boy named Louis. Throughout the series, Hélène is nearly as likely to assume a masculine identity as a feminine one: She is a Russian sailor in *L'Arrestation de Fantômas,* a valet in *La Guêpe rouge,* a jockey in *Le Jockey masqué,* and a Mexican cowboy in *La Série rouge.* Like her father, evasiveness is Hélène's foremost attribute.

The episodic nature of the series also requires that Fantômas cannot be arrested. In every novel, Juve and Fandor pursue Fantômas, discovering his various identities and connecting each and every horrific crime to him, to the point that by the end of each episode they engage him in a direct confrontation. But in some brilliantly executed dodge, Fantômas always escapes their grasp. This may be either an elaborately planned escape (such as the Valgrand exchange on the scaffold in the first novel), a clever ruse (such as the marquis de Sérac/Fantômas's claim before the police that Juve is Fantômas at the end of *Un Roi prisonnier de Fantômas*), or an implausibly fortuitous accident (as in *Le Policier apache,* when Juve and Fandor unknowingly step upon a bees' nest and run away as Fantômas escapes by standing perfectly still amid the bee swarm). Similarly, Hélène is constantly dodging someone; the familial appeals of her father, the long arm of the law (she frequently finds herself on the wrong side), and the unrequited affections of Fandor.

The perpetual escapes of Fantômas, in perpetual motion, in perpetuity, belie Fayard's claim on the book covers that "Each Volume Contains a Complete Story." The *fin* of each story is in fact an *à suivre* ("to be continued"). The existence of the series required a swerve of some sort —either an impossible pastiche of overlapping characters or an unrealistically contrived escape to the next episode. In this way, *Fantômas* functioned a popular corollary to a surreal dream text. Readers derived pleasure from the process of displacement itself, from a recurring, unending, and continually metamorphosing story.[34] *L'Insaisissable,* Fantômas is the dodge.

TRUQUAGE

The Genius of Crime is not simply, or even primarily, a "human monster." The scale of his crimes do not depend upon Fantômas's inner deformity, biological degeneration, or psychopathology. Rather, his audacity and violence are measured by the wide range of methods, devices and gadgets that he employs to commit those crimes. These *trucs*—technological gadgets or contraptions—form the basis of his outrageous exploits. Such *truquage* gives the series a distinctly modern flavor.

Fantômas loves to commit three kinds of crimes: violent murder, spectacular robberies, and large-scale disasters. Combinations of these recur in nearly every episode of the series. The first *Fantômas* novel provides illustrations of each type; the murder of the marquise, the theft of Sonia Danidoff's money and necklace, and the sinking of the steamship *Lancaster*. Notably, each of these crimes requires modern forms of transport and technology. An express passenger rail train makes it possible for Fantômas to reach the marquise's chateau in the Dordogne with sufficient time to commit the murder, return toward Paris, and then reboard a slower train from Paris in order to arrive back at the same chateau on the following morning. An elevator enables Fantômas to escape from the Hôtel Palais Royale after robbing Princess Danidoff. Blowing up the trans-Atlantic passenger liner *Lancaster* provides a way for Fantômas to rid himself of his Etienne Rambert identity; international newspaper reportage of the disaster guarantees wide circulation of the renowned businessman's death. In these ways, Souvestre and Allain used modern technologies to give the exploits of Fantômas a contemporary flavor.

Sometimes, these take the form of more-or-less stock devices from crime and detective fiction. Fantômas loves to put his victims under with poisons and soporifics and to tie them up with rope. Juve and Fandor are rarely without their revolvers. In other instances, seemingly mysterious events can be traced back to everyday inventions. In *Le Fiacre de nuit,* mysterious light rays in the Seine turn out to be the beam from an underwater flashlight. In *La Main coupée,* Juve determines that a Monte Carlo roulette wheel has been cleverly rigged and operated by a foot pedal. These kinds of devices are common in action-packed fiction of the era. More disturbingly, otherwise common objects can be put to nefarious uses. To punish Monsieur Chapelard of Paris Galeries, Fantômas outfits the department store with poisoned perfume aspirators, lines shoes with broken glass, and fills gloves with toxic chemicals, killing and wounding scores of shoppers. In these ways, small objects are intimately bound up in the Lord of Terror's violence. Such *truquage* provides uncanny slippage between the quotidian and the horrific.

Of equal interest are those gadgets cleverly designed by Fantômas himself. These extraordinary devices often assist Fantômas in some kind of miraculous escape, leaving the reader as baffled as Juve and Fandor. In *Juve contre Fantômas,* for example, Dr. Chaleck/Fantômas eludes the heroic duo by building a house with identical rooms, each completely outfitted with the same furniture and objects, to the bewilderment of the detective and the journalist. In *L'Agent secret,* Fantômas escapes by hiding in the secret compartment of a cleverly hollowed-out armchair. A secret compartment in *Le Fiacre de nuit* allows Fantômas to manipulate a corpse coachman atop the horse-drawn cab and evade capture by Fandor.

At times, the gadgetry in *Fantômas* becomes the foremost narrative element, as the story moves from one scary device or situation to another. *La Mort de Juve* is one of the most gadget-filled novels in the series. In this episode, bank notes mysteriously disappear from real-estate broker Hervé Martel's office whenever a mysterious wind is felt and heard. One of Juve's assistants, Inspector Michel, later discovers that a pneumatic air pump connected to the floor vents is sweeping the bank notes off the table and into the ventilation shaft (the discovery costs Michel his sight; his eyeballs are sucked out when he peers a little too closely at the vent's grill). Later in the episode, Fantômas, disguised as an armless man (*un manchot à deux bras*), murders Martel by means of a hat equipped with a mechanism that shoots out a knife.

At the climax of the novel, Inspector Juve, who has been feigning complete paralysis since the end of the previous episode, catches the Lord of Terror off-guard by lunging from his bed directly at the villain. Juve successfully wrestles Fantômas to the ground and then stakes him to the floor with nails and rope. With Fantômas immobilized, Juve calls out to a police officer on the street below to watch over the bound criminal while the detective goes to get some assistance (Juve is unable to telephone the police, because during his months of "incapacity" he forgot to pay the phone bill). Fantômas, however, has anticipated the possibility of Juve laying a trap for him; the attending police officer turns out to be one of the master-criminal's agents. When the false police officer decides to betray the Master of Horror by leaving him staked to the floor, however, the Genius of Crime lives up to his reputation: A timed firebomb explodes in the apartment building. Terrified, the double-crossing accomplice releases Fantômas, who tosses the unfortunate underling into the flaming stairwell before making his own escape by bounding through the apartment window.

The success of *Fantômas* as a thriller detective series depends upon such *truquage*. The monstrosity of the Lord of Terror is equal to his command of material technology. The world is rigged in favor of the Emperor of Crime; objective chance is not only possible, it is inevitable.

UNMOTIVATED VIOLENCE

Perhaps the most disturbing aspect of *Fantômas*, from a moral point of view, is the inability to explain what drives the villain to commit criminal atrocities in endless succession. In the first seven episodes, the tormented love affair between Gurn and Lady Beltham provides one kind of motivation. From the eighth forward, the contentious father-daughter relationship between Fantômas and Hélène, as well as Fantômas's frustration over Fandor's love (albeit largely unrequited) for his daughter, provides another. But such familial conflicts are more likely to suggest motivations for killing one another than for reveling in jewelry theft, monetary scams, gratuitous murder, or mass-scale destruction.

Further, most Fantômas aliases display none of the physical characteristics suggestive of biological or social pathology charted by criminal anthropology of the era. On the contrary, Fantômas is most often endowed with aristocratic, professional, and entrepreneurial characteristics. Throughout the series, Fantômas assumes lower-class identities only about twenty percent of the time, and he abandons them altogether after the first six novels. In contrast with the nineteenth-century popular-novel tradition, which associated underworld crime with the lower classes, the *Fantômas* novels show a distinct preference for aristocratic and bourgeois aliases. Descriptions of Fantômas *en cagoule* provide no clues to his criminal identity at all. In these passages, he is mysteriously healthy, faceless and athletic. The only explanation for his crimes, finally, is the invocation of the various names of Fantômas—Lord of Terror, Master of Crime, Genius of Evil. Fantômas is conjured up, not motivated.

In large part, the physical violence in *Fantômas* is either implied, as in the discovery of the corpse after the murder, or contrived through the use of gadgetry. On occasion, Souvestre and Allain graphically depict physical violence. In one such passage occurs in *Le Fiacre de nuit*, when the ruffian *Bec-de-Gaz* murders his prostitute-wife, *La Panthère*. Having discovered that his wife has allowed Raymonde (Hélène) to escape, the *apache* curses and beats her in a rage. The moment-by-moment description of *Bec-de-Gaz*'s fury and *La Panthère*'s unheeded cries for mercy until she is silenced by death, harkens back to the social origins of the nineteenth-century popular novel, which equated underworld violence with poverty and misery.

More often in the series, though, the power of the violence is delivered through impersonal descriptions. Sometimes that violence approximates a storyboard construction later associated with movies and comic books. The deadly confrontation between the *pègre* prostitute Nini Guinon and

Lady Beltham in *Le Pendu de Londres* provides an excellent illustration of this technique:

> All of a sudden, Nini Guinon's interrogator [Lady Beltham] let out a cry of terror.
>
> Momentarily losing sight of her adversary, quick as a flash the prostitute had flown to the neighboring room where baby Daniel slumbered.
>
> She was armed with a dagger.
>
> In a fit of anger, Nini flung herself upon the child, seized him, and in a frightful move drove the dagger into his chest.
>
> Before baby Daniel drew another breath, a torrent of bright blood spewed from his wound. Immediately, his lips went pale.
>
> "There!" shrieked Nini Guinon, "You wouldn't let me have him! Now, neither will you . . . "
>
> Nini Guinon said no more.
>
> A gunshot rang out. Uttering a cry, the unfortunate Nini collapsed to the floor.
>
> The blasts from Lady Beltham's revolver continued, until it was emptied . . .
>
> Within the space of a few seconds, two beings met with death.
>
> Abruptly, this delicate, charming, tastefully furnished little apartment had been transformed into a horrific theater of blood.[35]

The "quick-cut" technique of this passage, a succession of short images immediately following upon one another, suggests a cinematic construction. Souvestre and Allain utilize this series of quick juxtapositions to distance the reader from the action in a kind of mechanical, nonemotional manner, prefiguring the cinema's reliance upon the sensory immediacy of sound and image to portray violence. At the same time, numerous scenes are compacted into "the space of a few seconds," anticipating the elongation of time through montage.

The explicit violence in *Fantômas* is often the result of some *truquage*, particularly in such large-scale disasters as train crashes and deadly traps laid in department stores. In these instances, the horror of the violence depends upon, and is augmented by, the use of gadgetry. In *La Fille de Fantômas*, Fantomas kills the entire crew and passengers of an ocean liner by releasing plague-infested rats onto the ship while withholding the serum for himself alone. In *La Main coupée*, a severed hand keeps showing up in unexpected locations in a Monte Carlo casino. In *L'Arrestation de Fantômas*, Fantômas executes the double-crossing carcass-knacker (*équarrisseur*) Jean-Marie in one of State Executioner Deibler's guillotines. To increase the horror, Fantômas places his victim faceup in the guillotine, rather than facedown (the usual practice), so that Jean-Marie can witness his own execution. In *L'Évadée de Saint-Lazare*, Fantômas kills Blanche Perrier, the mistress of one of his previous victims, by catching her long hair in an automatic washing-machine ringer and scalping her alive. In these instances, the strength of the violence matches the gadgetry employed to accomplish it.

At other times, however, the contrivance is invoked to soften a genuinely terrifying moment. One striking illustration of this is the murder of Isabelle de Guerray by Fantômas in *La Main coupée*. Fantômas enters the bedroom of the Monte Carlo aristocrat, blindfolds her, and threatens to kill her unless she reveals the combination of her safe-box. Blinded, the woman feels the blade of a knife against her arm and the warm blood flowing from her body; she loses consciousness and dies. Afterward, Juve reveals that Isabelle de Guerray has died of fright: Fantômas did not cut her, but rigged her with a tube of flowing warm water, which the blindfolded Isabelle mistook for her own blood. In *La Livrée du crime*, Fantômas sets off a bomb in a placement bureau office filled with young women waiting their assignment posts. Souvestre and Allain revel in the horrific aftermath, amply detailing the mutilations incurred by the unfortunate women, but, as it turns out, no one has been hurt; Fantômas had set off bombs filled with blood, bone fragments, and bits of flesh, and the women were merely covered with the carnage. In these instances, the gadgetry is employed both to evoke a horrific responses and at the same time soften a truly horrific frisson within a contrived scheme.

At times, the line between entertainment and moral offense in *Fantômas* blended too thoroughly for social sensibilities of the era. The violent excesses of the novel series were toned down, for example, in Louis Feuillade's five *Fantômas* movies, 1913–14. From the outset, Gaumont redesigned the film poster, featuring the image of masked man in formal dress towering over the Parisian landscape, so that Fantômas lacked the deadly *poignard* held behind his back on the original book cover. Titles from the novel series were changed as well, to fit within social conventions. The novel's title, *Le Magistrat cambrioleur*, was rendered as *Le Faux Magistrat* in the film version. In both instances Fantômas falsely poses as a judge, but the implication that a judge could also be a criminal did not make it into the movie. The films even altered story lines to soften the violence. In the first Feuillade *Fantômas* film, Juve discovers the substitution of the actor Valgrand for Gurn before the execution and saves him, whereas the innocent and duped actor loses his head in Souvestre and Allain's novel. Such re-plottings of the *Fantômas* film adaptations suggest that the violently imaginative details of the novel exceeded the moral conventions of the era.

But the unmotivated violence in *Fantômas* was precisely one of the sources of entertainment for readers, perhaps especially for those with surreal predilections. Surrealists Georges Sadoul, Jacques Prévert, Raymond Queneau, and Yves Tanguy used to play a game in which one person would call out a title from one of the novels in the *Fantômas* series, and the others would try and recall how many murders the Lord of Terror had committed in that particular episode.[36] But the surreal appeal of *Fantômas* was equally inherent in its overabundance of masks, swerves, and nefarious objects. In the twilight of the Belle Époque, the surrealists saw the immense shadow of Fantômas spreading over Paris and the world. The wildly imaginary dimensions of *Fantômas* left nineteenth-century origins behind. Instead, the surrealists incorporated the images of *Fantômas* into a twentieth-century modern mythology.

FANTÔMAS AND THE SURREALISTS

The paper trail of surrealistic Fantômas is more fragmented and sparse than Souvestre and Allain's series.[37] Fantômas was only occasionally the object of surrealist and avant-garde projects. Some avant-garde and surrealist writers, including Blaise Cendrars, Jean Cocteau, Robert Desnos and Max Jacob, among others, dedicated poems or prose fragments to Fantômas. In a "Fantômas" poem of 1914, Cendrars proclaimed the popular series "The School Hymn of Brutish Humanity" (*"Alma Mater Humanité Vache"*), a contemporary plagiarization of Homeric epics. Jacob included two prose fragments in his 1916 collection of poems, *The Dice Cup* (*Le Cornet à dés*). In Jacob's "Fantômas," the central image is that of a well-polished silver door clapper with the alluring ears of a sailor or gorilla. In "Encore Fantômas," the Genius of Crime is a master chef who satisfies both epicures (*gourmets*) and snobs (*gourmés*). Mostly, avant-garde Fantômas-inspired works remained fragments of unrealized projects. Raymond Queneau is said to have wanted to write Fantômas film scripts, but the project was never realized. In 1934, Alain Resnais began an 8-mm "Fantômas" film, but the project was abandoned. The 1936 film-short, "Mr. Fantômas, Chapter 280,000," by Belgian surrealist poet Ernest Moerman was the only surrealist treatment to be realized on screen during the interwar period.[38]

Likewise, avant-garde visual images of Fantômas are rare. In Juan Gris's cubist still life *Fantômas (Pipe and Newspaper)* (1915), a generic copy of a *Fantômas* novel is one of a number of everyday objects scattered about a café table, including a copy of *Le Journal*, a sensational *fait-divers* daily newspaper. The fusing of fantasy with the banality of daily life nearly passes unnoticed in the collage. In an early painting by Yves Tanguy titled *Fantômas* (1925–26), a landscape of disparate objects and alienated human figures provides no direct correspondence between the painting's title and its imagery. A bloody corpse stretches out across the center of the landscape, but one would only recognize the shadow of Fantômas after first accepting that the Lord of Terror is the author of all horrific scenes.

Among surrealist painters, Belgian René Magritte was the greatest champion of Fantômas.[39] Often, Magritte selected his Fantômas imagery from Louis Feuillade's Fantômas films rather than Souvestre and Allain's novels. At the end of the second Feuillade Fantômas movie, *Juve contre Fantômas* (1913), Fantômas raises his arms in a gesture of victory, after having pulled a lever that set off an explosion in a house in which Juve and Fandor were trapped. Magritte makes use of these elements— the Man in Black, the lever—in his 1926 painting, "The Generous Man" (*L'Homme du large*). The composition of "The Foreboding Murderer" (*L'Assassin menacé*, 1926), is taken from Feuillade's third Fantômas movie, *Le Mort qui tue* (1913). In this painting, as in the film, two men lie in wait on either side of a doorway, ready to assault their unsuspecting victims with nets and clubs. In "The Barbarian" (*Le Barbare*, c. 1930), the masked face of Fantômas from the original book cover fades in and out of a brick wall.

Most often, *Fantômas* was treated as a subtext, as an ancestral member of the surrealist family. In the new series of *Littérature*, the quasi-dadaist literary review edited by Aragon, Breton, and Soupault immediately prior to *La Révolution Surréaliste*, Fantômas appeared in the genealogy of "Erutaréttil," or "Littérature" spelled backwards.[40] In his place on the underside of literature, Fantômas is a direct descendant of Lautréamont, a cousin of Arthur Rimbaud and Alfred Jarry, and a brother of Apollinaire, Jacques Vaché, and Raymond Roussel, all significant authors in the surrealist pantheon of origins. A similar sort of genealogy appears in a play by Breton, Desnos, and Benjamin Péret titled "What a Beautiful Day!" (*Comme il fait beau!*)[41] In a tropical forest, a monkey, who carries on a hallucinatory conversation with another monkey and a leaf-insect, bears a family coat of arms that includes the name of Fantômas. In these instances, Fantômas was acknowledged as an important influence on the collective heritage of the surrealist movement.

Fantômas was also an icon for a dark, mysterious, and familiar Parisian landscape. The expansive Fantômas shadow referred to in the final verse of Desnos's "Lament" was inspired by the Fantômas image on the original book cover—the masked gentleman bandit in top hat and formal evening dress, towering over the Parisian landscape. Casting his eyes at the reader, Fantômas rests his chin in his left hand in contemplation, and holds a dagger behind his back in his right in violent anticipation. In Pierre Prévert's compilation film, *Paris la belle*, a *Fantômas* novel is drawn from a *bouquiniste* box along the Seine and is displayed in front of the camera during the closing moments of the film.[42]

Sometimes the surrealists incorporated Fantômas iconography into their own projects. The final installment of the original novel series, *La Fin de Fantômas*, features the image of a ball mask, a familiar Fantômas icon, floating on the ocean in the foreground as the ocean liner *Gigantic* sinks in the background (carrying both Juve and Fantômas to their deaths). This same image of the Fantômas mask appears in Man Ray's 1928 experimental film, *Étoile de mer*. The eye-slits of the floating mask are juxtaposed with an intertitle reading "Beautiful, like a flower of flesh." In such instances, *Fantômas* was a subtext, a presence more felt than seen.

In a cubist collage by Juan Gris, "The Man at the Café" (*L'Homme au café*, 1914), Fantômas is not directly represented but lurks within the work. Here, a mysterious figure cloaked in a broad hat and overcoat reads, and is half-concealed by, the daily newspaper, *Le Matin*. The round wooden handles of the newspaper holder repeat in multiple images, resembling dripping blood from the sensationalist stories contained within the *fait-divers* daily. On the front page of the newspaper, Gris pasted the headline, *"Bertillonnage, on ne truquera plus les oeuvres d'art,"* proclaiming that police science has invented some new way of detecting faked art works. But the mysterious and elusive impression of the collage suggests that perhaps the followers of Alphonse Bertillon were no more effective than Inspector Juve in eliminating crime. For Gris and for the viewer, the headline is more a dare, a criminal challenge—an opportunity for exploit and counterexploit—than a message of order and security.

Fantômas was only one of many popular crime and detective stories from the turn of the century that appealed to the surrealists. Another surrealist favorite, the fictional American detective series *Nick Carter*, appears in Aragon's "Outline for a History of Contemporary Literature" immediately following the futurists and the *Ballets russes.*[43] Aragon's inclusion of *Nick Carter* recontextualizes the popular detective series by elevating it to the status of the contemporary *avant-garde*. But it was Philippe Soupault's *Mort de Nick Carter* (1926) that perhaps best fulfilled the agenda of releasing the crime fantasies of that detective series from their banal origins and redirecting them toward the surrealist revolution.[44]

The *Death of Nick Carter* is less an homage to the detective weekly than Soupault's attempt to exorcise the law-and-order mentality of the serial and to release its imaginative details. The story opens with a telephone call from investigator Patsy Murphy to his boss, Nick Carter, describing the details of a double murder at a country chateau. From an inventory of the premises, Patsy finds fourteen tables in the antechamber of the house displaying, in order, an orange and a knife, a green feather-duster, two seashells, a new Spanish coin, a blue-and-yellow handkerchief, a pair of scissors, nothing on the eighth table (the seventh is missing from the inventory), an oil lamp, a white carnation, a rose and a caramel, a full wine glass, an ivory elephant, and a calling card from the Shah of Persia; a sonnet lies on the floor in front of the last table. After further investigations, including the discovery of the corpses, Patsy waits in the garden until he sees the suspect—a black man dressed in a white uniform and gloves—returning to the scene of the crime.

From the address on a letter found near the bodies, Nick, his brother Chick, and Patsy head out to an insane asylum in the west of France. The inhabitants of the sanatorium run loose on the lawn, screaming like blind birds, laughing and crying out at imagined crimes and atrocities. One inmate chases after the shadow of an invisible enemy, shouting "Bang! Bang! Bang!" Inside the sanatorium, the patients' therapy room is painted red and covered with fine wool carpets. A hermaphrodite statue in the classical mode is framed in the room's single window. Thirty or forty watches and clocks hang on the walls, ticking so loudly that the room sounds like the inside of a sewing machine. From a local town official, Nick and company learn that a black man named Albert Martel previously worked as an orderly at the asylum for a couple of months. Martel was well liked by the patients, the concierge, children, the gardeners, and the other orderlies. That evening, a new orderly arrives.

Two weeks later, a large American automobile pulls into the clinic driveway. A black man, named Albert, gets out and inquires about a person spotted looking out the third-story window. The director replies that it is the new orderly. Shortly thereafter, a cry rings out as the orderly plunges from the window to his death. Inmates, who have been playing soccer on the lawn, scream and throw their shoes at each other. Gunshots ring out, and two vagabonds are found shot against the asylum wall. The inmates laugh and scream louder, attacking the newest of their fellow-patients, mortally wounding five of them. Albert Martel disappears.

The dead orderly is identified as Nick Carter, and the two vagabonds as his faithful companions, Chick and Patsy. At seven o'clock that same evening, newspaper hawkers on the boulevards shout, "Nick Carter Dies!" A black man with a bandaged hand buys a newspaper, and hands the kiosk owner a hundred-franc note. "Keep the change." In this surrealist appropriation, Soupault kills Nick Carter in full complicity with action and motifs of that detective series. What Soupault accomplished in so doing was the surrealist reformulation of the commercial detective story.

The French avant-garde and the surrealists, however, recognized that the *Fantômas* series had itself achieved some measure of surrealism. Guillaume Apollinaire, creator of the term "surrealism," first articulated this in his review of *Fantômas* in the *Mercure de France*.[45] Read in the proper spirit, Apollinaire argues, *Fantômas* provides the raw cultural material to re-create the imaginations of its readers. To achieve the full poetic effect of *Fantômas*, he suggests reading one of the novels straight through as quickly as possible—anybody can do it—and not only *Fantômas*, but the popular adventure novels of Dumas père and Paul Féval, and the American "epics," *Nick Carter* and *Buffalo Bill*, as well. From the standpoint of the imagination, Apollinaire concludes, *Fantômas* is inestimably rich. Future generations, he predicted, would find it an unequaled mine of *argot* and contemporary vernacular.

By the 1920s, the surrealists had claimed *Fantômas* as one of their own: a literary ancestor, an icon of a dark and mysterious Paris, a subtext of pleasure derived from unmotivated criminality. While the social origins of *Fantômas* were conservative and bourgeois, the overabundance of masks, swerves, gadgets, and horror in the popular series exceeded the restrictions of literary style and social order. Like Philippe Soupault, one could rewrite the detective story to release its fantastic elements into imaginative play. Or, like Apollinaire, one could simply read *Fantômas*.

Ultimately, the tremendous achievement of *Fantômas* rests on its own merits. As Roger Caillois would later articulate it, the effective crime and detective novel (*roman policier*) creates a powerful phantasmagoria of anarchy versus order, its revolutionary impulses equal to the power of conservatism and order to try to constrain it.[46] *Fantômas* was precisely such a compendium of the fantastic amid the changing landscape of everyday life, approximating what Aragon called a "modern mythology" in *Le Paysan de Paris*. Surrealists before the letter, Souvestre and Allain tied the imaginative exploits of *Fantômas* to the details and twists of the modern world, continuously reinvented every month, to the nearly total neglect of social propriety and literary style. With the brief exception of Desnos's "Lament," none of the surrealists' Fantômas projects came close to rivaling that renown.

3 Murder, Mirth, and Misogyny

THE DARK HUMOR OF HENRI DÉSIRÉ LANDRU,
THE BLUEBEARD OF GAMBAIS

In March 1921, the Paris dada group published a "literary value" chart in the review *Littérature*.[1] On a scale of -25 to $+20$, the chart ranked various public and artistic figures according to their creative merit. Naturally, the dadaists gave themselves the highest marks: Louis Aragon, André Breton, Paul Éluard, Philippe Soupault, and Tristan Tzara all scored in the $+12$ to 16 range. Literary forbears sympathetic to surrealism, such as Alfred Jarry and Guillaume Apollinaire, also received high scores, as did contemporary cultural iconoclasts, such as American entertainer Charlie Chaplin. The lowest marks were reserved for the bastions of the literary and political establishment. Académie Française poet Henri de Régnier, Nobel Prize-winning author Anatole France, and war hero Marshal Foch, all scraped the bottom of the barrel with scores of -18 to -22.90.

In addition to these renowned literary, entertainment, and political figures, the chart also included the names of three well-known criminals. The Belle Époque bandit Jules Bonnot, whose band of anarchists had funded their political activities through spectacular bank robberies, received the impressive score of +10.36. Also included was the nineteenth-century "elegant criminal," poet-assassin Lacenaire (Pierre-François Gaillard). Although he only received a score of +1.00 on the literary value chart, Lacenaire's merit would later be reaffirmed by his inclusion in André Breton's *Anthologie de l'humour noir.* Finally, the chart included the name of Landru, a presumed serial murderer, who had been languishing in prison since April 1919 and awaiting trial. The members of the Paris dada movement awarded the infamous "Bluebeard of Gambais," as Landru was popularly known, a score of +2.27.

Between April 1915 and January 1919, Landru swindled ten "fiancées" who had responded to his marriage offers in the newspaper. According to charges later brought against him, he murdered each of these women (and one woman's son) at one of two villas he kept outside of Paris, at Vernouillet and at Gambais. Since Landru's arrest in April 1919, dedicated readers had followed the details of the case in the daily press. Within the first week after his arrest, it was advertised that Landru was not only a crook and con-man (*escroc*), he was also a serial murderer. An overwhelming amount of circumstantial evidence was quickly amassed to support the serial-murder thesis. Clothing, furniture, jewelry, and other articles belonging to the disappeared women, were recovered from various garages around Paris where Landru fronted stolen goods. Also found were individual dossiers on the ten women, as well as on 273 other women who had responded to his false marriage offers in daily newspapers. The most tantalizing piece of evidence was Landru's *carnet,* his expense notebook, which provided an incomplete record of his comings and goings throughout the period. But neither the women themselves, their corpses, nor any identifiable body parts, were ever found. The physical evidence against Landru amounted to slightly less than a kilogram of ashes and bones that forensic experts identified in court as human. However, this evidence was recovered from Gambais two weeks after the original sweep of the villa, a somewhat suspect occasion, staged by the police with invited members of the press attending.

Two years later, when Landru's name appeared on the dada literary value chart, the state's case was substantially no further along than it had been in the few weeks after his arrest. Finally, on 7 November 1921, the trial in the *cour d'assises* (criminal court) began. Landru was charged with twenty-five counts of having robbed and murdered his ten mistresses (and one of the women's sons) by chopping off their hands, feet and heads, and cremating them in his kitchen oven. Throughout the trial Landru openly admitted that he had swindled some of these women (others were destitute), but he firmly denied that he had killed any of them. Yet the coincidence of ten missing women, whose only point of connection was Landru, proved too powerful not to conclude "murder." Moreover, the circumstantial evidence proved to be a sufficient foundation upon which horrific and murderous scenarios could be constructed, no matter how fantastic and incoherent the details. There was really never a question of "whodunit," only an impossible "how?"

On 1 December 1921, the international press declared, "Landru Condemned to the Guillotine!" After twenty-one court sessions, nine of twelve jurors from the *cour d'assises* in Versailles found Landru guilty as charged of all ten murders and on all but two counts of fraud. The penalty was death. But a shadow of doubt was immediately cast back upon the jury's declaration of "guilty"—and by no less than the jurors themselves. Directly after the verdict, another and more peculiar pronouncement followed: Landru's defense attorney filed an appeal for clemency with the presiding judge, signed by all twelve jurors, the two alternates, and the family of one of the disappeared women. It was a paradox: On the one hand, the jury had already found Landru guilty of being a liar and serial murderer; on the other, they appealed for clemency, without specifying any extenuating circumstances. Beyond rational reconciliation, the jury stood complicit in the aggrandizement of the Landru Affair to an unimaginable level of surreality.

This chapter examines the surreal cultural logic of the Landru Affair. The case stands out as a unique compendium of turn-of-the-century French criminal culture, ranging from criminal anthropology and police laboratory science to popular legends of "human monsters" and sensationalist journalism. This culture of criminality required an easy solubility between the material details of the case and the imagined violence of a "Bluebeard." Such displacements of the imagination were not, however, unique to the Landru case; they were in fact common to tales of criminality.

In the Landru Affair, however, the interplay between criminal fantasies and quotidian details escaped the constrictions of verisimilitude. In contrast to the realistic reconstruction of the scene of the crime, and its accompanying moral comfort in the triumph of law and order over anarchy and sensation, the Landru Affair generated a terrifying fantasy corollary to what André Breton called "dark humor" (*l'humour noir*).[2] The journalistic excesses built into the story of Landru constituted a kind of dream text, which required the participation of newspaper readers, and ultimately the court jurors, to coalesce into the image of the "Bluebeard of Gambais." The Landru Affair escaped "the paucity of reality" and entered into a hallucinatory world of collective fantasy, sustained only by the power of the imagination.

THE SECRET OF LANDRU

Landru was arrested on Saturday morning, 12 April 1919. The story was scooped by a sensationalist daily newspaper, *Le Petit Journal*, the next day:

> Yesterday in Paris, in the heart of Montmartre, thanks to some anonymous tips, a mobile police unit arrested an elegantly dressed man, nearly bald but sporting an impressive black beard. This man, who it is believed practices the science of hypnotism in the services of satisfying his base instincts, has been sought by more than ten judicial districts across France, under the various names of Dupont, Desjardin, Prunier, Perrès, Durand, Dumont, Morïse, etc.
>
> After an interrogation by the Sûreté, he finally confessed to being in reality Henri Nandru [*sic*], born in the 19th arrondissement of Paris in 1869. Nandru is currently charged with a number of frauds—theft, swindling, and abuses of confidence—all of which he denies, without the least explanation. To every question he replies, "I have nothing to say; you can take it up with my lawyer."

It seems that it might be more prudent for this sad person to be a little less reserved. In all honesty, soon he will be answering in court to charges much more serious than those he refuted today. On this score, much more weighty charges have already been presented against him.[3]

Many of the attributes of the affair—those that would eventually cost Landru his head—were established in this initial report. He was a known criminal with bourgeois pretensions. He utilized hypnotic powers to satisfy violent and sexual desires. He passed under numerous aliases. He refused to cooperate with the police. There were more mysterious and graver crimes attributed to this man than those already known.

Le Petit Journal continued its coverage on Monday morning: "The Mystery of the Gambais Villa. A New Bluebeard. Engineer Landru, man of a hundred names, suspected of having assassinated several women. Conscientious reportage by our special envoy continues."[4] The report was reprinted on the same day in another sensationalist newspaper, *Le Matin*.[5] The article returned to the summer of 1915, when an elegantly dressed driver of an automobile, identified as "Georges Dupont, Engineer," rented a villa from a Monsieur Tric in the quaint village of Gambais, situated at the edge of Rambouillet forest, seven kilometers from Houdan, southwest of Paris. Dupont appeared at the villa once or twice a month, but never for more than twenty-four or forty-eight hours at a time, and always with the same brunette woman, around forty-five years old. The following year, he brought another, younger woman with him, but no one ever saw her again. Nor the first.

When the families of these women notified the police, inquiries were made. Dupont, it seemed, was also known as Frémiet, Natier, and Cuchet. His real identity, however, was Henri Désiré Landru, who had outstanding arrest warrants in three different police jurisdictions. A search of his apartment following his arrest on 12 April turned up women's underclothes, jewelry, and locks of hair. A sweep of the Gambais villa on the same day produced boxes of revolver cartridges, traces of blood, unidentified trunks, and dog corpses. Landru's only reply to these developments was, "See my lawyer."

That same morning, *Le Journal* ran the story under the headline "Did Landru Kill His Four Mistresses?"[6] The article added a few new details:

Landru was born in the poor, working-class district of Belleville. The Gambais trunk contained the underclothes of a third woman; the dogs had belonged to a fourth victim. Traces of blood were found on the kitchen stove. Commissioner Bichon, in charge of the case, believed that the police had their hands on a modern Bluebeard, the folktale slayer of seven wives, or another Dumolard, the monstrous nineteenth-century murderer of female domestics.

This second day's coverage simultaneously refined and aggrandized a mere *fait-divers*, a news blurb, into a full-blown *affair*. The heart of Montmartre became the rue de Rochechouart and Belleville, locations frequently portrayed in the press and fiction as hotbeds of violent crime.[7] Landru's aliases and outstanding arrest warrants were reduced in number, but now fit into the well-established chronology of a known criminal. The "more weighty charges" turned out to be a series of missing women, two reported by their families, and the others inferred from evidence. The power of hypnotism was supplemented by stolen property and murder trophies. Behind the tight-lipped swindler Landru was a horrific identity—the modern Bluebeard, a sexually deranged slayer of women. From these numerous details, a host of fantastic stories began to emerge.

For the next two weeks, the daily press ran wild with the criminal possibilities suggested by Landru's arrest, and the story defracted into multiple images. Newspaper headlines varied according to their different approaches to the affair. Some referred to Landru as "Bluebeard," a term consistently used by the conservative French newspaper *Le Figaro* (*"Landru, dit Barbe-Bleue"*) and internationally by the *New York Times* ("French Bluebeard"). This association invoked both the Perrault folktale of Bluebeard and his seven wives, and the memory of Gilles de Rais, the notorious lieutenant of Joan of Arc who was burned at the stake in the fifteenth century for sodomizing and murdering boys.[8] *Le Journal* referred to Landru as *"Un Frégoli du crime,"* comparing his multiple aliases to the famous Belle Époque Italian entertainer Leopoldo Frégoli, who played as many as sixty characters, male and female, in a single performance. Other newspapers emphasized the enigma of the case, such as *"L'Affaire mystérieuse"* in the Catholic daily *La Croix*, *"La Mystérieuse existence de Landru"* in the moderate *Le Temps*, and the "Lonely House Mystery" in the *London Times*. The conservative *Le Matin* focused upon the secluded village of Gambais as the source of the mystery, initially as *"Le Mystère de Gambais,"* and after April 24 as *"Le Barbe-Bleue de Gambais."* While these early reports did not agree on the substance of Landru's crimes, they were all incantations of a powerful and terrible secret.

The press tracked Landru's murderous proclivities in daily installments, each constituting a "New Chapter in the Landru Novel."[9] Generating a list of female victims proved to be the major source of press fascination in the two weeks following Landru's arrest. From dossiers the police confiscated the day of his arrest, newspapers began to report that there were either ten or eleven missing women. Mesdames Cuchet and Buisson were known from the outset, having been reported missing by their families. On 15 April, Madame Collomb was identified by the "M.-P." initials embossed on a trunk which she had borrowed from her sister, Madame Pelat (Moreau-Pelat). On 17 April, Mademoiselle Marie-Thérèse Marchadier was identified as *"la dame aux griffons"*; the remains of her dogs had been found at Gambais on the day of Landru's arrest. Anna Pascal, reported missing by her niece, Madame Carbonnel, appeared in the press on the twentieth. The discovery of Landru's *carnet*, and the dossiers he kept on all 283 newspaper respondents, added the names of Mesdames Guillin, Jaume, and Héon to press accounts on 23–24 April. Three cryptic references in the notebook, "Brésil, Le Havre, and Mogador," were identified on 28 April as Mesdames Laborde-Line (Argentine, not Brazilian), Héon again (born in Le Havre), and Mademoiselle Andrée Babelay ("Mogador" being a possible reference to a shop in Belleville where Babelay and Landru presumably first met). Altogether, the women victims comprised seven widows, one divorcée, one prostitute, and a teenage domestic (table 1).

But this list of ten women is the tidy one, corresponding to the list of murder charges finally presented by the state against Landru. The list generated by the press was greater. Nearly any woman reported missing during the month of April 1919 seemed yet another of Landru's victims, and the press suggested various possibilities. On 18 April, *Le Matin* featured a front-page photomontage of the heads of Cuchet, Buisson, and Collomb, vertically aligned and superimposed upon a field of question

Table 1 Landru's Victims as Compiled by Interrogating Magistrate Bonin

Name	Age	Profession	Disappearance
1. Jamast, Jeanne. Veuve Cuchet	39	laundry owner	January 1915
1b. Cuchet, André Georges	17	son	January 1915
2. Turan, Thérèse. Veuve Laborde-Line	47	unemployed	June 1915
3. Pelletier, Marie. Veuve Guillin	52	public assistance	August 1915
4. Henry, Berthe-Anna. Veuve Héon	55	unemployed	December 1915
5. Moreau, Anna. Veuve Collomb	44	former cook	December 1916/ January 1917
6. Babelay, Andrée-Anne	19	domestic	April 1917
7. Laire, Célestine. Veuve Buisson	44	cook	November 1917
8. Barthélemy, Louise. Veuve Jaume	36	seamstress	December 1917
9. Pascal, Anne-Marie. Divorcée Gabriel	36	laundry owner	April 1918
10. Marchadier, Marie-Thérèse	39	prostitute	January 1919

SOURCES: Colin, "L'affaire Landru," *Mercure de France* (1920); Béraud, *L'Affaire Landru* (1923); Fleuriant-French, *Le Secret de Landru* (1930); Bardens, *The Ladykiller* (1972); Damon, *Landru* (1994).

marks, with the headline, "How will he respond to a new crime?"[10] The question referred to an unidentified woman's corpse discovered at the end of February in Morlaye, in the Chantilly region where Diard-Cuchet-Landru had once lived. The same day, *Le Petit Parisian* suggested that "Ketty," a friend of Mademoiselle Marchadier who had been missing from her residence in Versailles for more than a year, was yet another of Landru's victims.[11] The following day, *Le Journal* asked "Who are these girls?" referring to two pretty, blond, twelve-year-old girls that Madame Cuchet's concierge claimed had Landru met in 1914. "More victims, perhaps?"[12]

In addition to these imagined victims, there were who-knew-how-many "escapees" who were portrayed in the press has having slipped through Landru's clutches. On April 27, both *Le Petit Parisian* and *Le Journal* picked up the story of a Mademoiselle Deschamps, who claimed

Landru approached her in the Métro on Saturday morning, 12 April, at
10:00 A.M.[13] Supposedly, the two agreed upon a rendezvous back at the
Métro on the following morning. Deschamps claimed that she was about
to write Landru on Sunday evening to apologize for having failed to keep
their appointment earlier that day, when she saw his picture in the
evening paper. Neither of the newspapers running the story bothered to
point out that Landru had already been arrested by the time Deschamps
claimed to have met him in the subway. Further, she could not have seen
his picture in the paper at the time she claimed to have written her letter
of apology, for the first press photos of Landru did not appear until Tuesday, 15 April. The fantasy of Landru had already begun to take precedence over the known realities of the case. As far as the sensationalist
press was concerned, all women were potential victims of Landru. It did
not matter whether they were young or old, working-class or *légères*,
propertied or penniless, known or unknown, alive or dead. The press
had a seemingly limitless story in Landru's missing women.

Yet not all murdered women had died at the hands of Landru, however much the Parisian dailies suggested otherwise. On 27 April 1919,
a woman's corpse was discovered in a sack in the Craponne canal in
Moule. The corpse was soon identified as that of Félicité Benoît, owner of
the Montmartre Palmarium club, who had been missing since May 1918.
Not only the *fait-divers* papers, such as *Le Journal* and *Le Petit Parisian*, but
also the conservative *Le Figaro* and the moderate *Le Temps* claimed that
Benoît was yet another of Landru's victims. She had plenty of money, and
Landru had been seen in Tarascon with a woman about the same time she
disappeared. But other facts did not square with the press fantasy: No
one in Gambais recognized Benoît's photograph. Toward the middle of
June, a Monsieur Durand, an *artiste lyrique* friend of Madame Benoît, convinced the Sûreté investigators that the former club owner had never
known Landru.[14] Perhaps Landru preyed on women, but he had no mo-
nopoly on murder.

Two other women *not* murdered by Landru posed problems, not so
much for the press as for the coherence of the image of Landru as an in-
satiable serial murderer. One was his wife, Marie Landru (*née* Rémy),
who lived in Clichy with Landru's four children and was financially sup-

ported by him throughout the period of the women's disappearances. Although estranged from her husband, throughout his trial Madame Landru insisted that he was a dutiful family man. The other important non-victim was Landru's final mistress, Fernande Segret, who had lived with him at the 76 rue de Rochechouart residence for over a year and a half. Simply put, there was no denying that Landru and Segret had been truly affectionate companions (the intimacies of their relationship were later published as the highly embellished "Memories of an Escapee").[15] Even more than his wife's claims of Landru's bona fides, Segret's continuing affection for Landru worked against police efforts to construct a profile against him as a compulsive, psychopathic murderer of women.

After the initial flurry of speculations about the hideous and heinous serial murderer, the still unsolidified image of the Bluebeard of Gambais began to deteriorate. The press was somewhat disappointed when they finally got a look at Landru, during his transfer from the Mantes prison to *La Santé* in Paris on 27 April:

> Dressed in a black suit, wearing a beige overcoat and bowler hat, Landru did not make a good first impression. Of average height, a bit small perhaps but broad shouldered, with his head drooped down around his shoulders, he seemed nervous and depressed. He walked with an uncertain step, bewildered by the flash of camera bulbs. He turned his head, raised his hand, hid his eyes. Finally, he covered his face with a large red checkered handkerchief. This final movement allowed us to see his strong hand with its long and flat thumb, characteristic of Lombroso's criminal thumb.[16]

Although this reporter for *Le Journal* managed to find a "criminal thumb" on Landru—other papers commented on his hypnotic eyes—the basic impression was one of complete ordinariness. Of average or even small stature, confused and a bit alarmed by the media presence, Landru did not fit the popular image of a violent killer with a bestial, deformed, or powerful physical constitution. On the contrary, during his incarceration the press reported that Landru had a weak stomach and that he abstained from tobacco and alcohol. The actual man was less than his legend.

Yet in the sensationalist press, the legend could create the man. If the police were slow in coming up with the evidence against Landru, the press found they could generate quite a bit themselves. Through *correspondents particuliers* and *envoyés spéciaux*, sensationalist dailies such as *Le Matin* and *Le Petit Parisien* began to conduct their own inquiries.[17] Articles penned by these "special correspondents" paraded a steady stream of the missing women's neighbors, relatives, and above all concierges, ready to give their impressions of Landru. While a few of these acquaintances found Landru gentlemanly, most thought him a shady and suspicious character. The inhabitants of Gambais and Vernouillet readily volunteered stories to the press about the stench from the smoke coming out of Landru's chimney. Bones were discovered in his burn piles, and the press proclaimed them pieces of skulls, ribs and tibia (actually chicken, mole, mutton, and rabbit bones). Some had witnessed Landru burning trunks in the backyard. Others had seen him dump cloth-covered parcels into nearby ponds in the middle of the night. Thanks to investigative journalism, for two weeks after Landru's arrest the relationship between facts and fantasies remained in flux.

Toward the end of April, however, press fantasies converged with police inquiries as the state stepped up its activity on the case. On Friday, 25 April, after nearly two weeks of public access, the police finally secured Landru's villas. Two days later, Landru was transferred from the prison at Mantes to Paris, for Judge Bonin to conduct the interrogation trial in the jurisdiction of the Seine-et-Oise. State prosecutors Lescouvé and Scherdeline were brought in to develop the case against Landru. The investigations of the mobile police unit under commissioners Bichon and Dautel were augmented by that of commissioner Tanguy of the judicial police (*Sûreté générale*). Laboratory police were organized under the guidance of forensic expert Dr. Paul.

On Sunday, 27 April, *Le Journal* reported that a new sweep of the Gambais premises was scheduled for the following Tuesday morning.

> It's very likely that Tuesday, Judge Bonin will travel to Gambais in the company of Dr. Paul, the Sûreté commissioner, and Landru. An excavation team has already been put together to carry out further research.
>   Perhaps it won't take as long to produce results as one might suppose. At the Gambais property, under a cover next to the house, there is

a huge pile of leaves that Landru had untiringly piled up. It was under this slightly burned pile of leaves that the three darling pets of Mademoiselle Marchadier were found.

What will be found under this pile of leaves? When Landru was taken there on the day of his arrest, certain individuals remarked that the accused frequently looked over in that direction.

Is that where they will find his victims? We will know soon enough.[18]

Two days later, on 29 April, the new police investigation at Gambais was carried out. The press and the curious, notified in advance, were waiting when the police arrived at around eight o'clock in the morning. Contrary to the information given in Sunday's article, Landru was not present.

Not surprisingly, this second investigation revealed a trail of ashes and bones leading from Landru's oven in the basement to his burn pile in the yard.[19] Dr. Paul, the forensic expert, led journalists into Landru's basement to view the oven. Rummaging among the ashes in the fire-box, Dr. Paul pulled out two or three pieces of bone, which he immediately declared pieces of human skull—the upper jawbone. Next, the journalists were taken down a few stairs to the wine cellar. Dr. Paul noticed brown stains on the ground. He took a pinch of soil, rubbed it between his fingers, and proclaimed, "It appears to be blood!" Monsieur Beyle, a forensic technician, stated that it was very likely human blood. Several strands of women's hair were found in the cellar, as well as a meat cleaver in the corner. From there, the investigation moved out to the leaf pile next to the house. At first, nothing suspicious. Then, a small pile of bones was discovered in corner of the shed, containing what looked like a big toe and a molar, as well as a piece of a corset and a hairpin fused into a piece of melted glass. Later that day, when the police and journalists visited the ossuary at the cemetery adjoining Landru's villa, Dr. Paul found nothing noteworthy. The only suspect bones, it appeared, were those *chez* Landru.

The results of this search provided the only physical evidence that the state would present against Landru. From slightly less than two pounds of ash and bone fragments, laboratory police experts, under the guidance of Dr. Paul, later declared that, on the basis of calcium content, the remains were indisputably human. During the November 1921 trial, forensic experts testified that the debris included pieces of skull, fingers, and teeth, and it represented at least three and possibly five persons. Further, they testified, the remains were most likely female, given the small size of the teeth, although there seemed to be some room for debate on the point. But direct connections between this physical evidence and any of the missing women were never established. For his part, Landru claimed that the ashes were not human, and that the high calcium content came from oyster shells he threw on his burn pile.

In the aftermath of the 29 April 1919 police sweep, Landru commanded front-page press coverage for a week. Further investigations were carried out at Landru's villa in Vernouillet. Ponds near Gambais, where witnesses said they saw Landru dump parcels, were drained and searched, but the police turned up nothing. Again, in the absence of police results, the press began to generate its own. More of Landru's neighbors and his victims' relatives were interviewed. More missing women became possible victims. A Gambais fisherman, Monsieur Barreau, claimed that once he caught a human arm on the end of his line, but lost it out of fright.[20] Readers were instructed on Dr. Locard's fingerprinting methods, which improved upon Alphonse Bertillon's anthropometric system, and the press admonished the police to employ the methods of the Lyon school of police laboratory science to the case.[21] But press coverage of Landru dropped off during May and June, and became intermittent over the next two years.

The summer of 1920 found the state no further ahead in preparing its case than it had been the previous year. At one point it even considered dropping the murder charges and settling for multiple counts of fraud, which would have sufficed to imprison Landru for the remainder of his life.[22] Finally, on 7 November 1921, two and a half years after his arrest, Landru was brought to trial on twenty-five combined charges of first-degree murder and fraud. The families of Mesdames Pascal and Cuchet pressed civil charges as well. Attorney Moro-Giafferi, renown for his defense of the Bonnot anarchists in 1912, represented Landru. In twenty-one court sessions, the spectacle created in the press two years earlier was recreated in the Versailles *cour d'assises.*

The prosecution spent two weeks reconstructing scenarios about how Landru deceived and murdered his eleven victims, based largely upon inferences from his own records and from the "witness testimony" of more than one hundred friends and relatives of the missing women. Fernande Segret, Landru's mistress, was the primary witness for the defense, but her fainting on the stand made more of a lasting public impression than her testimony. For the better part of a week, medical experts testified to Landru's sanity and police laboratory scientists to the authenticity of the human bone fragments found at Gambais. Lawyers for the Pascal and Cuchet families were given a day to present their civil cases against Landru. Prosecutor General Godefroy spent a day summing up the state's case. Defense attorney Moro-Giafferi spent one and a half days arguing for acquittal. After a two-hour deliberation, on 30 November 1921 the jury returned a verdict of guilty. After being refused a stay of execution, Landru was guillotined by State Executioner Deibler on 23 February 1922. He maintained his innocence to the end.

IN THE IMAGE OF BLUEBEARD

The week after Landru's execution, Philippe Soupault published an interview with Landru's defense attorney, Moro-Giafferi, in the first issue of the new series of *Littérature*.[23] During the course of the trial summation, Moro-Giafferi had felt it necessary to provide an alternate explanation for the disappearance of the ten women. He suggested that Landru had sold them into prostitution. In the *Littérature* interview, he admitted that such a claim was patently false. But then again, he continued, so was everything else about the case. "Never in the annals of the law has someone been presumed to have committed so many crimes on so little proof," Moro-Giafferi maintained. "The disappearance of all those women, it's an extraordinary thing. Much has been said about it, and nearly all of it untrue. . . . "

As *Le Temps* noted on the eve of his trial, it was not one or another murder scenario that made Landru's case remarkable but the "personal imprint" attributed to his crimes.[24] The "true crime" story of Landru reported in the daily press concentrated a common *fin-de-siècle* repertoire of criminal signs, established through criminal anthropology, police laboratory science, and legends of "human monsters," into one terrifying persona—the Bluebeard of Gambais. What was distinctive about the Landru affair was not the "fact" of serial murder, but the power of its terrifying story to capture the imagination. The powerful image of the Bluebeard of Gambais assembled in the daily press proved fatal in the courtroom.

Early in the affair, the communist daily *L'Humanité* was virtually the only newspaper openly hostile to the press's sensationalistic treatment of Landru's case. In a sarcastic editorial titled "The Philosophy of the Landru Affair," Victor Snell attacked what he saw as a collaboration between the press and police, whereby the two created through fantasy what was lacking in fact.[25] First of all, Snell noted, there was an enchanting quality to those two names, "Landru! Gambais!" If one believes Balzac's ideas about the predestination of names, he suggested, then perhaps there is a necessary connection between Landru and Gambais, and a bloody enigma between them. It may be extreme to execute a man simply for being named Landru, Snell acknowledged, but once an affair of this sort begins . . .

Next, Snell addressed the fact that no corpses had been found in the gardens of Vernouillet and Gambais. All the better, he asserted: it only made the case more interesting, and simply proved how thorough and tricky Landru really was. No doubt there are plenty of other gardens without corpses buried in them, "but that's not the same thing." Some absences are quite revealing, while others are concealing. Third, he continued, that peculiar phrase, *corps du délit* (the French phrase meaning "evidence," but literally "body of the crime"), contained its own profound justification: *"On recherche le corps et même les corps du délit."* Not only were the bodies missing; the police were missing the actual evidence of murder as well. If need be, Snell suggested, the synthetic power of language could provide the proof.

Finally, Snell asked, what do you think about that tooth they found when rummaging around the other day? Whose tooth was it? If Georges Cuvier could reconstruct an antediluvian monster from a single molar tucked away in some geological layer, he suggested, shouldn't it be mere child's play for experts to identify that Gambais tooth? If it turns out to be a man's tooth, rather than a woman's, don't be surprised Snell warned, it will simply "extend the field of investigation."

Within a short two weeks, Snell had recognized the fantastic nature of the Landru Affair, particularly its linguistic possibilities. Landru was an *homme dru*, a hard man, and a tough nut to crack—*filandru* as a spectator later called out during his trial.[26] The name was excellent for a crook and murderer. Further, the objects reported by the press as recovered from Landru's various outlying garages and villas—ranging from revolvers, rifles, ropes, and chopping tools on the one hand, to jewelry and articles of women's clothing on the other—provided an endless source for the combination and recombination of the nefarious activities of the Bluebeard of Gambais. The condensations and displacements of the affair became sinister, "four women, four aliases, four residences."[27] While factually suspect, such serial associations made for easy slippage from one mysterious criminal detail to another.

Yet as any writer or reader of murder mysteries knows, the story begins with a corpse. In the absence of bodies, Snell perceptively saw how language itself could create the illusion of presence. *Le Matin*'s labeling of Landru as an *escamoteur de femmes* illustrates Snell's point about synthetic language connections well.[28] *Escamoter* means to fleece someone, or to make something subtly disappear by means of a ruse. An entire range of criminal activities, connecting the swindler and the murderer, were represented by calling Landru an *escamoteur* of women: He ran a false marriage racket, he fleeced the women, he made them disappear, and he did all so cleverly that he didn't leave a trace. But while Landru may have been an energetic crook, somewhat clever at dodging the police with aliases, he wasn't subtle. The ease with which the police came up with Landru's *carnet*, dossiers, files, and the women's possessions, suggests that he was at best a sloppy *escamoteur*. He had been previously sentenced to prison on five occasions between 1904 and 1914, for fraud (*escroquerie*) and breach of trust (*abus de confiance*). At the time of his arrest, Landru had outstanding warrants for those same crimes. Evidence of Landru's swindling abounded after his April 1919 arrest, and he freely admitted to those activities, in full awareness that it would send him back to prison for life. But the known reality of the man took a back seat to the synthetic power of words.

Snell's most powerful insight concerned what would qualify as evidence in the affair. No matter what the police found, he believed, it would become an indication of murder. The criminal fantasy determined the meaning of objects, not vice versa. The surreality of the Landru Affair lay in the ability of the story to configure disparate material elements into the singular irrational image of the "Bluebeard of Gambais." However, the objective framework which supported that criminal scenario was not derived from an irrational fantasy, but was first developed in the supposedly scientific realms of criminal anthropology and police laboratory science.

To be identified as a criminal in the Belle Époque, it helped to look like one. In his foundational 1871 work, *L'uomo delinquente* ("Criminal Man"), Dr. Césare Lombroso established the discipline of criminal anthropology as the science of physiognomy, the deciphering of external body markings as signs of internal pathologies. According to Lombroso, physical deformities and irregularities were atavistic signs of evolutionary inferiority. A hereditary propensity toward criminality, Lombroso believed, originated in the inheritance of an aberrant biology, a theory supported by the claim that the bodies of criminals and the insane, those with known social and psychological pathologies, readily displayed such irregularities. Throughout Europe, criminal anthropologists were united in their attempt to develop a science of reading body signs as symptoms of character disorders.

In France, criminal anthropology traced its historical origins to the medical and psychiatric "nosology" of Pinel, Esquirol, Morel, and Charcot and was organized in the late nineteenth century by Alexandre Lacassagne through the *Archives d'anthropologie criminelle*. In a series of international congresses on criminal anthropology (Rome 1885, Paris 1889, Brussels 1892), Lacassagne's French school of criminal anthropology drew a clear distinction between itself and the followers of Lombroso.[29] In contrast to the biological determinism of Lombroso, the French school of criminal anthropology considered the individual a "social organism." Those physiological characteristics crucial to Lombroso's system, such as an unusually shaped skull, a small brain, a weak constitution, and enlarged sexual organs, were considered insufficient measures of the "criminal type" by the French school of criminal anthropology. Such physical "abnormalities," it was argued, were prevalent not only in prison populations, but among the general public as well. The number of individuals identified through physiognomy as biologically inferior in the Lombrosian sense were few, French criminal anthropologists concluded.

At the same time, the French school readily concurred that criminals displayed high rates of physical abnormalities and unusual body markings. In *Les Habitués des Prisons de Paris* (1890), Dr. Emile Laurent detailed the degenerative physical and mental disorders found in male prison populations.[30] The maladies of habitual criminals, Laurent claimed, did not originate in biology, but in the circumstances that first led a person to commit a crime, usually an underdeveloped moral sense resulting from insufficient training. Habitation in a criminal environment, alcohol consumption, and engaging in suspect sexual practices reinforced the criminal personality through the repetition of crimes. With repetition, the argument continued, the combined effects of criminal activity and a degraded environment produced a kind of Lamarckian evolutionary regression toward physical deformations and mental inferiority. Therefore, one was not born with criminal features; rather one grew into them through a lifetime of criminal activity.

In practice, the French school of criminal anthropology had it both ways. On the one side, if the criminal's life was not predestined by biology or heredity, he was responsible for his criminal acts. While recent historiography has focused upon the *crime passionnel* or "crime of passion," which absolved murderers of responsibility for their actions, the issue of passion versus responsibility in cases of crime was very much contested by French criminal anthropologists and legal jurists of the era.[31] Criminal anthropologist Emile Laurent affirmed that the fear of imprisonment was intended precisely to curb those whose passions were stronger than their intelligence and that all criminals should be held responsible for their actions (with the possible exception of most severely insane).[32] Jurist Louis Proal concurred that crimes of passion extending to the sphere of irresponsibility were extremely rare. "Whether due to passion or not," Proal emphasized, "crime is always crime."[33]

On the other side, French criminal anthropologists regarded the individual as a "social organism," whose inheritance was the product of both biological and social factors. The unchecked activities of individual

criminals, French criminal anthropologists argued, exerted a degenerative influence not only on themselves and their progeny but upon society at large. So while body signs were in themselves insufficient guides
for identifying criminal types, French criminal anthropologists heartily
supported the invocation of those same signs to stigmatize criminals.
Once an individual was a known criminal, irregular physical features,
sexual perversities, alcoholism, and even tattoos became expressions of
his degraded condition.

The practice of connecting body signs to criminality was reinforced
by the invention of the anthropometric fiche, introduced by Alphonse
Bertillon in 1882 as a method of identifying recidivists.[34] Because a person could alter his or her physical appearance, Bertillon developed a catalog system that detailed a wide range of information about an individual upon arrest. Photographs of a suspect were recorded on his or her
fiche, in front and side portraits. But since outward physical appearances
changed over time, more stable body measurements were recorded as
well—height and body type, measurements of the skull, ears, nose,
middle finger, and big toe, notations about eye and hair color, unusual or
distinguishing marks such as birthmarks or tattoos, as well as general observations about the individual's features. The criminal's anthropometric
records were then conserved in two places: first, a personal file, containing the collected photographs and measurements of the individual; second, a collective file in which the individual's measurements were broken
down by the various body parts and grouped with those of other individuals. Through a comparison of the two files, positive identification of
a recidivist could be established when the cross-referenced measurements conserved in the collective file matched an individual fiche. In this
system, the crucial file was the collective one, representing a new approach to establishing a specific criminal identity through the accumula-
tion of fragmented body parts.

In Landru's case, the ability to piece together a criminal identity
proved more important than his actual appearance. His personal anthropometric fiche failed to advertise his criminality. Marcel Coulon, who
covered the Landru Affair for the *Mercure de France*, noted that Landru
simply wasn't ugly enough to be stigmatized by his anthropometric

profile.[35] He had some missing teeth, but they were molars, and therefore not visible. He was bald, but in a distinguished sort of way. His beard was a bit more suggestive, Coulon conceded, resembling a paste-on beard. But the feature that ultimately proved Landru "monstrous," Coulon accurately predicted, was his *silence.* In the absence of stigmata, and given his refusal to admit to murder, Landru's persona as a serial killer was pieced together from data in the collective anthropometric file.

In the press, Landru's physiognomy became completely plastic, assembled and rearranged to suit the sensationalist needs of a particular article. The most descriptively stigmatizing depiction of Landru appeared in *Le Journal.*[36] According to Dr. Pactat, Professor of Physiognomy and a disciple of Gall and Lavater, Landru exhibited the conoidal skull of *l'homme aux finances* (a world play on *l'homme au fiancées,* a phrase often used in press coverage of the Landru affair). This skull of "the man of finances," Pactat explained, indicates a sanguine and brutal nature but at the same time practical and enterprising. A protuberance on Landru's forehead, however, indicated obstinacy and lowered intelligence. According to Pactat, Landru's bushy eyebrows were signs of a domineering, irascible, and unsocial character. The profile of his nose showed courage, but the nostrils and mouth were excessively sensual and lascivious. Above all, Pactat concluded, it was Landru's strange fixity of gaze that fascinated his victims.

While Dr. Pactat's description was unabashedly blatant in its fabrication of Landru's appearance, the Parisian press generally engaged in similar divinations of his supposed criminal features. Like his anthropometric fiche, the initial photographs of Landru in the press were fairly nondescript, the portrait of a man with a trimmed beard, thin hair, and fair complexion.[37] But soon, photographs of Landru varied substantially according to the needs of a particular article. Some photos darkened Landru's eye sockets and retouched the eyes to produce the sparkling gaze of an underworld seducer of women.[38] In others, Landru had a large mustache and unkempt beard, a pointed ratlike nose with flared nostrils, and heavy eyelids, suggestive of the deranged slayer of women.[39] In yet other portraits (pl. 5), Landru was formally attired, well groomed and elegant, the bourgeois husband-pretender of grief-stricken widows.

Plate 5.   Landru and Fernande Segret on the cover of *Détective* magazine, 1930. (Collection: Bibliothèque Historique de la Ville de Paris)

The fluidity of Landru's appearance reached its supreme expression on the eve of his trial in a photo-illustrated article in *Le Matin*.[40] Without a doubt, the article began, Landru is irresistible, so much so that his fiancées burned for him. Still, the article conceded, Landru's actual appearance may not please all women. Therefore, "Which Landru do you prefer?" Composite portraits and descriptions of various Landrus followed: romantic or austere? domineering or delightfully old-fashioned? sporting a "conquering mustache," full beard, or clean-shaven? thick or thin hair? with or without glasses? Perhaps, the article suggested, Landru changes his social position and appearance for each woman. Which is preferable? "It really doesn't matter," the article concluded, "so long as it is He!" In the sensationalist press, Landru's actual appearance mattered less than those features that exerted his supposed effect on women.

To complete the image of the Bluebeard of Gambais, however, not only Landru's appearance but everything associated with him had to become saturated with signs of criminality. Here, the path was prepared by police laboratory science. Whereas criminal anthropology and anthropometrics sought the signs of criminality on the body of the accused, forensic analysis shifted the field of investigation to the much wider realm of objects upon which the criminal had left his mark. In the early twentieth century, Dr. Edmond Locard was director of the technical police laboratory in Lyon, and was perhaps the most esteemed forensics expert of the era. Thanks to modern police science, Dr. Locard wrote in *Policiers de roman et policiers de laboratoire*, the incredible ratiocinations of Edgar Allan Poe's Auguste Dupin, Emile Gaboriau's Detective Lecoq, and Arthur Conan Doyle's Sherlock Holmes had become a reality.[41] Crime endowed the world with traces of criminality, and the police laboratory science methodically collected and interpreted those signs to discover the culprit.

In *L'Enquête criminelle et les méthodes scientifiques*, Locard made a strong argument in favor of police science.[42] Through laboratory analysis, the signature of a criminal's activity could be found in a wide range of materials, including fingerprints, footprints, teeth imprints, blood stains, traces of sperm, feces, urine, mucus, dust, ink, paper, clothing, threads, handwriting, and cryptograms. The advantage to the technical analysis of these materials (*preuve indicale*), Locard argued, was that it established a direct rapport between the crime and the accused. The rapport was contingent, he admitted, but it was far more reliable than witness testimony. While direct confession remained the "queen of proofs," the corroborating evidence of technical analysis made the case against the accused stronger.

In the Landru Affair, however, criminal fantasy proved stronger than corroboration. The most intriguing piece of circumstantial evidence against Landru was his *carnet*, his daily expense notebook, which became crucial in making the swindler-murderer connection. The principal finding from the *carnet* was that Landru was extremely tight with his money; he noted even a few *sous* paid out for alms candles. The fact that Landru number-coded some of the entries, in order to protect the nature of his business transactions, leant an additional air of mystery to the document.[43] Tantalizing entries in the *carnet* included train ticket purchases to Houdan, near Gambais, which corresponded to the disappearances of Mesdames Collomb and Babelay. In these instances, Landru had purchased two outgoing tickets, but only one return. Cryptic references to dates of entry, the names of Collomb, Babelay, Buisson, Jaume, and Pascal, and various times of day were widely interpreted as Landru's record of each victim's time of death. In addition to the *carnet*, the police recovered files from his garage in Clichy containing 283 responses to his newspaper marriage advertisements, as well as Landru's responses to more than 150 of them. Such excessive numbers, so carefully documented, made it much easier for the press to speculate on the Bluebeard of Gambais's possible crimes. Still, neither the *carnet* nor the dossiers shed any direct light upon the fate of the ten missing women.[44]

But the absence of direct connections was precisely where Snell's point about "plenty of other gardens" applied. Even everyday objects such as stoves, coal, burn piles, and cutting tools became sinister signs when discovered on Landru's property. The outlying locations of Landru's villas, *The Lodge* at Vernouillet and *La villa Tric* at Gambais, and various garages around the periphery of Paris—in Clichy, Neuilly, and Saint-Ouen-l'Aumône—were mysterious by virtue of their seclusion. The horrific fantasies associated with these objects and locations made them compelling, whether they really were used in the commission of murders or not.

The most infamous, and technically opaque, sign of Landru's crimes was his kitchen oven, which was displayed in court during his trial in November 1921 (pl. 6). From early press reports about bones and ashes in burn piles, blood stains on Landru's oven, and the stench coming from the chimney, the story quickly developed that Landru had burned his

Plate 6. Landru's oven in court. From F. A. Mackenzie, *Landru* (Charles Scribners' Sons, 1928).

fiancées in the oven at Gambais. Once this scenario had captured the imagination, everything known about the oven and its accessories became "proof" of the cremation theory. The fact that Landru had an oven meant that he could have burned the women. But since the oven was very small, he had to chop them up first. Landru could have used the cutting tools found at Gambais to cut them up. Also, Landru had ordered coal for his oven, and had been seen by witnesses carrying sacks of coal, so he could have used to coal to cremate the women. Since he did not order very much coal, he burned only parts of the women. Because the head, hands and feet are the most easily identifiable parts of the body, those were the parts he burned. The fact that the experts had cremated a sheep's head in an oven similar to Landru's meant that the same thing could have happened to the women's heads, feet and hands.

But such a ratiocination of "facts" only appeared convincing when the
foregone conclusion was that Landru had burned the women in his stove.
Other facts should have seriously put into question the fantastic deduc-
tions developed around the "evidence" of the oven. From the outset,
doubts were raised about the ability of Landru's small stove to reach tem-
peratures necessary to cremate human bodies, a test never established in
fact. No blood stains at Gambais were ever identified as human. The
cause of death for any of the women— even the fact of death—was never
established. These issues were never resolved and remained outside the
fantasy.

Yet the ultimate proof of Landru's murderous crimes was the simple
assertion that he was the "Bluebeard of Gambais." To stabilize his identity as a murderer and infuse his possessions with lethal intent, Landru
required a monstrous persona. Again, the known attributes of the man
made it difficult to establish such a personality. Landru's previous criminal record as a swindler (*escroc*) was not of much use to the police in trying to prove him a murderer. Given Landru's otherwise fairly ordinary
existence (an altar boy at the Ile de St-Louis church, an unremarkable
stint in the military, a technical engineering degree from the École des
Arts et Métiers), the police found nothing in Landru's past to suggest he
was a serial killer. By contrast, Landru fit the con-man profile perfectly—
a fifty-year-old male, married with children, urban, educated, technically
trained, with a known criminal record of swindling, but with no record
of violent crime.[45] *Escroquerie*—forging signatures on bank notes, selling
the property of others, fronting stolen goods, breaches of trust—was the
scenario most consistent with the available evidence against Landru. It
accounted for his use of so many aliases, his many residences, and his refusal to cooperate with the police when he had outstanding prison sen-
tences to serve under the name of Landru.

Neither did Landru exhibit an "aberrant psychology." During his previous incarcerations, medical reports from psychiatric experts (*médecins
aliénistes*) in 1904 and 1906 concurred that, although Landru possessed
some worrisome hereditary and personal pathological antecedents—
his father's suicide, mental depression during his previous incarcerations
—he was nonetheless psychologically normal.[46] When psychiatrists

reached the same conclusion during his 1921 trial, Landru considered it a point in his favor. "I would like to most sincerely thank these esteemed experts," Landru said, "for explaining that the monstrosity of the crimes which have been attributed to me suggests a perversity that stems from complete insanity. Since they have declared me psychologically sound, it means that I couldn't have possibly committed such crimes."[47] Even newspaper editorials noted that Landru was basically a pathetic little man, lacking the physical power or charisma of the mythic Bluebeard. "An entire legend stands between the awful little hovel at Gambais and Bluebeard's castle," as *Le Figaro* put it.[48]

Yet if Landru personally lacked a murderous personality and a record of violent crimes, this did not restrain the press. Both Landru's persona and his activities could be pieced together from a vast repertoire of infamous nineteenth-century "human monsters." Immediately after his arrest, Police Commissioner Bichon associated Landru with Dumolard, who had murdered at least two servant girls between 1859 and 1860.[49] Over the course of two years, Landru was linked to other famous murderers as well. He was compared to Jean-Baptiste Troppmann, who, in 1869, murdered the entire Kinck family in Pantin, a northeastern suburb of Paris.[50] Landru's ability to influence lonely widows recalled the 1882 case of Euphrasie Mercier, who befriended, murdered, burned, and buried the widow Elodie Menetret in the victim's own suburban house in Villemomble, east of Paris.[51] Landru was also compared with Carrara, who in 1897 murdered a bank messenger and, together with his wife, cremated the man's body in a large furnace in their mushroom cellar.[52] This gallery of nineteenth-century monstrous criminals provided the press with the range of horrific activities attributed to Landru.

However, it was the case of Albert Pel upon which Landru's story was most closely modeled.[53] Until he became a murderer, Pel had led an unremarkable life as a part-time watchmaker and chemist on rue Rochechouart. Then, between 1871 and 1884, the women in his life began to die mysteriously. First was his mother, Madame Pel, who died of "electrical shock." Next was his fiancée, Eugénie Meyer, who suffered from diarrhea, vomiting, colic, and intense thirst before dying. His wife, Eugénie Buffereau, died after displaying the same symptoms. The subsequent fiancée, Madame Mura-Belliste, wisely left Pel after the onset of such maladies.

But it was the death of Pel's final mistress, Elise Boehmer, that established the scenario used in the Landru affair. After Boehmer set up house with Pel in the Parisian suburb of Montreuil in 1884, no one ever saw her again. In the middle of July, some of Pel's neighbors were sickened by disgusting smells emanating from his chimney. Others saw great flames lighting up his apartment widows. Upon closer inspection, they could see Pel stooping over the glowing furnace, stoking the fire. Some noticed a great quantity of white cinders in Pel's ash-box. The police were notified and, after a judicial investigation, Pel was arrested. Forensic experts conducted an experiment in a stove similar to the one owned by Pel. They dismembered a corpse and burned it over a forty-eight hour period, recovering about six kilos of ash similar in appearance to that found in Pel's furnace. In his 1885 trial, Pel was found guilty of the murder of Elise Boehmer and was sentenced to death. But an appeal commuted his sentence to life imprisonment with hard labor, since no direct connection was ever established between the collected ashes and Boehmer. Nearly all of the details elaborated upon in Landru's case were first established in the Pel trial.

This repertoire of "human monsters," sensational murders, and trials provided the press with a complex cultural system from which to fashion the image of the Bluebeard of Gambais. Criminal anthropology and forensics had provided a multitude of criminal signs that could be poured into the imaginary image of Landru, itself a composite identity fashioned out of a late nineteenth-century popular tradition of human monsters. The real Landru paled in comparison, more an "everyman," as Carolyn Dean has characterized him, than a "monster."[54] Yet by maintaining his silence in the presence of those criminal fantasies, the actual Landru was reformulated into the surreal image of the Bluebeard of Gambais. The oversaturation of images and signs of criminality circulated in the press and replayed in the courtroom helped the majority of the jurors in the *cour d'assises* abolish the antinomies between the known small-time crook Landru and the fantastic stories about the Bluebeard of Gambais, and they found him guilty of imagined murder.

SURREAL MURDER

Was Landru guilty? Any other response seems inconceivable. The circumstantial evidence against him was overwhelming: the endless testimony, the mysterious *carnet* and multiple dossiers, trunks of clothes and garages of furniture, the coincidence of ten disappeared women, and Landru the only point of intersection between them. Yet a consistent story could never be established—neither in motivation (why Landru killed) nor in fact (a poverty of causes in relation to the multiplicity of effects). The question of "whether" Landru murdered the women was displaced by a far more fascinating question: "how?"

For what was most compelling about the Landru Affair was not the fact of murder, but the sadistic, excessive, and macabre fantasy that transformed a small-time crook into a serial murderer of monstrous proportions. From across the English Channel, an editorial in the *Outlook* questioned the larger significance of the trial: "[T]he puzzle of the Landru case is less the mentality of the criminal than the character of the popular interest taken in his deeds." The key to that puzzling popular mentality, the editorial continued, was a kind of humor. "It is not a morbid interest in the fate of Landru, or a shuddering curiosity concerning his victims. Landru is a joke. The murdered women are a joke. The whole atmosphere is that of cynical levity."[55] What was most distinctive about the affair was neither the murderer nor his victims, but the dark humor of the surreal story of the Bluebeard of Gambais created and circulated by the press.

"I'm a crook, that's understood. But prove that I'm a murderer! A lover leaves his mistress; they get into a fight, and never see each other again. But that doesn't make me a murderer."[56] Landru's line of defense had been simple enough: Prove me a murderer. Despite the formidable circumstantial evidence against him, Landru may have well hoped that even if he were found guilty, like Pel his sentence would be commuted to life imprisonment. On the one hand, the police had collected less than a kilo of bone ashes for ten bodies, as opposed to six kilos for a single body in Pel's case. In addition, French law required an eighteen-year waiting period before a missing person could be presumed dead. Even then, the presumption of death was considered insufficient evidence in murder cases, points that defense attorney Moro-Giafferi eloquently argued (albeit in vain) during his closing summation before the jury.

But Landru's defense was a miscalculation. For the jury that listened to his case, a conviction verdict was not established through the evidence presented in court but from within the consciences of the jurors themselves. Since the French Revolution of 1789, a trial system based upon the "personal conviction" (*conviction intime*) of the jurors had replaced the Ancien Régime legal burden in capital cases of two corroborating pieces of unrelated evidence presented before a judge.[57] Even more that the weight of evidence, the jurors were instructed by the presiding judge to examine their consciences to the full extent of their rational capabilities, and render a verdict of guilty or innocent. On the final day of November 1921, the jury reached its verdict. By a vote of nine to three, they found Landru guilty on all charges of murder, and all but two of breach of trust (*abus de confiance*).

But then a curious thing happened. At the instigation of defense attorney Moro-Giaferri, immediately following the verdict the jury presented the presiding judge with *un recours en grâce,* an appeal for clemency, to be forwarded to the president of the Republic, Alexandre Millerand. The appeal was signed by all the jurors, the twelve plus the two alternates, as well as one of the civil parties, Madame Fuchet, representing the disappeared Madame Pascal. The reaction among members of the press to the contradictory responses of the jury — on the one hand affirming that Landru was the horrific murderer of ten women and one adolescent boy, and then unanimously appealing for clemency on the other—was one of confusion and disbelief. "What went through the minds of those twelve honest citizens?" asked Emile Vuillermoz, who covered the trial for the conservative weekly, *L'Illustration.*[58] They had already passed judgment on Landru—guilty of murder on every count—Vuillermoz emphasized, so why did they refuse to assume responsibility for inflicting the deserved punishment? In an unusual display of insight, *Le Journal* suggested that by signing the *recours en grâce,* the nine steadfast jurors who voted guilty were in fact less than certain about the verdict and in this way actually affirmed the three votes for acquittal.[59] Still, there was something deeply disturbing about a verdict of guilty mixed with a unanimous appeal for clemency; as Vuillermoz also pointed out, no extenuating circumstances had been invoked on behalf of Landru.

Instead, a surreal dark humor accounts for the paradoxical judgment of the jurors in the Landru Affair. André Breton described dark humor (*l'humour noir*) as an unconscious process of the pleasure principle. Situated, as Breton put it, at the intersection of the "black sphinx of objective humor" (unconscious pleasures whose origins we do not understand) and the "white sphinx of objective chance" (known coincidences which are equally beyond rational explanation), dark humor accords psychic power to the individual against the logic of external reality.[60] It is the gallows humor of the condemned man who, when led to the scaffold on Monday morning, declares, "What a way to start the week!"[61] Confronted with overwhelming circumstances, such humor derives self-pleasure by denying authority to physical reality or social order.[62] The pleasure the individual derives from such humor is far from comic, however; it is more likely to be psychologically disturbing and physically convulsive.[63] A surreal, dark humor provides an interpretive key toward understanding, as Vuillermoz put it, what went on in the minds of those jurors.

The development of the dark humor of the Landru Affair followed the same stages as those that Breton noted in Léon-Pierre Quint's *Le Comte de Lautréamont et Dieu:* sadism, imaginary excess, and ironic negation.[64] Before the jury even entered the courtroom, the surreal story of the Bluebeard of Gambais had been created and circulated by the press. Throughout the periods of Landru's arrest and trial, sensationalist newspaper coverage emphasized sadism as Landru's dominant attribute. Yet in the aftermath of the jury's pronouncements, the press deflected its own part in the creation of such sadistic fantasies; instead it chastised newspaper readers and court spectators for their own morbid fascination with Landru. According to many Parisian dailies, the trial proceedings took place in a milieu of crime and vice. The courtroom spectators were characterized as underclass riffraff (*la pègre*), who laughed and munched bonbons throughout the proceedings. Most newspaper accounts characterized the courtroom crowd as composed of overly excited women pressing in front

of one another to get a better view of Landru. The press also noted the
courtroom attendance of literary and entertainment celebrities (author
Colette and *chansonnière* Mistinguett) and international dignitaries (Per-
sian prince Mohammed Hussan Mirza, Chinese minister Tchen-Loh, and
Spanish ambassador Quinones de Léon). This carnivalesque combination of high society and lowlife proved too much for the Catholic daily
newspaper, *La Croix*. The paper admonished its readers, "Respectable
people, who due to devotion to fashion were mistakenly dragged into
this immoral crowd, have nothing to brag about by having followed the
proceedings of the Landru Affair!"[65]

The press attributed a particularly unseemly fascination with Landru
to female courtroom spectators. "It is a superb Punch and Judy show
(*théâtre grandguignolesque*)," *Le Journal* noted, "and the elegant women in
the audience hang on every word, with little shivers of delight running
down their necks."[66] Robert Dieudonné complained in *Le Figaro* that the
large number of curious and unruly women in attendance had turned
the court into a bawdy spectacle. Their outbursts, laughter, exchange of
pleasantries, he claimed, were a direct expression of women's poor command over their emotions. Right down to the final court session, Dieudonné concluded the article, these women continued to treat Landru as
an entertainment personality.[67] Yet by claiming that it was the women in
the audience who had turned the trial into a shameful spectacle, the press
in effect merely completed its own sadistic story of Landru with a reciprocal insinuation of masochism.[68]

Such attention devoted to the courtroom *spéctatrices* in the press revealed little about Landru, his female victims, or the actual women in attendance, but expressed a great deal of the dark humor of the story itself.
By connecting feminine desire to Landru's sadism, the press retold the
masochistic story of desired punishment. In *Le Figaro*, Camille Mauclair
wrote that history is rich in legends about the punishment of feminine
curiosity, not only the seven wives of Bluebeard, but Eve, Lot's wife,
Pandora, and Psyche as well.[69] The promise of punishment nourishes an
all-powerful feminine curiosity, he affirmed, and yields a disturbingly
shocking delight (*une joie étrangement frissonate*). The unfortunate woman
who is actually killed by a cold-blooded monster for having looked

MURDER, MIRTH, AND MISOGYNY

through the keyhole, Mauclair judged, does nothing more than the millions before her, the centuries-old sign of woman's nature.

Throughout the affair, the press had suggested that Landru's victims were to blame for their own fates. Professor Pactat, who analyzed Landru's physiognomy for *Le Journal* in May 1919, required nothing more than photographs of the missing women to declare them masochists: "On being shown the photographs of the alleged victims the man of science waved them contemptuously away with the remark: 'Defenseless women, credulous, round-faced—therefore easy to deceive.' The professor paused, seized Mme Buisson's photograph, and corrected himself. 'That is one who ought to have resisted. She has a square face. She ought to have drowned Landru.'"[70] Landru may have been a sexually deranged murderer, but according to the press his task would not have been accomplished so easily had his female victims had not desired such punishment.

The press further attributed such a masochistic yearning to newspaper readers generally. At the outset of the affair, shortly after Landru's arrest, popular novelist Clément Vautel wrote about lovelorn older women seeking marriage or remarriage in his *"Mon Film"* column for *Le Journal.* The same skeptical and suspicious woman who will not even lend her best friend ten francs, Vautel wrote, becomes the most ingenuous and naive person in the world once she has been struck by "marriage fever." Such women, he claimed, were easy prey for Landru:

> "Marriage Offer Fraud." The most banal kind of *fait-divers* . . . Yet it led Landru to murder. Why? Dumolard assassinated women servants, Landru his women patrons. He has killed perhaps a dozen of them. . . .
> What astonishes me is that there aren't fifty or a hundred. But it's also true that the investigation has only just begun.
> I hesitate to say it, but it seems to me that all eligible bachelors over forty years old are somewhat the accomplices of Landru.[71]

Vautel caricatured Landru's "victims" as utterly suggestible and emotionally unstable women. Further, Landru's crime was peculiarly modern, a combination of a swindling scheme committed daily by means of the press, and murder (although it lacked the powerful passionate violence of the nineteenth-century "human monsters").

But Vautel's most suggestive criticism was that the newspaper readers who followed the affair were, to some degree, passive participants in Landru's banal sadism. For once the qualifiers were removed—Landru was neither "eligible" nor a "bachelor," and the fact of his fifty years held no direct relationship to the varied ages of the missing women—"all eligible bachelors over forty-years old" boiled down to passive men. In the gender-stereotyped system that opposes passionate men to suggestible women, such enervated men are hardly men at all, complicitous in imagining both the sadistic exploits of Landru and the masochistic fates of his victims.[72] This emphasis upon masochistic victims and readers completed the sadistic story of the Bluebeard of Gambais, while the press deflected its own role in its creation.

This slippery move, whereby the press cast its own sado-masochistic fantasy back upon the public, was noted in the anarchist weekly, *Le Libertaire.* As early as the second week of the trial, an article by a *célèbre inconnu* attacked *Le Journal* editor Edouard Helsey for charging a "bestial public" with indecency.[73] The sensationalist daily, this famous unknown pointed out, had already served up all the spicy details (*croustillants*) of crimes, killings, murders, and rapes that one could possibly imagine. The article took particular aim at *Le Journal*'s publication (a week before the trial) of Fernande Segret's embellished "memoirs", which provided more than enough fuel to heat up (*chauffer*) public opinion. If the public remained ignorant about the real issues involved in the Landru Affair, the article concluded, it was the bourgeois press that kept it so.

In the same anarchist journal, French feminist Madeleine Pelletier pushed the critique further.[74] However strange the notion might sound, she claimed, the Landru trial actually supported the feminist cause. Whether Landru was guilty or not, such a notorious "Fantômas" was only possible, Pelletier asserted, because of the actual subservient condition of unmarried and widowed Frenchwomen. Isolated, socially ridiculed as old maids, jealous of younger women rivals, and desiring a middle-class "sweet home," such women, Pelletier pointed out, had few options outside marriage. The women who responded to Landru's marriage offers, she claimed, were merely following the principle of the legal guardianship of husband over wife, before being cast into his oven. The press's fascination with Landru's victims, Pelletier maintained, had only diverted attention away from real economic, social, and legal inequities between the sexes in French society. This scenario would only change, she concluded, when liberated women no longer required masters. Such a critique was obscure, however, in the daily, mass, sensationalist press.

Recounting the imagined sadistic exploits of Landru in newspaper articles, and their supposed masochistic enjoyment by a female public, constituted one level of *l'humour noir*. To augment the effect, the daily press, since Landru's arrest and investigation in 1919, supplemented the sado-masochistic fantasies with an excess of anecdotal humor, the second quality Breton noted in Quint's *Lautréamont*. In April, *Le Temps* reported that Monsieur Henri Landru, exporter, manufacturer, and recipient of the Medal of the Legion of Honor, wanted it made a matter of public record that he bore no relation whatsoever to the accused murderer.[75] In May, Mademoiselle Gilberte Marty from Aubin denied press reports that Landru had sent her horse carcasses to be ground into sausages.[76] And throughout the Sûreté's investigatory trial of Landru, the press reported witticisms from the accused directed toward his interrogating judge. In one instance, after the day's interrogation, Landru's attorney suggested that his client wear a headband to protect his watery, inflamed eyes. Landru reportedly responded, "You want me to look like Justice?"[77] Such witticisms were recounted throughout the 1921 trial as well.

Yet the anecdotal humor generated by the press exceeded mere reportage. Especially noteworthy were cartoons displayed on the cover of *Le Journal* throughout Landru's trial. One cartoon format involved a juxtaposition of cartoons, split left and right on either side of the newspaper masthead. In one, the left cartoon portrays Landru and a woman standing in front of an oven ("Have a seat, Fernande"), with a caption that reads, "Pay attention Ladies! At Gambais, you risk being shot by Landru (*le coup de feu*)." The cartoon on the right shows a woman in the courtroom, reaching out toward Landru in the dock, "But at Versailles you risk being struck by love-lightning (*le coup de foudre*)."[78] Another shows Landru in the dock between two guards in the left cartoon, proclaiming, "You cannot condemn me without proof!" The cartoon on the right shows Landru skewered on a pitchfork, as Satan promises, "As he sinned, so he will be punished."[79]

Other cartoons stood alone. In one, a street *clochard* asks another, "If he is acquitted, do you think he will find a new companion?" The other responds, "No doubt! Lots of women like to hang on the arm of a famous man."[80] In another, titled "Everything is Explained," a very devilish Landru, with large knitted brows, a formidable mustache, and a long inverted-triangle beard, roasts a pig-faced woman on a skewer over an open hearth, apologizing, "She's the one who asked for a broach (*broche*, or brooch) for her engagement present."[81] In yet another, a man dashing out the front door—coat, briefcase, and umbrella in hand—turns back to his wife, who is holding a baby, and asks, "What did he say? Papa? . . . Mama?" . . . "No," the woman replies: "Landru."[82]

Other forms of humorous excess appeared as well. Both *Le Matin* and *Le Journal* ran "The True History of Bluebeard" features, in verse and play formats, during the trial.[83] The week before his trial, *Le Journal* published a note supposedly written by Landru to his interrogating judge, requesting that he be allowed to attend the afternoon matinee performance of *"Paris en l'air"* at the Casino de Paris on All Saints' Day.[84] Advertisers made use of the trial to boost sales. The Eldorado theater suggested that Landru should change lawyers and come see the performance of their renowned defender, Trambi, in "The Cobbler's Crime" (*Le Crime du Bouif*).[85] In these hyperbolic diversions, the imaginary exploits of Landru were multiplied and further circulated.

Yet the carnival of the Bluebeard of Gambais could not be sustained forever. Eventually, the *humour noir* reached that critical moment when the violent and excessive fantasy began to question itself, confirming Breton's final inspiration from Quint's *Leautréamont*— that of ironic negation. The Parisian press's fantasy began to collapse immediately following the jury's verdict. Afraid that there might be something peculiarly French about the Landru Affair, Robert Dieudonné asserted in *Le Figaro* that "all men are similar." The Chinese engage in torture, he claimed, the Spanish run in front of bulls, and the Germans excel in the atrocities of war. The Landru Affair, Dieudonné concluded, is not so much an expression of modern times or French customs as it is an expression of our degraded human nature (*la bête humaine*).[86] Despite the self-serving nature of his interpretation, Dieudonné's comments shifted the focus of the affair upon human nature as degraded and morally culpable, and away from the horrific fantasy.

Other newspapers expressed fears that the persuasive power of the daily-installment newspaper story (roman-feuilleton) might save the convicted murderer from the scaffold rather than send him to it. In a farcical story adapted from the Dreyfus affair, La Croix asked the reader to imagine Landru deported to Cayenne, where he becomes an dutiful accountant.[87] After a year or so, one of his fiancées reappears, and his case is reopened. He becomes a martyr, then a member of the Chamber of Deputies, and even the minister of finance. He dies at a ripe old age, honored and respected. Then, one day, the editorial continued, his memoirs will reveal an ironic confession: I did not kill ten women, only nine. At that point, the editorial concluded, the credulous reader of newspapers will finally lose any faith he might still have in human justice. Despite the duplicity of generating yet another chapter in the story of the new Bluebeard, the editorial ironically illustrated how press fantasy and judicial process had become inexorably intertwined in Landru's trial.

As the fantasy of the Bluebeard of Gambais began to dissolve in the aftermath of Landru's trial, jokes in the press assumed the status of gallows humor. On the eve of his execution, Landru reportedly asked the prison barber to trim his beard especially well, "to please the ladies one last time."[88] A variation on the story added that during the final shave, the barber remarked that Landru's glasses (lunettes) were too small to fit properly, to which Landru replied, "It doesn't matter. A few hours from now, Deibler will give me another fitting" (une autre lunette, a reference to the aperture of the guillotine).[89] Stories were also circulated that just before mounting the scaffold, Landru was offered a shot of rum, which he politely refused, "No thank you, I don't drink." And similarly, for the final cigarette, "No thank you, I don't smoke."[90]

Yet such jokes paled in comparison to the darkest humor of all, the execution of Landru. The scene invited ironic juxtapositions. Landru, sentenced to death for having killed widows, was in turn killed by "The Widow" (la Veuve, a nickname for the guillotine). The only confirmed corpse, however, was Landru's. The "public" execution was performed in the outlying locality of Versailles, and in the early hours of the morning. Preparations for the execution—wheeling in the guillotine and constructing the scaffold—were all done under the cover of darkness, so that Landru could be executed at dawn. To complete the macabre effects, candles adorned and illuminated the scaffold.[91] The humorous negation only lacked actual execution.

Parisian literary figure André Salmon, founder of the *Archives du Club Onze* and a participating poet in some of the early dada performances organized by Breton and others at *Littérature*, covered Landru's execution for *Le Matin*.[92] It is a strange sight, Salmon commented, to see these workers beginning their day, and farm wives on their way to market, milling around the platform in silence, craning to get a good view. Once fastened to the guillotine plank, Salmon noted, Landru had become so thin and light that, despite a strong push, his body did not trip the guillotine's automatic mechanism. Another second or more, and the blade fell. "The sound . . . the terrible sound—unlike anything else!—of the heavy blade in motion . . . Did anyone see it? . . . Can anyone confirm? . . . In a moment, everything is over. It is 6:04 in the morning." The darkest humor of all—the truth about the Bluebeard of Gambais—was the silence after the excitement had passed.

Two years after Landru's execution, literary and popular novelist Pierre Mac Orlan ruminated about Parisian murderers in the *"Chronique de Paris"* column of the literary review, *Mercure de France*.[93] In modern Paris, he noted, violent crime is an everyday occurrence. Magazines and newspapers are filled with stories about women chopped to pieces, he complained. In particularly sensational murders that excite the imagination, Mac Orlan believed that "The Spirit of Evil" (*l'Esprit de Mal*) mingled together atmosphere, details, and astonishing tales of murder, in a completely literary and plastic way. The monstrous personalities of certain murderers, he reflected, seem to emit the luminescence of a nightmare, although the nature of that light had nothing in common with the clarity of an electric lamp. Among Parisian murderers, he remarked, none had caught the popular imagination more than Landru. We have a fond weakness for the taste of the nocturnal life of such murders, Mac Orlan lamented. With or without the aesthetic fineries, he concluded, we are truly a generation accustomed to violent death.

Landru also received a passing reference in Aragon's *Le Paysan de Paris*. As he strolls through the Opera Passageway, Aragon contemplates the shop sign of "Vodable, *Tailleur mondain*." At the base of the sign, he imagines an advertisement that reads, "At court as in town, Monsieur *Landru* is outfitted by The Gentlemen's Tailor."[94] All Landrus still undiscovered, Aragon speculates, will converge upon this tailor shop. The inside joke: Vodable was dead, and his shop was being run by his widow.[95]

4 Is Suicide a Solution?

SURREALIST QUESTIONS AND *FAIT-DIVERS* RESPONSES

> If, as it is often said, man is double, it is because social man
> superimposes himself upon physical man. This social identity
> necessarily implies a society, which it expresses and serves.
> When this dissolves, however, . . . it leaves us devoid of all ob-
> jective foundations. All that remains is an artificial combina-
> tion of illusory images, a phantasmagoria made unconscious
> at the slightest reflection. . . . Consequently, we lack motives
> to live; for the only life we possess no longer corresponds to
> anything in reality. . . .

Emile Durkheim, *Le Suicide* (1897)

> Suicide is a poorly formed word—that which kills is not the
> same as that which is killed.

Théodore Jouffroy, quoted in André Breton,
"Is Suicide a Solution?" (1924)

The first number of *La Révolution Surréaliste* was issued on 1 December
1924. The cover announced, "We must realize a new declaration of the
rights of man." The inside cover identified Pierre Naville and Benjamin
Péret as the directors of the Central Bureau of Surrealist Research, "open
daily from 4:30 to 6:30, 15, rue de Grenelle." On the bottom third of the
second page, in large and bold typeface, the journal announced the first
surrealist *enquête*:

Inquiry

The *Surrealist Revolution* indiscriminately appeals to everyone to respond to the following open inquiry:

We live, we die. What is the part of the will in all of this? It seems as if we kill ourselves the same way we dream. This is not a moral question we are asking:

Is Suicide a Solution? [1]

The next month's issue not only published the responses but clarified in part what the surrealists had been up to. Many respondents were offended by the suggestion that suicide was a solution. But if you think about it, the surrealists countered, not so very long ago we were killing ourselves en masse—a thinly veiled reference to the one and a half million French soldiers killed in the Great War. Since 1919, war commemorations and memorials had become an everyday feature of French cultural life, in daily newspapers, illustrated weekly magazines, and even in automobile travel guides such as the series of "Michelin Illustrated Guides to the Battlefields (1914–1918)," dedicated to the memory of the Michelin factory workers and employees who had died gloriously for France.[2] "If suicide is not a solution," the surrealists asked, "what are all these heroic rumblings and legendary hazes floating about?"[3] Eight double-column pages of responses to the inquiry followed. The article concluded with an extract from a letter by Fernand Fontaine, Class of 1916, killed on 20 June 1915, "This is not as entertaining as I thought it would be. . . . And if I die, know that it will be against France."

On one level, the surrealists were railing against a hypocritical society that praised the millions of men who had voluntarily marched into slaughter during the course of the war but morally condemned anyone who died by his or her own hand. Such a critique is nearly self-evident, however, and fits firmly into a now-familiar thesis of the surrealists as yet another group of angry young men from the generation of 1914.[4] The first issue of *La Révolution Surréaliste* was formulating the germ of another critique as well: Beyond the easy target of the European conflagration of war, the surrealist inquiry into suicide drove toward irreducible paradoxes of modern existence as experienced at the level of everyday life.

In addition to posing the question "Is suicide a solution?", the premiere issue of *La Révolution Surréaliste* reprinted short *faits divers*, sensationalist newspaper accounts, of suicides originally published in newspapers (see the appendix to this chapter). Most were *faits divers en trois lignes*, that is, accounts contained in a single sentence, or two or three at the most. In one, a middle-aged woman with a lantern and umbrella threw herself down her neighbor's well. In another, a feverish young woman, wearing lingerie marked with a W, drowned in the Seine near the quai des Célestins. In a hotel room on rue Crébillon, a twenty-three-year-old American man "planted a bullet in his head" and left three suicide letters, including one for a Monsieur Frédéric Crébillon. In a report titled "A Strange Suicide," an artillery sergeant gathered his comrades in the canteen, lit three candles, and "blew his brains out" shortly thereafter.

This chapter explores the cultural significance of suicide in turn-of-the-century France in general and seeks in particular to illuminate what was surreal about suicide *faits divers*. By juxtaposing the question "Is suicide a solution?" with news tidbits about actual suicides, the surrealist inquiry extended beyond a mere condemnation of the senseless slaughter of the Great War. Through the paradoxical issue of suicide, simultaneously social and radically individual, the surrealists pushed their critique into the realm of everyday life. As critical and discriminating consumers of mass culture, the surrealists carefully selected their *faits divers* in order to emphasize the fundamentally sensational and fragmented nature of modern identity.

In the last quarter of the nineteenth century, French medical case studies of suicide amounted to little more than highbrow sensationalist literature, in substance indistinguishable from what the public read in press accounts. In *fin-de-siècle* medical literature, the details of bizarre suicides provided doctors and psychiatrists (*aliénistes*) with a didactic forum for delivering moral lectures about the degenerative social effects of alcohol, "criminal contagion," hereditary insanity, and improper education. These vices, the medical experts claimed, were most readily displayed among the lower social echelon of *la pègre*: the "lazy classes" of beggars, thieves, drifters, swindlers, gamblers, pimps, and prostitutes. In the early twentieth century, by contrast, sociologists and psychologists were increasingly coming to view suicide as an expression of an intensely felt alienation in otherwise normal individuals.

Yet the persistence of suicide *faits divers* into the interwar period simultaneously challenged earlier moral judgments and contemporary rational explanations of suicide. As "unclassifiable information," such *faits divers* constituted a form of daily mana or cultural excess that disrupted the normalcy of everyday life.[5] Produced from within the mass-culture industry of the press, these short accounts provoked paradoxical responses of revulsion, fascination, and compassion in newspaper readers. The surrealists hoped that the psychic disarray implicit in suicide *faits divers* would both undermine messages of social order and promote the surrealist revolution in consciousness.

THE HIGH ROAD TO SUICIDE: FROM MEDICINE TO SOCIOLOGY

According to many medical doctors and criminal anthropologists of the late nineteenth century, the moral implications of suicide left little room for uncertainty. Most suicide victims, they maintained, belonged to *la pègre*, which, as a class, lacked evolutionary verve in "the struggle for life." Studies by physicians, psychiatrists, and criminal anthropologists nearly always emphasized the debilitating effects of a familiar range of "socially degenerate" factors among suicide victims—alcoholism, laziness, hereditary madness, physical deformities, the mental and physical inferiority of women and children, uncontrollable animal passions, and insufficient moral development. Further, they believed that high rates of suicide among these "lazy classes" exercised a degenerative effect upon the whole of French society.

Those nefarious effects were spread through the "contagion of suicide," that is, through the mass circulation of accounts of bizarre suicides reported in the daily press. The theories of sociologist Gabriel Tarde were propounded by criminal anthropologists and medical experts who believed that hereditarily weak individuals, possessing underdeveloped physical constitutions or poor moral character, were susceptible to the

social contagion of suicide.[6] Hypnotically reenacting the details of suicides graphically recounted in the press, these individuals thus killed
themselves by imitation. Accounts of sensationalist suicides were found
not only in the daily press, the experts emphasized, but also in romantic
literature and in popular novels written in "bad" French and full of slang
(*l'argot*).[7]

  Yet in late nineteenth-century France, many medical and psychiatric
"case studies" amounted to little more than *faits divers* themselves,
dwelling on the morbid details of suicide to a greater degree than many
newspaper accounts. Within the context of their "scientific" studies,
however, these experts argued, such horrific and striking details served
the cause of proper moral training. The purported moral authority of
criminal anthropologists and psychiatrists regarding the topic of suicide
was challenged by the publication in 1897 of Emile Durkheim's *Le Suicide*,
which linked suicide to a lack of social integration, not heredity or imitation. Yet the moral debate over suicide was deeply rooted.

  At the end of the nineteenth century, the contagion of suicide was seen
as a veritable epidemic. "Suicide is the issue of the day," Dr. Paul Moreau
de Tours wrote in *Suicides et crimes étranges* (1899), "and not a single social class escapes its deadly influence."[8] In this remarkable work, Moreau
de Tours described dozens of bizarre suicides in all their astonishing and
horrific ferocity. For the purposes of this discussion, *Suicides et crimes
étranges* stands out as a representative compendium of the medical and
psychiatric interpretation of the social contagion of suicide at the turn of
the century. Consequently, the contours of that work warrant retracing in
some detail.

  Moreau de Tours's stated rationale for exploring accounts of extraordinary suicides was to determine the correlation (if any) between the
mental states of suicide victims and the methods they employed to accomplish suicide. Thus, he divided *Suicides et crimes étranges* into a series
of categories—suicides by criminals, suicides resulting from a morbid
compulsion, the suicides of *aliénés* (individuals suffering intense psychological alienation because of romantic disappointments, physical
maladies, or alcoholic stupor), suicides among the *franchement aliénés*, or
"completely insane" (those unhinged by hallucinations, religious de-

mentia, depression, hereditary madness, or monomania), "impulsive" or inexplicable suicides, and, finally, suicides attributable to "anesthesia."[9]

First, Moreau de Tours examined the cases of condemned criminals who committed suicide to avoid the scaffold. In 1887, in a Chicago prison cell, the anarchist Lingg stuck an explosive cartridge in his mouth and lit it with his cell candle. The terrible explosion blew off pieces of his throat, neck, chin and face, and he languished, blood flowing from his gaping wounds, until he died a few hours later. In Liverpool, in March 1888, a prisoner asphyxiated himself by tapping into an overhead gas pipe. In China, "some years ago," a man who had seduced his brother's wife, killed himself as punishment for his crime. With the entire family gathered, he tied a rope around his feet, braided a weight into his hair, and hoisted himself to the ceiling; blood filled his head, veins bulged, eyes burst out of their sockets, and blood gushed from his ears until he died. This type of suicide by criminals, Moreau de Tours asserted, occurs in all cultures.

Next, Moreau de Tours considered those who committed suicide due to a morbid compulsion (*une impulsion maladive*). Though seemingly in complete possession of their mental faculties (*sains d'esprit*), these individuals meticulously planned out their suicides in minute detail (often influenced, he suggested, by the details of suicides recounted in the press). Their line of work sometimes inspired their choice of method. An artillery lieutenant shot himself in front of a cannon. A toy maker, Madame C——, shot herself in the head with one of her toy cannons (as did her twelve-year-old son). The suicides of several metalworkers were particularly gruesome: One impaled himself with a heated iron tube, another lay on the ground and dropped a 550-pound anvil on his head, and a third crushed his head in a stamp press. These deaths, Moreau de Tours noted, were remarkable for their bizarre and graphic details.

Various groups of *aliénés* constituted a third category of suicide victims—those who experienced intense psychological alienation. A fifty-year-old man, jilted by his younger mistress, slashed his throat and then strangled himself with a red silk scarf; when he was found dead, his hands were still clutching the tourniquet's baton. Two young lovers, their marriage thwarted by their parents, tied themselves together on the beach at low tide and drowned as the tide came in. A young medical student from Clermont-Ferrand, suffering from an unspecified incurable illness, tried to kill himself with an overdose of morphine. Finding that the drug acted too slowly, the young man tried to cut out his own heart with a scalpel; he died of the resulting hemorrhage. In another case of suicide motivated by terminal illness (which Moreau de Tours called "a little on the comical side") a hatter from Passy suffocated himself with a special hat of his own creation that stretched all the way down his neck. Once again, these detailed case studies emphasized sensational descriptions of suicides.

Moreau de Tours cast an aspect of nearly Gothic horror upon his examples of suicides among the *franchement aliénés*. One night, the chronically alienated Lady H. W——— rose from her bed, put on her nightgown, and started a fire in the hearth. She stepped into the flames, silently stood still until her nightgown had entirely burned, and then returned to bed. Denying any knowledge of what had occurred, she died the following evening. Another woman in her thirties, whose sister had committed suicide, managed to kill herself only after trying several means: First, she covered herself in creosote. Then she tried drowning. She succeeded at last by choking on a sharp rock. At the autopsy, the examiners recovered a wooden rake tong from her stomach, and three nails, a wood screw, and three pieces of a sewing needle from her intestines.

Moreau de Tours also discussed suicides thought to result from religious dementia among the *franchement aliénés*. Mathieu Lovat, a Venetian shoemaker, was convinced that God wanted him to die on the cross. For two years he planned out his self-crucifixion, preparing the cross, the crown of thorns, and loincloth. When the time came, he suspended the cross in the transept of a church, mounted a small ledge that he had built at the bottom of the cross, and placed his hands (in which he had driven holes before ascending) over pegs in the crossbar. In another religiously inspired suicide, a man identified as C——— from Castellamare, a religious fanatic (and a glutton to boot), guillotined himself with a hatchet that slid down runners. Like the previous case, C——— had taken two years to construct his ingenious device.

Suicide attributed to drunkenness and alcoholism constituted yet another subcategory of the *franchement aliénés*. La fille B———, brought to a local police station drunk and with a bad case of the shakes, unsuccessfully attempted to drown herself in the prison toilet. An elderly female alcoholic from Loison was found dead on her blood-soaked bed, having cut her abdomen open with a pair of scissors. B———, a former bell ringer who had lost his job because of intemperance, fell into a drunken melancholy and was found hanged in his room, strung head to foot between the door handle and a window. Suffering intense anguish or dementia of one form or another, the *franchement aliénés* appeared fixated upon the idea of suicide.

However, Moreau de Tours found the category of "impulsive" suicides the strangest and most incomprehensible. Suicidal impulses came instantaneously upon these individuals, producing overwhelming confusion and mental disorder, and "opening all the pores of the spirit to madness." Moreau de Tours suspected that brain lesions lay at the origin of such morbid impulses. Even so, he argued, it was a "lack of moral faculties" that ultimately rendered the "impulsives" susceptible to suicidal thoughts. Moreau de Tours maintained that such persons were bored and disgusted with life (*tædium vitæ, complètement dégoûté de la vie*). Some of these impulsive suicides were triggered by some personal catastrophe, despair, or sorrow, but many impulsive suicides, Moreau de Tours asserted, were simply "inexplicable." In one case, a woman walking along the Pont au Change suddenly climbed the bridge railing and threw herself into the Seine. In another instance, a man at a dinner party suddenly began stabbing himself with his table knife; he then ran upstairs to his room and blew his brains out. An individual tranquilly smoking his pipe along boulevard Barbès suddenly turned his pipe around, swallowed it, and choked to death. Sieur E——— killed himself "in the most horrific manner imaginable," by crawling into a hot bread oven. A woodcutter ended his life "under terrible circumstances," by hanging himself by a belt above the fireplace hearth until the belt burned and he fell into the fire. A theater spectator ignited a piece of dynamite in his mouth, killing himself and seriously wounding the woman sitting next to him. It was the details of these "unmotivated," impulsive suicides, according to Moreau de Tours, that made them particularly remarkable.

Moreau de Tours's final category comprised suicides provoked by "anesthesia." In contrast to compulsives, *aliénés*, and impulsives, all of whom felt overwhelmed by morbid feelings that drove them to suicide, "anaesthetics" felt nothing at all. Some "curious examples" of such suicidal anesthesia included a melancholic who slashed his throat with a piece of porcelain, a man who chopped at his legs and left arm until he broke them, and a five-year-old girl who lit herself on fire after first attempting to hang herself. In each case, the victims claimed to have felt no pain at all. But the difficulty with this final category of suicides, Moreau de Tours conceded, was that often anaesthesia victims were *aliénés* as well, so their motivations for killing themselves were mixed.

The discussion had thus come full circle. "Here we must stop," Moreau de Tours concluded, "for we have no further recourse along such a questionable line of inquiry. We must simply confine ourselves to saying that there are as many ways of killing oneself as there are people."[10] Under the guise of a medical and psychological work published by the Société d'Éditions Scientifiques, *Suicides et crimes étranges* shed little explanatory light upon the causes of suicide. Instead, it accorded a large amount of space to anecdotal accounts of suicide. Moreau de Tours had established various categories of suicide victims, but all the suicides were astonishing in the same degree. More than the mental or physical state of the victims, what was compelling in these accounts (as Moreau de Tours frequently noted) were the bizarre details of their deaths.

At the same time, Moreau de Tours expressed a strong moral and social condemnation of these suicide victims. While conceding that a few of these individuals were "healthy" (*sains d'esprit*) to all appearances, he characterized the great majority as alienated, criminal, physically degenerate, or mentally unstable. After detailing instances of bizarre crimes, as well as suicides, Moreau de Tours concluded that there was a real analogy between the two.[11] While on the surface there may seem to be differences between criminals (who, he claimed, display abnormal intelligence and revel in their animal passions) and suicide victims (who may appear healthy and in control of their mental faculties), do not be fooled by such appearances, Moreau de Tours warned; rummage around in the lives of their ancestors, he suggested, and you will find that both criminals and suicide victims always reveal some hereditary trait of unhealthy vice (*une tare morbide*). From a medical and psychological point of view, Moreau de Tours admonished his readers, suicide victims are dangerous people. And society, he affirmed, has both the right and the need to defend itself against the degenerative influence of their spontaneous impulses and irresistible passions. Inherited morbid biology and abnormal psychology do not render these individuals blameless, Moreau de Tours insisted: On the contrary, this is why we put the insane in asylums and criminals into prison.

As a cultural artifact, *Suicides et crimes étranges* makes for bizarre reading. But in fact, it was neither overly anecdotal nor exceptional compared to other medical studies of suicide and works of criminal anthropology at the turn of the century; on the contrary, Moreau de Tours was frequently quoted as an expert on suicide. His work occupied a secure place within a wider cultural realm that fused criminality, heredity, insanity, improper moral education, and physical abnormality with suicide.

In *L'Anthropologie criminelle et les nouvelles théories du crime* (1893), for example, Dr. Emile Laurent listed suicide among other forms of crime.[12] While noting that "incorrigible criminals" hardly ever committed suicide, Laurent affirmed that leading authorities on criminal anthropology concurred that crime and suicide went hand in hand. Laurent pointed out that Henry Morselli had demonstrated in *Suicide* (1879), that "[w]here . . . the annual average of voluntary deaths offers a very perceptible increase, a synchronous increase of crime is also generally seen."[13] Morselli's explanation was that the human "struggle for existence" in a rapidly modernizing Europe, had made social competition more fierce. On the losing side of that struggle, suicide victims were counted among the less well fitted, exhibiting earlier stages and correspondingly lower functions of human evolution.

Criminal anthropologists concurred, with slight modifications, in Morselli's judgment.[14] Cesare Lombroso, founder of the Italian school of criminal anthropology, believed that both criminals and suicide victims suffered from an "analgesic indifference" (*insensibilité analgésique*) that destroyed their will to live. Alexandre Lacassagne, founder of the French school of criminal anthropology (which traced the origins of "hereditary degeneration" to social anarchy rather than to biological defects, as did the Lombrosian approach), viewed suicide as a variant of homicide—the murder of oneself (*le meurtre de soi-même*). But irrespective of biological or social origin, the judgment was the same: Suicide victims lacked competitive evolutionary muster in the "struggle for life."[15] Along lines similar to Moreau de Tours, Laurent concurred that suicide victims suffered from a infirmity of mind and character that rendered them particularly susceptible to acting upon their violent impulses.[16]

This underdeveloped consciousness and conscience supposedly rendered suicide victims susceptible to suicide by "contagion." *Suicides et crimes étranges* had grown out of Moreau de Tours's own doctoral thesis, *De la contagion du suicide* (1875). That work in turn inspired Dr. Paul Aubry's study in criminal anthropology, *La Contagion du meurtre* (1896).[17] In a chapter devoted to suicide, Aubry also affirmed that suicide had become an epidemic in France. The underlying cause, he concluded (along with other criminal anthropologists), was an hereditary predisposition toward suicidal obsessions. Drawing on a notion of "social somnambulism" of imitation put forward by Tarde, Aubry believed that the contagion of suicide was spread largely through the details of suicides recounted in the newspaper.[18] Provided on a daily basis with ideas for choosing their mode of death, he argued, individuals predisposed to suicide were incapable of resisting the imitative force of press accounts. Such contagious suicides, he argued, had an analogy in the *suicide à deux*, in which the passive receptor (*le succube*) acts out the nefarious suggestions implanted by the active sower of vice (*l'incube*).[19] Suicides, he concluded, follow the logic of crimes of passion, in which a predisposed and passive character becomes the victim of another's will. Not a week passes, he added, without some sensational newspaper story prompting yet another suicide.

Suicide by contagion was also taken up by Dr. Séverin Icard in an article in *La Nouvelle Revue*, "De la contagion du crime et du suicide par la presse."[20] Whenever a newspaper recounts the details of some sensational crime, Icard predicted, another crime or suicide will follow shortly; the connection, he argued, is obvious and banal. The causes of such contagion lie in the workings of the brain itself.[21] According to Icard, the brain registers all sensory perceptions perfectly, either consciously or unconsciously. Whether weak or strong, these direct impressions leave indelible traces upon cerebral matter, which then lie latent. The publication of sensational stories in the press activates these latent impressions in beings with underdeveloped morals. The contagion of crime and suicide, Icard claimed, is particularly evident in animals (Icard cites the mass suicide of sheep in Rabelais), the ancients, primitives, persons with hereditary defects, and women during their menstrual periods.

The best defense against the contagion of crime and suicide, Icard asserted, is a sufficiently strong counterdose of "moral contagion": the combined positive effects of physical health, proper moral education, and inspiring literature. Further, stories of sensationalized violence should be eliminated from the press entirely. "If we are committed to promoting and glorifying the good," Icard emphasized, "then we must kill evil and enforce a silence around it." [22] Censoring stories of murder, rape, suicide, infanticide, and jealous violence—acts loosely assembled under the rubric of *crimes passionels*, he argued, will spare enfeebled minds from suffering the deteriorating effects of sensational contagion.

While conceding that contagion through the press might precipitate a suicide, medical authorities located the propensity toward self-destruction within the individual himself. In *De l'automutilation, mutilations et suicides étranges* (1909), one Dr. Lorthiois argued that suicide was essentially an intensification of mutilation directed against oneself. [23] Although self-mutilation and suicide are quite different, Lorthiois maintained, they are connected serially. Suicide victims, he pointed out, often have previously mutilated themselves several times. The means of nonfatal self-mutilation and "successful" suicide—striking or hitting the body, cutting oneself or a part of the body (particularly the sexual organs), combustion, consumption of foreign substances, weapons directed against the body—are often the same, he asserted. For Dr. Lorthiois, self-mutilation and suicide differed in degree, not in kind. [24]

Late nineteenth-century criminal anthropologists, physicians, and psychiatrists were united in advancing a "similarity in kind" argument that linked crime, biological pathology, and suicide. While ostensibly scientific, their ideas—rhetorically, if not theoretically—in effect constituted a closed and self-referential moral system. An overriding belief in qualitative similarities between social plagues and biological pathologies established the moral basis for condemning suicide. These presumably scholarly works associated suicide with a range of maladies—alcoholism, criminal activity, hereditary or racial degeneracy, insanity, laziness, prostitution, religious dementia, unbridled passions, insufficient moral training, and the inferior biology of women and children—and in so doing thoroughly muddled causes and effects.[25] These authorities charged the press with playing a particularly nefarious role in spreading suicide: A biologically or psychologically sick individual may be predisposed to suicide, but the latent obsession with killing oneself, the experts argued, is activated by the printed word. Printing bizarre and startling details of sensational crimes, suicides, and other acts of violence without sufficient moral reflection was viewed as a failure of social responsibility. These same authorities situated their own recounting of bizarre and gruesome suicides, by contrast, within the context of proper moral training.[26]

It was against this hermetically sealed moral world—a closed circuit in which biological inferiority, social degeneration, and moral condemnation reinforced one another—that sociologist Emile Durkheim's groundbreaking study, *Le Suicide,* appeared in 1897. In the first section of that work, Durkheim systematically dismantled this presumed biological, social, and moral nexus through the sociological analysis of suicides in order to demonstrate that the supposed relationships were either in error or superfluous. Further, the morality or immorality of suicide had no bearing on whether it was socially "normal" (i.e., statistically true), or even whether it might serve some useful purpose (in Durkheim's case, as an indicator of *anomie* or the social strains produced by modernization). For Durkheim, suicide was a "social fact" with moral ramifications rather than a problem of biological or moral insufficiency producing social ills.

Durkheim did not pioneer the collection of statistical data on suicide ("moral statistics" studies had been conducted by De Guerry, Tissot, and Etoc-Demazy more than a half-century earlier during the July Monarchy).[27] Nor did he question (indeed he affirmed) the basic finding suggested by nearly all suicide studies: that the incidence of suicide had increased throughout Europe over the course of the nineteenth century.[28] Rather, Durkheim's innovation lay in conceiving of suicide as a *sui generis* social phenomenon. That is, the social significance of suicide was un-related to an individual's moral character or pathology—and vice versa. "Perhaps, individual circumstances might make this or that isolated person kill himself. . . . " Durkheim admitted, but "[a]s they are not attached to a specific kind of social organization, they do not have social consequences. They concern the psychologist, not the sociologist."[29] For Durkheim, suicide was a collective social fact that could be explained in relation to other social phenomena.

The opening section of *Le Suicide* makes it clear that Durkheim did not consider "extra-social" factors relevant in the statistical consideration of suicide. French *départements* that displayed high rates of insanity or alcoholism, for example, did not always have high suicide rates. Conversely, certain *départements* with high rates of suicide had low insanity and alcoholism rates. Since neurasthenia and mental alienation were considered quintessentially female disorders by medical and psychiatric authorities, Durkheim reasoned, one should find higher rates of suicide among women; in fact, the rates were higher among men. Durkheim also found that biological arguments failed to produce social correlations. Race and heredity provided unreliable correlations with suicide, while nationality and age (both socially, rather than "innately," established) yielded consistent measures. Catholics, frequently mentioned in cases of "religious dementia," had lower suicide rates than Protestants. Jews, noted by Durkheim as having a higher incidence of "insanity" than either Catholics or Protestants, displayed lower suicide rates than either Christian group.

Durkheim advanced a twofold argument against the purported contagion of suicide by imitation:[30] First, he argued, imitation involves copying behavior that is direct and largely unreflective. The idea that someone "imitates" a press story, for Durkheim, ignores the multiple mediating processes that must occur for the reader to read, understand, and digest a story—a procedure much more complicated than simple imitation. Second, imitation by "press contagion" could not be statistically demonstrated. Durkheim showed that suicide rates in Paris, where population density and newspaper circulation were extremely high, were surpassed by the suicide rates of more than 166 *communes* in the more isolated rural *département* of the Maux. If imitation by way of the press was truly a factor, Durkheim reasoned, the highest rates of suicide should appear where newspaper and population density are greatest, and no such correlation existed.

"In sum, while it is certain that suicide is contagious from individual to individual, we never see imitation affecting the overall suicide rate."[31] Durkheim thus reversed received medical wisdom that pathological individuals infected society through "social contagion." Far from being a cause of social disintegration, individual suicide became one of its symptoms. The incidence of suicide, Durkheim asserted, was a function of the extent of an individual's social integration, usually established through religion, marriage, or citizenship. Those lacking such social integration were most susceptible to suicide. The individual lacking a place within society was susceptible to egoistic suicide. The individual whose sense of social integration was greater than his individual identity was susceptible to altruistic suicide. The individual who was incapable either of determining or meeting the status requirements of his social position was susceptible to "anomic" suicide (characteristic of a modernizing Europe at the turn of the century, according to Durkheim). Yet whatever the type, Durkheim argued, a society's tendency toward suicide had more to do with whether individuals were socially integrated than whether the biological or psychological maladies of immoral people exerted a nefarious influence upon others.

While Durkheim's sociological concept of suicide is not without its own critical problems,[32] as an historical and cultural event, Le Suicide ruptured a long-standing medical and psychological linkage between individual and social pathologies. Durkheimian sociology had broken apart the biological, social, and moral nexus so long assumed by French doctors, psychiatrists, and criminal anthropologists. In its place, an individual's lack of social integration sufficed to explain why someone committed suicide. In response to the sociological interpretation of suicide, the medical establishment invoked its own expertise and continued to insist upon the biological origins of nervous and mental disorders among suicide victims. Debates over whether suicide was primarily a psychological or social issue continued into the interwar period.[33] But whatever position one took, suicide had become less an ethical problem than a social or clinical "fact" of modern existence. Through this intellectual turn, recounting the details of suicides lost the ability to teach moral lessons. Only sensation remained.

THE LOW ROAD TO SUICIDE: THE *FAIT-DIVERS* PRESS

If medical and psychiatric authorities resoundingly condemned suicide, the moral status of self-inflicted deaths recounted in the daily newspaper was more ambiguous. According to ethics philosopher Albert Bayet in *Le Suicide et la morale* (1922), the press played a crucial role in creating uncertainty and confusion concerning the moral implications of suicide.[34] On the one hand, the press reported suicide as criminal activity and described it in terms of horror and repugnance. At the same time, the press often characterized suicide victims as "desperate" (*désespéré/e*) or "unfortunate" (*malheureux/euse*), terms that played to the reader's compassion. This affective characterization of suicide victims did not escape the surrealists in their assemblage of *faits divers,* in which the terms *désespéré/e* and *malheureux/euse* appeared with far greater frequency than in the Parisian press at large. As connoisseurs of suicide *faits divers,* the surrealists emphasized the psychic disarray implicit in drawing together these sentiments of dread and sympathy.

The apogee of the sensationalist *fait-divers* press in France occurred at the turn of the century. Sensationalist stories of crime, murder, natural monstrosities, and political scandal have an enduring fascination, and printed accounts of crime, in fact and fiction, have been in continuous circulation in France since the sixteenth century.[35] During most of the nineteenth century, sensational crime stories were marketed to readers along lines of social class. Newspapers, notably the *Gazette de Tribunaux,* recounted the details of trial proceedings for a bourgeois reading audience, while broadsheet *canards* recounted the "horrible details" of crimes and the "lamentations" (*complaintes*) of criminals for the common classes in story, verse, and woodcut images.[36] It took the late nineteenth-century development of the *quatre grands journaux*—*Le Petit Parisien, Le Petit Journal, Le Journal,* and *Le Matin,* the four leading daily newspapers—to constitute a mass *fait-divers* press that crossed all social boundaries.

Two factors were central to this development. First, was the innovation of the daily paper priced at one *sou* (five centimes), introduced by *Le Petit Journal* in 1863.[37] At five centimes, amounting to about one-eighth the price of a kilo of bread, the newspaper became a common denominator of cultural literacy throughout France. Along with the reduction in price, the newspaper format was reduced as well. A single, large page, folded in the middle, yielded four pages. The four-page daily newspaper constituted what was known as the *petite presse*. Initially, the *quatre grands* were all sensationalist newspapers within this "petite" press. After the turn of the century, these daily newspapers increased their size to six or eight pages, the per-issue price rose to fifteen centimes, and more of their content became "newsworthy." But the *fait-divers* tone was already well established.

If circulation figures are any indication, the sensationalist *quatre grands* were enormously successful.[38] By 1910 they accounted for three-quarters of the market of the nearly five million Parisian newspapers consumed daily. The daily circulation of *Le Petit Parisien* alone (1.4 million copies) exceeded the remaining quarter of the market, comprised of seventy newspapers. It took the next eight most widely published Parisian dailies combined—*La Croix, L'Echo de Paris, L'Eclair, L'Humanité, L'Instransigeant, La Liberté, La Petite République,* and *La Presse*—to match the daily output of *Le Matin* (670,000 copies), the least widely distributed of the *quatre grands*. By the eve of the Great War, the *quatre grands* not only dominated the Parisian press but accounted for forty percent of the daily newspaper market throughout France as well.

The second change crucial in the development of the mass press in France was the Law of 29 July 1881, particularly Article 68, which established a historically unprecedented degree of freedom of the press in France.[39] Article 68 superseded all previous edicts, laws, and ordinances regulating the production and circulation of printed matter, from book publishing and the periodical press, to the occasional press and posters. The article guaranteed the right to sell all forms of printed matter in public and to publicize the details of crimes and other infractions of the law. Henceforth, the only binding regulatory laws upon the freedom of the press would be those included in the Law of 29 July 1881 itself and subsequent legislation. The new law thereby embodied two principles: the liberalization of all past laws restricting freedom of the press and the legislative right to promulgate laws concerning the press.

The combination of cheap prices and editorial freedom made it possible for the *quatre grands* to disseminate sensationalist news to all levels of French society, at a price affordable by all, and without fear of legal reprisal. While the content of the *quatre grands* was self-represented as informative, culturally edifying, politically neutral, and up-to-date—the masthead caption of *Le Matin* proclaimed to "see all, know all, and tell all"—in practice all four newspapers had *fait-divers* reputations.[40] Some of the more renowned sensational stories from the late nineteenth and early twentieth centuries that were circulated by the press included the suicide of General Georges Boulanger (1891), the Panama Canal scandal (1892), the exploits of the *bande-à-Bonnot* anarchists (1911–12), and the trial of Madame Caillaux on the eve of the Great War (1914). Such spectacular crimes and scandals were the exception, however, not the rule. Daily catastrophes and common crimes constituted the mainstay of the *fait-divers* press.

Common *faits divers* included such diverse items as unusual weather, natural disasters, assaults, robberies, petty thefts, suicides, and, increasingly in the opening decades of the twentieth century, automobile accidents. If notable enough, the *fait divers* was developed into an article. If sensational enough, it received front-page coverage. Especially spectacular *faits divers* were featured in illustrated weekly newspapers, such as *Le Petit Journal's Supplement Illustré.* But the majority of newspaper *faits divers* were short announcements, gathered in a column as *Nouvelles Divers* or simply *Faits Divers.* Sometimes these news columns were broken down by geographical location: *À travers Paris, Environs de Seine-et-Oise,* or *Dans les départements.* Such columns were not limited to the *quatre grands* but were a regular feature of most daily newspapers—even those generally considered more moderate and reputable in their coverage, such as *Le Figaro* or *Le Temps.* The radical political press, both right and left, scarcely covered *faits divers.*

In the late nineteenth century, suicide constituted one of the major categories of sensationalist journalism.[41] By the 1920s, suicide had been reduced to an occasional feature, reported less frequently than details of criminal arrests, thefts, or automobile accidents. Some daily newspapers did not cover suicides at all in their *fait-divers* column, notably *La Croix*, the major Catholic daily newspaper (although some suicides may have been buried within its *accidents mortels* column). Still, sensationalist papers such as *Le Journal* and *Le Matin*, suicides were included in the *fait-divers* column every day or two, and in more informative papers, such as *Le Figaro*, they were reported once or twice a week.

Used as filler to avoid blank column space, many of these suicide reports were limited to a single sentence or two, amounting what the newspaper profession called a *"fait divers en trois lignes."* [42] According to Paul Bringuier, a newspaper reporter and columnist for *Détective* magazine, writing *faits divers* constituted the basic training for budding journalists.[43] On any particular newspaper staff, novice reporters were assigned to cover two or three of Paris's twenty-one *arrondissements*. Instructed that no detail was too insignificant, each was responsible for reporting such items as burglars seen on rooftops, petty thefts from small shops, and elderly ladies hit by cars, which gave them a reputation as *chien écrasé* ("road-kill") reporters.

The actual production of a *fait divers*, however, was less an eyewitness account than a form of automatic writing. According to Bringuier, the astute apprentice reporter quickly discovered that one rarely witnessed such accidents personally, and that "pounding the pavement" was unproductive. Instead, hourly rounds to the secretaries of local police stations, four per *arrondissement*, provided the best source of information. Bars and cafés, where reporters would share information on a *quid pro quo* basis, were also good locations for collecting *faits divers*. The reporter relayed the information to newspaper telephone operators, who typed the details directly onto slips of yellow paper. These slips were reworked by layout editors, who fit them to the column space available. Somewhat analogous to a surrealist writing game, *fait-divers* reportage was an impersonal form of literary production that owed everything to the coincidental arrangement of its sentence elements.

Within this mode of production, these short *faits divers* achieved surreality by juxtaposing material elements of uncertain meaning. While the sensational details were drawn from everyday life, the simultaneously saturated and fragmented structure of these *faits divers* both exceeded and eclipsed realist explanation.[44] Among the suicide *faits divers* selected by the surrealists, for example, the story of Madame Billiard, who drowned in her neighbor's well, included the extraneous—indeed excessive—elements of an umbrella and a lantern, which created a sense of mystery about the relationship of these objects to her suicide. A sense of excess also infused the story of a young American man who shot himself in a hotel on rue Crébillon after writing a letter to Monsieur Frédéric Crébillon. Beyond the mysterious coincidence of names, the letter, left anonymously at a post office, suggested a possibly illicit connection between the American and the Frenchman. (Crébillon was also the name of an eighteenth-century pornographer, Crébillon *fils*. Whether the staff of *Le Petit Parisien* made the connection is uncertain, but the literary-minded surrealists might well have.)

Yet even when the details were deciphered, the mystery remained. An agitated young woman, whose lingerie was marked with the letter *W*, drowned in the Seine. She was identified subsequently as a Swiss student named Elisa Wally, but, as the follow-up *fait divers* concluded enigmatically, "Her body has not been recovered," and solving the mystery of the *W* provided no clue to the enigma of her suicide. The causes of suicide remained elusive even when the details appeared closely related to the account. Knowing, for example, that Sergeant Bessieux waited until the three candles had burned out and his comrades had left the canteen before shooting himself in the head still did not explain why the military man killed himself. Although the coincidence of the elements told a more coherent story, the sensational effect was still produced by the juxtaposition of details rather than by causal explanation.

Nonetheless, the "morass of confabulation" created by suicide *faits divers* rested upon a familiar system of cultural signs for their intelligibility.[45] Repetition of the means of suicide provided one anchor. From suicide accounts reported in four Parisian daily newspapers during the same period as the surrealist collection of *faits divers*, self-inflicted shooting was the single most frequently reported method, accounting for one in three suicides (table 2). Hanging, asphyxiation, jumping, and drowning together accounted for nearly half of reported suicides. The balance of *fait-divers* suicides were attributed to poisoning, slashing, or setting fire to oneself. On the whole, most suicides were accomplished by everyday and well-advertised means.[46]

Table 2   Suicide *Faits Divers* Comparisons (1): Reported Methods

Method	Men	Women	Combined
Gunshot (revolver)	30	6	36
Head	16	1	
Chest	1	1	
Heart	3	1	
Abdomen	1	2	
Unspecified Region	7	1	
Rifle, unspecified	2	0	
Hanging	13	2	15
Asphyxiation	7	6	13
Gas	3	3	
Coal/Charcoal	2	1	
Unspecified	2	2	
Jumping	7	5	12
From a Height	4	2	
Under/From Train	3	3	
Drowning	3	8	11
River	1	6	
Well or Basin	2	2	
Poisoning	4	4	8
Noxious substance	2	3	
Overdose	2	1	
Slash	4	2	6
Knife	3	1	
Razor	0	1	
Glass	1	0	
Self-immolation	0	3	3
Method Unknown	5	0	5
TOTAL METHODS	73	36	109

Total methods employed exceeds the number of total suicides (104) due to the use of multiple methods in four instances.

SOURCES: *Le Figaro* (Oct./Nov. 1924), *Le Journal* (Oct./Nov. 1924), *Le Matin* (Oct./Nov. 1924), *L'Instransigeant* (Nov. 1924).

The motives that drove victims to suicide were much less easily classified, however. Reported motivations were many, while the repetition of any single motive was low. "Neurasthenia," a vague category encompassing a wide range of symptoms from migraine headaches and digestive disorders to depression and sensory hyperstimulation, was the most frequently invoked motive in four major Paris dailies, accounting for slightly less than one-tenth of reported suicides (table 3). "Amorous disappointments" (*chagrin d'amour*), drunkenness, personal problems (*chagrins intimes*), and madness, followed neurasthenia as a motive, collectively adding up to about one-quarter of suicides. But by far the largest single category was *mobile inconnu*, where no motivation was provided at all, accounting for forty percent of all suicide *faits divers*.[47] Further, at times these unmotivated suicide victims were sympathetically described as "desperate" (*désespéré/e*), "unfortunate" (*malheureux/euse*), or simply as the "suicide victim" (*suicidé/e*). Thus, while the means of suicide were fairly predictable, the mixed motivations for an individual's suicide reported in short *faits divers* rendered the cultural meaning of suicide ambiguous.

In this way, the suicide *fait divers* was the textual equivalent of an uncanny juxtaposition in a surrealist image, whose the elements may be easily identifiable but whose uncertain meaning provokes anxiety.[48] As ethics philosopher Albert Bayet astutely understood, the contentious issue was not moral—for or against suicide. Rather, the critical issue involved the establishment of a cultural space that precluded such judgments: "Newspapers disclose a space of confusion, from both the depths of common opinion and ambiguity. Crime produces horror, misfortune stimulates compassion. Suicide invokes a sense of horror and compassion at the same time. In the uncertainty resulting from this conflict, journalists nearly always automatically abstain from anything which might resemble a moral judgment."[49]

The surrealists played upon this psychic conflict of horror and compassion by juxtaposing the question "Is Suicide a Solution?" with actual suicide *faits divers*. Far from evoking simple moral condemnation, newspaper reportage of suicides combined revulsion for the criminal act with a fascination for mysterious details and a compassion for its victims. Of

Table 3   Suicide *Faits Divers* Comparisons (2): Reported Motives

Reason	Number	Keywords
Neurasthenia	10	neurasthénique; accès de neurasthénie
Amorous disappointments	8	jealoux/euse; chagrin d'amour; abandoné/e
Alcohol	7	alcoolique; ivre; accès d'ivresse
Personal sorrows	7	chagrins intimes
Madness	6	fou/folle; aliéné/e; la folie
Criminal behavior	4	manoeuvres criminelles; vol; meutrier/ère
Heated argument	4	discussion; drame conjugal
Financial loss	3	misère; mal récolte
Desire to end life	3	finir la vie; fin à ses jours
Incurable illness	3	incurable; souffrance
Loss of family	2	mort de mari; mort de fils
Single instances	8	fièvre chaud; négligence; persuasion; fatal oubli; menace; semonce; sans billet; affolée
REASONS GIVEN	65	
Unknown		
"Desperate"	7	désespéré/e
"Unfortunate"	3	malheureux/euse
"Suicide"	8	suicide
Unspecified	23	
REASONS UNKNOWN	41	

In two instances, two reasons were included in the same *fait-divers*, making the known/unknown total 106 (of 104 suicides).
SOURCES: *Le Figaro* (Oct./Nov. 1924), *Le Journal* (Oct./Nov. 1924), *Le Matin* (Oct./Nov. 1924), *L'Instransigeant* (Nov. 1924).

these three elements—revulsion, fascination, and compassion—the last was the subversive element. Identifying with the suicide victim created a mental and ethical opening, rather than closure.

IS SUICIDE A SOLUTION?

The loss of a moral frame of reference, combined with the linguistically unstable construction of *faits divers*, illuminates the cultural and historical significance of the responses to the suicide *enquête* assembled in the second issue of *La Révolution Surréaliste*. In reviewing the responses reported in that issue, the surrealists seem to have adhered to a version of the social-isolation thesis; it is certain that they rejected the moral interpretation of suicide. But unlike Durkheim, who identified suicide as a reflection of social disorder, surrealists ascribed the importance of suicide to its singular ability to disrupt the order of French society and culture—like a short *fait divers*. The impulse toward suicide opened a realm of individual phantasm that, they hoped, could break through into consciousness. It remained an open-ended issue, however, whether the profane illumination thus achieved would promote the surrealist revolution or end in actual suicide.

When reviewing the "indiscriminate responses" that the *enquête* had solicited, the surrealists found a few quite thoughtful arguments.[50] Poet Pierre Reverdy considered suicide a weakened form of rebellion, one that placed an unwarranted confidence in the power of death to provide peace. Monsieur Claude Jonquière suggested that suicide was as much a solution as a natural death. Among other respondents, the surrealists also found a number of humorous and ironic insights, whether so intended or not. Monsieur Louis de Russy, they noted, had a particularly bizarre understanding of suicide: "The only case of suicide: Rimbaud." Doctors Gorodich and Guillot de Saix suggested that suicide was more a dissolution than a solution. Monsieur Georges Fourest replied "Why not? A solution of arsenic, perhaps?" Monsieur Michel Corday stated that it was only a solution for a very limited number of times (*à tirage limité*). Monsieur Pierre de Massot quoted a poster from his bedroom wall, "You may enter without knocking, but please kill yourself before exiting."

But in their comments on those who took a moral position against suicide, the surrealists were vicious. Monsieur Josef Florian was ridiculed for being "as Catholic as possible" in his insistence that Church doctrine unequivocally states that suicide is a moral issue. Doctor Maurice de Fleury and Professor Paul Lecène were called "sinister imbeciles" for wrapping their moral condemnation of suicide in the pseudo-intellectualism of psychological and philosophical opinions. The surrealists found *Le Journal* columnist Clément Vautel's response, a sort of vulgarization of Pascal's wager that the afterlife might be even more uncomfortable than this one, "equally technical." What was lacking in these abstract and detached responses, the surrealists insisted, was any human resonance with the experiences of furor, disgust, and passion that one finds among the writings of those who have considered suicide, and in some cases have actually killed themselves.

On this score, the surrealists had well-established suicide credentials.[51] Jacques Vaché, the literary autodidact who had been a psychiatric ward patient under André Breton's care during the war, as well as Breton's mentor in *l'humour noir*, killed himself with an opium overdose in 1919. Arthur Cravan, dadaist forger of Oscar Wilde manuscripts under the pseudonym "Dorian Hope" and an inspirational figure for the Paris dada movement, disappeared without a trace in 1918, the consensus being that he likely committed suicide. In the years following the *enquête*, Jacques Rigaut, dadaist author of the *Agence Générale du Suicide* who attempted suicide on various occasions, finally succeeded in bringing an end to his life in 1929. In a posthumous article published in *La Révolution Surréaliste* later that year, Rigaut proclaimed, "Suicide must be a vocation."[52]

Among the surrealist respondents to the 1924 suicide *enquête*, René Crevel was the only one to affirm, "A solution? . . . Yes." Reckoning himself the product of a "despotic moral and religious education," Crevel considered everyday life, as he accepted it, the most terrible argument against himself. Each day, he felt, brought him closer to the *élan mortel*. With regard to his own contemplation of suicide, Crevel judged, "I want to keep the door open, and not close it." In a moment of extreme personal crisis, the result of growing political antipathies between the surrealists and the communists, Crevel committed suicide in 1935.[53]

Most of the surrealists who responded to the *enquête* considered suicide an option—but not theirs. Maxime Alexandre demanded another solution. Pierre Naville considered suicide a theft rather than a solution. Antonin Artaud thought that suicide remained a hypothesis. A related thread of reasoning worked through the responses from these authors: The meaninglessness of contemporary social life had, for all purposes, already killed their individual existences. Yet unrealized impulses toward love and the marvelous kept each of them on this side of actual suicide. As Marcel Noll put it, although he was already among the walking dead, he was not yet a *désespéré* and his blood flowed quite well. It remained an open issue whether and exactly how suicide served the cause of surrealism.

The only individual known to have joined the surrealist movement as a result of the suicide *enquête* was an ex-priest named Jean Genbach, or the Abbé Gegenbach.[54] In July 1925, Genbach wrote a letter to Breton in the style of a *fait divers*, "A few days ago, a young man attempted suicide by throwing himself into Lake Gérardmer. Until a year ago, this young man had been the Abbé Gegenbach, and he had resided at the Trocadéro Jesuit Seminary at 12 rue Franklin . . . I am that young man."[55] (See pl. 7.) Defrocked for his amorous liaisons with a young actress from the Odéon music hall, Genbach felt that the Church had turned him into a *désespéré*, a revolutionary, and a nihilist. While recovering from his suicide attempt, Genbach came across a copy of the surrealist suicide *enquête*. After a personal interview with Breton, Genbach was accepted into the surrealist fold and his correspondence was occasionally published in *La Révolution Surréaliste*.[56]

But individuals represented in the suicide *faits divers* from the first issue of *La Révolution Surréaliste*, with the frequent invocation of "the desperate ones" belong among the surrealist entourage as well. As the surrealists had stated in their original formulation, suicide was not so much a moral question as one of unconscious, human resonance. This is precisely what had drawn Genbach to surrealism: "In your suicide inquiry, I saw anguished cries expressing the desire for nothingness, or perhaps a nostalgia for another life that escapes this miserable one, a life in which we can finally be *free*."[57] The surrealists critically exploited the subversive possibilities of suicide *faits divers* when they asked their readers to consider whether suicide was a solution. Given daily and mass circulation in newspapers, these brief suicide announcements provoked paradoxical feelings of horror, fascination, and sympathy in ordinary readers —feelings that lay outside the assurances of ethical judgments or rational explanations. The unstable combination of dread and compassion in short suicide *faits divers* advertised the human revolt against the meaningless and oppressive conditions of modern life. Whether or not the inquiry attracted new adherents to the surrealist movement, these *faits divers* shared affinities with the surrealist revolution in daily life.

Plate 7. "... I am that young man." Photograph of an anonymous priest published with the Abbé Gegenbach's letter to André Breton in *La Révolution Surréaliste* (1928).

APPENDIX: TRANSLATIONS OF SHORT SUICIDE
FAITS DIVERS IN THE FIRST ISSUE OF
LA RÉVOLUTION SURRÉALISTE

"An Inconsolable Widow." Blois, 5 November.—Unable to console herself after the death of her husband, a railroad worker accidentally run over on 21 September at Vernouillet (Seine-et-Oise), the widow Besnard, born Collin, 33 years old, living with her mother in Mazangé, hanged herself. *Libertaire*

"Desperate Woman with an Umbrella" Compiègne, 5 November.—In Margny-les-Cerises, Madame Billiard, born Marie Thiroux, 53 years old, got up during the middle of the night, gathered her lantern and umbrella, and then threw herself down the well of her neighbor, Madame Villette, where the corpse was later recovered.

"The Desperate Ones." Arriving on the morning of St. Sebastian's day, Monsieur Pierre Régnier, 39 years old, vestments tailor, attempted suicide yesterday afternoon in a hotel room, at 26 boulevard de l'Hôpital. The desperate man, who had slashed his throat several times with a razor, has been taken to the Hospital de la Pitié and is in serious condition.

"The Desperate Ones." Police officer Boussiquier, from the tenth arrondissement, recovered from the Saint-Martin canal, opposite 110 quai Jemmapes, the corpse of Mademoiselle Eulalie Paquet, 30 years old, a domestic employed on the rue de la Pompe, who, following personal problems, killed herself. *Petit Parisien*

"The Desperate Ones." Toward 4 o'clock in the morning, a tall, slender woman, around 25 years old, walking feverishly along the quai des Célestins, suitcase in hand, suddenly headed down the embankment and, abandoning her parcel, threw herself into the water. Passersby vainly called out for help. No one was able to get her out. After the preliminary inventory by the local police superintendent, the only things found in the suitcase were a few pieces of lingerie marked with the initial *W. Petit Parisien*

"A Young American Kills Himself in a Hotel Room." A young American, Monsieur William Shorr, 23 years old, killed himself by embedding a revolver bullet into his right temple in a hotel, 4 rue Crébillon. The desperate man left three letters, one addressed to his mother, Madame Shorr, 29 Schenk Avenue, Brooklin [sic], New York; the second for Monsieur Karl Bloodgood, at Cook's Agency, and the last addressed to Monsieur Frédéric Crébillon, to be claimed at the receiving office (*poste restante*), rue du Louvre. *Petit Parisien*

"The Desperate Ones." Quai de la Marne, Madame Savin, 55 years old, transient, without permanent address, threw herself into the canal de l'Ourcq. She was rescued from the water, safe and sound, by a sailor.

Monsieur Georges Lachelais, 50 years old, hostler, hanged himself in his home, quai de la Charente.

Monsieur Giacomi, 65 years old, living at 35 boulevard St-Michel, attempted to asphyxiate himself using a charcoal-burning stove. He has been admitted to Cochin hospital in a disquieted state.

Thanks to the suitcase abandoned on the canal bank, the desperate woman has been identified who, last Monday, threw herself into the Seine from the quai des Grands-Augustins. She was Mademoiselle Elisa Wally, a student, Swiss nationality, 27 years old, living at 29 rue de Verneuil. Her body has not been recovered. *Petit Parisien*

"The Desperate Ones." Taking advantage of the fact that his mother had gone out, young Paul Philipick, 17 years old, living at 127 rue Saint-Honoré, while in a state of neurasthenia, asphyxiated himself with the aid of the gaslights.

Following some personal problems, Mademoiselle Jeanne Vellee, florist on the rue des Gravilliers, threw herself from quai Vahny into the Saint-Martin canal. She was retrieved, safe and sound, by police officer Boussiquier of the tenth arrondissement.

On the quai de Passy, Mademoiselle Yvonne Blanchard, a domestic working at 102 rue de Longchamp, threw herself into the Seine. Some sailors were able to retrieve her from the river, safe and sound. Boucicaut.

Monsieur Louis Jager, 32 years old, 30 boulevard de la Villette, following some personal problems, drove a knife into himself, near his heart, while in an establishment on the same boulevard. In the Saint-Louis hospital, his condition is serious. *Petit Parisien*

Monsieur Lemaire, 26 years old, lay down on the railroad tracks near the Bercy-La Rapée station terminus and was cut in two by a train. *Libertaire*

"The Desperate Ones." Monsieur Charles Guyot, 19 years old, living in a hotel on rue Saint-Maur, walked up and down the rue de la Présentation for nearly thirteen hours. Suddenly, he went up the staircase of a building, and on the fourth-story landing, shot himself in the head. He has been admitted to the Saint-Louis hospital in a desperate condition. Personal problems. *Petit Parisien*

"Did This Soldier Kill Himself?" Nancy, 5 November 5. Toward 11 o'clock in the evening, a body was recovered from the Meurthe River in Nancy, identified as André Bloc of the twentieth train supply squadron, on leave. Eighteen hours earlier, Bloc had been working at the recruitment office. Notwithstanding the mystery that has developed around the affair, stemming from the declaration that the soldier must have accidentally fallen into the water while going to look at the rising river, it is not impossible that the unfortunate man, weary of military slavery, killed himself. *Libertaire*

"A Strange Suicide." Sergeant Bessieux, of the tenth artillery regiment in Nimes, while in the canteen, lit three candles and forbade any of his comrades to leave. When the candles had burned out, he told his comrades to leave quickly, which they did. The sergeant followed them, and then blew his brains out. An inquiry has been opened to establish the circumstances of this strange suicide. *Eclair*

"An Evil That Spreads Terror." Monsieur Alfred Boniface, 76 years old, boarder at the Bicêtre hospice, hanged himself in his room.

Mademoiselle Marguerite Rochas, 21 years old, stenographic secretary, living with her father 225 rue de Charenton and afflicted by an incurable illness, shot herself through the heart with a bullet from a revolver. She died.

Conclusion

Today, I supply you with an astonishing narcotic, brought
from the borders of consciousness, from the frontiers of the
abyss. . . . It outstrips your cravings, stirs them up, and brings
out new, insane desires. Have no doubt: longings released by
this potent philter are the enemies of order. They circulate in
secret, under the noses of the authorities, in the form of books
and poems. The assuaging pretext of literature provides you
this deadly enzyme at an unbelievably low price, and it's high
time for its universal application! It's a genie in a bottle, safe
as poetry in the bank. Buy it! Buy the damnation of your
soul! Finally, you're going to be corrupted. Here's a machine
to capsize the mind. I present to humanity, this most grandi-
ose *fait divers*——a newly born vice, yet another madness be-
stowed upon man——*Surrealism*, son of frenzy and shadow!
Come in! Come in! Here's where the realms of the instantaneous begin!

Aragon, "The Imagination's Speech" (1924)

What does "modern" mean today? From the moment one de-
parts from a materialist social determinism, the world as it
appears imposes itself upon us. I no longer have the power to
change that. I've been to the movies. I've strolled down the
streets. I read the same newspapers as everyone else. And all
I see are the signs of a violently new epoch. Today, the "modern" is no longer in the hands of the poets; it's in the hands
of the cops. . . .

Aragon, "Introduction to 1930"

Three years after the publication of *Le Paysan de Paris*, Aragon publicly raised doubts as to whether his novel had exercised much of an effect upon the reading public. "It is regrettable that my recent masterpiece, I'm talking about *The Paris Peasant*, didn't receive the kind of acclaim, praise, in a word, encouragement, it had the right to expect," Aragon lamented in his *Traité du style*.[1] In this treatise, Aragon revised and invigorated his ideas about the cultural and political aims of surrealism. He more virulently attacked the French literary establishment and the bourgeois social order—in rude and scathing terms. He expressed disgust with commercial culture generally and with the press in particular. But above all, Aragon called for a new rigor within the surrealist movement itself. Surrealism, he emphasized, is not reducible to an artistic or literary style; not any old smut is the equivalent of surrealist poetry. But neither is surrealism indifferent to style, Aragon insisted. The surrealist, he emphasized, demonstrates a superior control of language. He does not write to express an inner fancy, but to describe reality. The literary and political value of surrealism is not determined from within but from without. Surrealism is not the product of one's arbitrary perspective, Aragon concluded; it is an objective revelation.[2]

In the 1920s, the surrealist movement had drawn inspiration from a shadowy side of mass culture. The unbounded Parisian landscape, the immense shadow of Fantômas, the dark humor of the Bluebeard of Gambais, an unconscious human resonance written into suicide *faits divers*, these and other sources of mass culture had inspired the surrealists along with their more well known artistic and literary forbears. As the shifting cultural and political context of the 1930s unfolded, however, the surrealist movement became increasingly preoccupied with its own activities and more distanced from its affinities with the culture at large. In the *Traité du Style*, Aragon articulated two contentious historical legacies of surrealism that have particular implications for the relationship of the movement to mass culture.

The first was that the surrealist revolution had to continually reinvent itself in order to avoid being co-opted or marginalized by the very culture it despised. As the 1930s progressed, the press and public grew increasingly accustomed to the antics of the surrealists. Elyette Benassaya has shown that over the course of the interwar period surrealism became gradually accepted by the mass press.[3] The daily newspaper *Le Journal*, which in 1930 had found Buñuel and Dalí's *L'Age d'Or* "an unprecedented scandal . . . overflowing with Bolshevik excrement," later found the International Surrealist Exposition of 1938 "mysterious, but inoffensive."[4] Perhaps even more damaging to the surrealist revolution, as the initially hostile press on the political right begrudgingly began to tolerate surrealism, the communist left, after its early support, increasingly distanced itself from the movement.

The surrealists were themselves at least partially responsible for their growing commercial success. An early surrealist foray into general cultural acceptance involved their participation in the production of a special issue of the journal *Variétés*, titled "Surrealism in 1929," a collaboration whose wisdom Breton later questioned in the "Second Surrealist Manifesto."[5] But even earlier, the surrealists had begun courting esteemed literary publishing houses such as Gallimard and José Corti, and an increasing number of Parisian galleries were displaying surrealist art. Surrealism finally achieved official-culture status with the advent of Albert Skira's highbrow arts journal, *Minotaure*, 1933–39. In the first issue, Breton proclaimed that "*Minotaure*, the revue *à tête de bête*, distinguishes itself from all other publications headed by some institute member or museum curator."[6] Other contributors, however, admitted that the existence of the journal constituted no less than the *embourgeoisement* of surrealism. As participating photographer Brassaï noted, "This sumptuous publication, with a limited issue of 3,000 copies . . . completely inaccessible to anyone on a working-class budget, can only speak to a disgruntled bourgeoisie, a milieu of titled and monied snobs, the initial collectors and patrons of surrealist works."[7] Surrealism was becoming accepted and woven into the fabric of the very culture it despised.

Aragon's second insight was that, in order to maintain its avant-garde status, surrealism would have to redefine its cultural and political mission. In the immediate postwar period, the dada and surrealist movements had been nearly alone among the Parisian avant-garde in their nonconformist ire and anti-establishment diatribes.[8] By the 1930s, in the face of growing fascism within France and without, the position of the movement and its membership had shifted enormously. During this decade of historical transition, the surrealist movement had splintered into various factions. By the time André Breton assumed the position of *La Révolution Surréaliste*'s sole editor, many of the movement's earlier adherents, such as Antonin Artaud, Robert Desnos, Michel Leiris, André Masson, Pierre Naville, Philippe Soupault, and Roger Vitrac, either had been expelled from the movement by Breton or had resigned of their own accord. Some ex-surrealists found their way to the first counter-surrealist journal, *Documents*, directed by Georges Bataille, 1929–30. Others lambasted Breton in *Un Cadavre* in 1930, "One day he cried out against the priests, the next he took himself for a bishop or the Pope in Avignon. . . . "[9] Breton had adopted the role of the rigorous inquisitor of the surrealist faithful, but he could not control the fold or the independent activities of other writers and artists.

In response to this fragmentation, Breton redoubled his efforts in the cause of surrealism. In the final issue of *La Révolution Surréaliste*, Breton published a "Second Surrealist Manifesto." In the second manifesto, Breton reconfirmed surrealism's avant-garde mission, only this time in the service of the Marxist social revolution. This renewed commitment led to the launching of a new periodical, *Le Surréalisme au service de la révolution*, 1930–33. But from the beginning, the surrealist movement had shared an uneasy coexistence with the French socialist and communist left. Disagreements between the surrealists and the Marxists began with Pierre Naville's *La Révolution et les intellectuels (Que peuvent faire les surréalistes?)* in 1925, and ties were severed altogether when the surrealists were barred from participating in the Popular Front Congress of Writers for the Defense of Culture in June 1935.[10] Thereafter, the surrealists were on the fringe of the French political left. Aragon, who had joined the Communist Party in 1927, abandoned the "inevitable rigor" in surrealism he had advocated in the *Traité du style*, and he threw in his lot with the literary cause of socialist realism during the Popular Front.

Within this shifting political context, surrealism cut many of its ties with mass culture as well. The final issue of *La Révolution Surréaliste*, published in December 1930, contained a number of statements expressing disappointment over the intersection of surrealism and the reading public at large. "Why do we continue to bother ourselves with meaningless gains (*à faire les dégoûtés*)?" Breton asked in the "Second Manifesto." Through its public activities, the surrealist movement attracted "a former policeman, a few warm bodies, two or three literary catches (*maquereaux de plume*), quite a number of disturbed persons, an idiot, some 'those-who-aren't-against-us-are-for-us' types . . . an amusing and inoffensive little group. Doesn't it add up to the very image of life itself, a team of men who pay out to play the game, and then think they're winning when they score points? *Shit!*"[11] In the "Introduction to 1930," Aragon railed against mass media newspapers and magazines as nothing less than the triumph of a police-state mentality over the entire population. "It's the triumph of censorship over the unconscious," he wrote. "Just glance through what's being published: *Détective, Jazz, Vu*, to mention a few. . . . From all sides, you'll find what we've always declared repugnant: The victory of the police!"[12] If earlier the surrealists had glorified the sensationalist press and popular literature for its imaginative possibilities, the surreal potential in mass culture now appeared insufficiently rigorous. A change of tactics was in order. With this final issue of *La Révolution Surréaliste*, Aragon claimed, the dadaist era of surprise and shock had come to an end. The modern world was in the hands of the police, not the poets.

The surrealist case against mass culture was made most forcefully in Georges Sadoul's diatribe against *Détective* magazine, titled "Happy New Year! To Your Health!"[13] *Détective*, the "Great Weekly Magazine of *Faits Divers*," began publishing in 1928, and within two years, to Sadoul's chagrin, it had achieved the astounding circulation figure of 800,000 issues weekly. In sixteen-page installments, the magazine's photo-illustrated articles recounted the details of sensational crimes and fiction from France and around the world.[14] Regular features included articles on the *grands procès* of criminal prosecutions and the *petites causes* of individual vindications. A *grand fait divers* was featured in the center spread.

Occasional columns included "Science versus Crime," by Edmond Locard, director of police laboratory science in Lyon, and "*Crimes d'autrefois,*" about sensational crimes and famous criminals from the distant past. Recurring themes included the wily ways of criminals, suspicious disappearances, serial killings, and executions. These regular sensations were supplemented by articles about exotic American gangsters, bootleggers, the Ku Klux Klan, and occult stories about weird cults and vampires. In addition, there were regular cartoon columns ("*La Lanterne Sourde*," "*Partout/Pour Tous*"), and a *Grand Concours Hebdomadaire*, in which fabricated criminal trial or mystery serials were accompanied by weekly quizzes and cash prizes awarded to readers who correctly solved the cases.

Sadoul's response to *Détective* was less than enthusiastic. In his view, the magazine constituted no less than a "Detective Club" for society at large. "*Détective* is an agent provocateur," Sadoul proclaimed, "and the murders committed in its pages only serve to make the police stronger and more effective."[15] Far from turning criminal fantasies toward social revolution, the magazine further consolidated commercial interests within the established social order.[16]

Yet Sadoul's condemnation of *Détective* magazine may have had more to do with the shifting terrain of the surrealist movement itself, and changes within its cultural and historical milieux than with sensationalist mass culture. In the first two decades of the twentieth century, members of the Paris dada and surrealist movements had not embraced mass culture indiscriminately. Rather, as the chapters of this book have shown, the surrealists were discerning connoisseurs of disturbing and insolent currents running through mass culture. That the cultural and political agenda of surrealism shifted in the 1930s does not mean that those currents no longer flowed. Rather, it may mean that the surrealists had ceased to be a useful group for finding the pulse of a popular dynamism within mass culture.

If Aragon and Sadoul were convinced that *Détective* magazine was contributing to the consolidation of a law-and-order mentality, other contemporary voices were far less assured. It is even possible that criminal fantasies exerted a greater impact as affective cultural forces than as expressive ones. In the nineteenth century, French criminal culture had been closely wed to the underworld of Paris. Books three and four of Maxime du Camp's multivolume *Paris,* for example, first published in the opening years of the Third Republic, were devoted to criminals, the indigent, and the institutions that regulated them.[17] In du Camp's account, the underclass—*la pègre*— was a social product of the lower strata of the Parisian environment. While roguery already had a long popular history in France, du Camp emphasized that in the nineteenth century *la pègre* especially flourished among the dirty commercial byways and along the periphery of Paris, in such disreputable drinking establishments as the *Bibine du père Pernette.* Despite the elimination of dark and tortuous streets through Haussmannization, the widening of the boulevards, and the introduction of gas lighting, du Camp believed in a "persistence of customs" among Parisian criminal and indigent classes, maintained in *bals,* cafés, and cabarets.[18] The *malfaiteur* was seen as the victim of his animal passions, and these low-life environments nourished his bestial pleasures.

In the 1920s and 30s, however, the criminal underworld began to overflow Parisian class and geographical boundaries to create a *pègre internationale.* The criminal element ceased to be an inferior cadre of humans, the product of biological degeneracy or environmental squalor, and instead assumed the status of a *parallel society,* whose machinations operated at all social levels. The most dreaded criminals in the reconstituted "army of crime" were no the longer working-class ruffian muggers, nor the small-time swindlers dressed in overcoats and bowler hats—nor even the notoriously violent Parisian *apaches.* Rather, the most dangerous criminals of the 1930s were the "smiling man" of bank scams (*l'homme souriant*), the "elegantly dressed" heroin dealer (*l'homme en habit*), and the suave drug-lord (*l'homme en robe de soie bleue*).[19] "There are crooks among millionaires, just as there are crooks among beggars," warned true-crime author Xavier de Hauteclocque in *Pègre et police internationales.*[20] Every level of society, he lamented, produces its particular *bêtise* or vice.

The new *Haute Pègre,* as Hauteclocque called it, constituted a vast network of international evil. Bootleggers and gangsters in America,

"Underworld Columns" in Germany, master-thieves in England, the criminal milieux of Paris and Marseille—for Hauteclocque all were part of a global organization. This world-confederation of criminality, he emphasized, lived according to its own rules, recognized no national boundaries, and, thanks to the technological developments of wireless radio transmission and airplane travel, was in constant communication with its various constituencies. *L'International de la Pègre*, Hauteclocque warned, constituted no less than an "anti-society," opposed to and fleecing the society of honest people.

While not so alarmist or conspiratorial in tenor, the former prefect of the Paris police, Alfred Morain, had similar worries about contemporary criminal activities. "The army of crime is no longer composed of a cohort, easy to distinguish by their marks," Morain lamented, "but consists of a numerous confraternity whose members are difficult to distinguish because they work in secret."[21] Morain was deeply disturbed by the thought that the police had lost the ability to distinguish who did or did not form the constituency of *la pègre*—that criminals today passed through legitimate society *incognito*. Well clothed and well housed, he noted, the modern criminal, displaying the superficial air of the respectability of a business man, but whose profession remained hidden, had replaced the easily identifiable, lower-class Parisian *apache*. Further, Morain complained that a high degree of professional organization, sophisticated weaponry, and scientific knowledge had placed the criminal underworld nearly at parity with the police. The only way for the police to maintain its advantage over this new criminal underworld, he insisted, was through adding specially trained agents to its ranks.

While Hauteclocque and Morain obviously had strong commercial and professional motivations for writing such things, this belief in an *international, invisible,* and *omnipresent* world of criminality marked a significant break with the nineteenth-century closed system of criminal signs established by criminal anthropology and crowd psychology.[22] Instead, imaginary realms of criminality had become spectacular and international. In terms of commercial production, the 1920s and 30s were a golden age of crime and detective novels, not only in England and America, but in France as well, with the creation of more than sixty-five new

series of crime and detective novels during the interwar period.[23] Firms
such as Fayard, Ferenczi, and Tallandier, the main publishers of adventure and detective fiction earlier in the century, continued to exert a major influence on the French publishing market in the twenties and thirties.
One new series alone, *Le Masque*, comprised nearly three hundred detective and mystery novels, all published between 1927 and 1939. Moreover,
firms with a more "literary" reputation, such as Gallimard and Nouvelle
Revue Française, also began to publish their own popular crime and police series. "True-crime" publications boomed as well, in new weekly
magazines like *Détective* and *Voilà*, dedicated to the exploitation of criminal and glamour sensationalism.

Such increased interest in mass-culture criminality was not limited to
the profit motives of publishers and the morbid fascinations of a tabloid-
reading audience. During the 1920s and 30s, French writers and intellectuals were drawn to the realm of crime and *faits divers* as never before,
drawing together tabloid journalist and literary author, criminal and intellectual. In the 1930s, literary paragon André Gide added *faits divers* to
his corpus.[24] In *La Séquestrée de Poitiers*, Gide presented a collection of
documents regarding the trial of a illegally confined woman (he had
served as a member of the jury). Not only was the book published by an
esteemed literary firm, Nouvelle Revue Française; it received double-
column advertising space in *Détective* magazine.[25] Other leading French
intellectuals of the era, such as Georges Bataille and Jacques Lacan, drew
upon the realms of criminal transgression in the development of their
social and psychological theories.[26] Even the surrealists, while disdain-
ing the likes of *Détective* magazine, continued to glorify unmotivated
criminality through such criminal *causes célèbres* as the eighteen-year-old
parricide Violette Nozières and the von Papen sisters, who murdered
their employer.[27]

It would be premature to accept the surrealists' judgment that in the
1930s sensationalist mass culture had placed the modern world into the
hands of the police. From the alternative perspective of Blaise Cendrars,
avant-garde poet, war *mutilé*, and sometimes journalist, modern-day life
was, more than ever, saturated with imaginary criminal dangers. In his

1935 *Panorama de la Pègre,* Cendrars drew together entertainment and psychological disturbance in a new zone of criminal terror—*gangsland.*

> The passage between the reality of the street and the blazing artificiality of a bar happens so easily, and so unexpectedly. . . . You feel a sense of vertigo. Suddenly, you are hanging on to your table for dear life, like a wreck tossed about a tidal wave of dancing couples in a hot-jazz club. The first shot of alcohol down, overwhelmed by the abstract decor, nothing can help you figure out where you are, or how you got there.
>
> Are you in Shanghai? In Buenos Aires? In a New York "speak-easy"? Or are you in Paris?
>
> Without being aware of it, you have landed, simply and completely, in *gangsland*—a cynical and triumphant spectacle of neon lights in a miserable little room, where nothing is a mystery, but everything is disturbing.[28]

For Cendrars, *gangsland* was a metaphor for the spectacle of modern life. Superficially similar to Hauteclocque, Cendrars wrote about the international *pègre* of Parisian gambling-dens, Marseille drug smugglers, Shanghai opium exporters, and an "international mafia" of con-men, jewel thieves, and hit-men operating from London to Berlin, and beyond. Also like Hauteclocque, Cendrars seemed troubled by statistical evidence which suggested that the activities of organized crime were on the rise.

But unlike his law-and-order counterpart, Cendrars was fully aware of his own complicity in writing a "panorama" of the *pègre.* A sense of excitement about this international criminal milieu, and an imagined social solidarity among its members, pervaded his writing. Further, Cendrars recognized certain irrepressible features of *gangsland.* What poor customs official, on his meager salary, could possibly refuse the material benefits of payoffs? Who could really fault a con-man for plying his profession when there are so many suckers (*poires*) in this world? Ostensibly recounting "true crime" stories, Cendrars lavishly illustrated his book with photographs from *Détective* magazine and stills from Pathé feature films. Intentionally or not, even the book's cover (pl. 8), emblazoned with lurid typography and graphics (PanoraMA de la PÈGRE, "*ma* pègre") hinted at Cendrars's complicity in the spectacle. As everyday culture,

Plate 8. Cover of the first edition of Blaise Cendrars, *Panorama de la Pègre* (1935). (Collection: Doe Library, University of California, Berkeley)

criminal fact and fantasy had become thoroughly blurred, a development as entertaining as it was disquieting.

In 1924, Aragon had announced that "*Surrealism*, son of frenzy and
darkness," constituted a sensationalist threat to law and order. The success of surrealism, he imagined, lay in its capacity to be circulated in secret, under the noses of authority—even with their permission in the
form of books. A decade later, however, Aragon had broken with surrealism and had thrown in his lot with the politically committed socialist
realism of the Popular Front of International Artists and Writers. On an
altogether different trajectory, Cendrars recognized that imagined criminality in mass culture continued to exercise a disquieting attraction for
its popular-reading audience. From "true crime" stories in detective
weeklies and the daily newspaper, to the *policiers* of popular fiction and
the movies, public fascination with criminal sensationalism challenged
messages of law and order and continued to constitute a popular mentality. While surrealism became more preoccupied with its self-defined
cultural and political rigor, disturbing and provocative tendencies still
inhabited the byways of mass culture.

The surrealist revolution never occurred. At our end of the twentieth
century, surrealism has been safely secured within French official culture, in Bordas readers and in national museums. Yet wildly fantastic,
imaginative, sensationalist, and violent forms of mass culture, embedded
in such print forms as *polars* and *bandes déssinées*, are denied official-
culture status within France, marginalized as *paralittérature*.[29] Given
the legacy of general antipathy among French intellectuals against mass
culture, as a hegemonic economic and ideological force in everyday life,
it seems unlikely that mass culture will become a springboard for serious cultural critique within France anytime soon.[30] Nonetheless, nearly
seven hundred detective and crime novels are published annually in
France, and the substantial majority are by French authors.[31] The popularity of sensationalist mass culture remains strong in France, even if its
popular attributes remain largely subterranean.

À-propos surrealism, a popular story has been recounted concerning
the sidewalks crossing the park above "The Forum," an underground
shopping mall in the center of Paris, built after the destruction of Les

Halles public market in 1970.[32] Where the belly of Paris used to be, the *allées* of today's open-air park suggest nothing of a *passage*. These garden paths are marked with street signs named after early twentieth-century Parisian writers, among them André Breton. Some unknown individual altered Breton's plaque, crossing out the letter *r* and adding an *accent aigu,* so that it read *Allée André Béton* ("concrete"). With surrealism set firmly within official culture, the tasks of invoking the marvelous and the transformation of everyday life have returned to the realms of popular culture.

Notes

INTRODUCTION

1.   "Anniversaire d'un coup de pioche. Le boulevard Haussmann est arrivé rue Laffitte," *L'Intransigeant,* 15 February 1924, 1. Throughout the book, translations are my own unless noted otherwise.

2.   Louis Aragon, *Le Paysan de Paris* (Paris: Le Livre de Poche, 1966), 21–22; "La Grande Trouée du Boulevard Haussmann," *L'Intransigeant,* 3 September 1924, 1.

3.   Recent works in the history of French technology that support this "new and overlapping" thesis include Henry Bakis, "Formation et developpement du réseau téléphonique français," *Information Historique,* vol. 49, no. 1, 1987, 31–43; Alain Beltrain, "Du luxe au coeur du système. Électricité et société dans la région parisienne, 1880–1939," *Annales ESC,* vol. 44, no. 5, 1989, 1113–36; Patrice Carré, "Le reseau téléphonique entre Paris et banlieue, 1880–1939," *Cahiers de l'Institute d'Histoire du Temps Présent,* no. 12, 1989, 63–70; Dominique Larroque, "Transporte urbaine et transformations de l'espace parisien," *Cahiers de l'Institute d'Histoire du Temps Présent,* no. 12, 1989, 41–56; Jean-Jacques Ledos, "Les Débuts de la radio en France: Des 'Merveilles de la science' à la confiscation," *Gavroche,* no. 56,

1991, 10–15; Rosalind Williams, "When the Eiffel Tower Was New," *Technology and Culture*, vol. 32, no. 1, 1991, 102–5; and J.-P. Williot, "Naissance d'un reseau gazier à Paris au XIXe siècle: Distribution gazière et éclairage," *Histoire, Économie et Société*, vol. 8, no. 4, 1989, 569–91.

4.   Aragon, *Paysan de Paris*, 15–16.

5.   Donald M. Lowe, *The History of Bourgeois Perception* (Chicago: University of Chicago Press, 1982); and Stephen Kern, *The Culture of Time and Space, 1880–1918* (Cambridge, Mass.: Harvard University Press, 1983).

6.   Works that have done a great deal to popularize the idea that the Great War was the primary force in shaping a modernist mentality among Europeans include Modris Eksteins, *Rites of Spring: The Great War and the Birth of the Modern Age* (New York: Doubleday, 1989); Paul Fussell, *The Great War and Modern Memory* (Oxford: Oxford University Press, 1975); and Eric J. Leed, *No Man's Land: Combat and Identity in World War I* (Cambridge: Cambridge University Press, 1979).

7.   On the historical milieux of the surrealists, and the intersection of culture and politics, see Alain Jouffroy, *La Vie réinventée: L'Explosion des années 20 à Paris* (Paris: Robert Laffont, 1982); Helena Lewis, *The Politics of Surrealism* (New York: Paragon House Publishers, 1988); Herbert Lottman, *The Left Bank Writers, Artists, and Politics from the Popular Front to the Cold War* (Boston: Houghton Mifflin Co., 1982); Jerrold Seigel, *Bohemian Paris: Culture, Politics, and the Boundaries of Bourgeois Life, 1830–1930* (New York: Penguin Books, 1986); Roger Shattuck, *The Banquet Years: The Origins of the Avant Garde in France, 1885 to World War One*, rev. ed. (New York: Vintage Books, 1968); Kenneth Silver, *Esprit de Corps: The Art of the Parisian Avant-garde and the First World War, 1914–1925* (Princeton: Princeton University Press, 1989); and John Willet, *Art and Politics in the Weimar Period: The New Sobriety, 1917–1933* (New York: Pantheon Books, 1978).

8.   On the leading role of André Breton in the surrealist movement, see Anna Balakian, *André Breton: The Magus of Surrealism* (New York: Oxford University Press, 1971); Anna Balakian and Rudolf E. Keunzli, eds., *André Breton Today* (New York: Willis Locker and Owens, 1989); Henri Béhar, *André Breton: Le Grand indésirable* (Paris: Calmann-Lévy, 1990); Dominique Bozo, *André Breton: La Beauté convulsive* (Paris: Editions du Centre Pompidou, 1991); Mary Ann Caws, *André Breton* (New York: Twayne Publishers, 1971); Mark Polizzotti, *Revolution of the Mind: The Life of André Breton* (New York: Farrar, Straus and Giroux, 1995).

9.   Writings on surrealism are extensive. The best introduction to surrealism remains Maurice Nadeau, *The History of Surrealism*, trans. Richard Howard (Cambridge, Mass.: Harvard University Press, Belknap Press, 1989), originally published as *L'Histoire du Surréalisme*, 2 vols. (Paris: Éditions du Seuil, 1944–48). Other standard introductions include J. H. Matthews, *An Introduction to Surrealism* (University Park: Pennsylvania State University Press, 1965); William S. Ru-

bin, *Dada and Surrealist Art* (New York: Harry N. Abrams, 1968); and Robert Short, *Dada and Surrealism* (London: Octopus Books, 1980). For edited anthologies of surrealist writings, see André Breton, *Manifestoes of Surrealism*, trans. Richard Seaver and Helen Lane (Ann Arbor: University of Michigan Press, 1969); Henri Béhar and Michel Carassou, eds., *Le Surréalisme* (Paris: Librairie Générale Française, 1984); Marcel Jean, ed., *The Autobiography of Surrealism* (New York: Viking Press, 1980); Robert Motherwell, ed., *The Dada Painters and Poets: An Anthology*, 2nd ed. (Cambridge, Mass.: Harvard University Press, Belknap Press, 1981); and André Breton, *What is Surrealism? Selected Writings of André Breton*, ed. and trans. Franklin Rosemont (New York: Monad, 1978). On the much-neglected subject of surrealism and women, see Mary Ann Caws, Rudolf E. Kuenzli, and Gwen Raaberg, eds., *Women and Surrealism* (Cambridge, Mass.: M. I. T. Press, 1991); and Whitney Chadwick, *Women Artists and the Surrealist Movement* (New York: New York Graphic Society, 1985). Principal scholarly reviews devoted to surrealist criticism and research are *Mélusine*, Cahiers du Centre de recherches sur le surréalisme (Paris VII) (Lausanne: L'Age d'Homme, 1978–present); and *Dada/Surrealism* (Iowa City: University of Iowa, 1971–present).

10.   For English readers, all are available in translation: Louis Aragon, *Nightwalker (Le Paysan de Paris)*, trans. Frederick Brown (Englewood Cliffs: Prentice-Hall, Inc., 1970), or *Paris Peasant*, trans. Simon Watson Taylor (Boston: Exact Change, 1994); André Breton, *Nadja*, trans. Richard Howard (New York: Grove Press, 1960); Philippe Soupault, *The Last Nights of Paris*, trans. William Carlos Williams (Boston: Exact Change, 1992). Throughout this book, however, citations refer to French editions unless noted otherwise.

11.   André Breton, "Manifesto of Surrealism," in *Manifestoes of Surrealism*, 26.

12.   The surrealist practice of *désenchaînement*, or "ideological unchaining," is explored in depth in Margaret Cohen, *Profane Illumination: Walter Benjamin and the Paris of the Surrealist Revolution* (Berkeley and Los Angeles: University of California Press, 1993), 107 f.

13.   Breton, "Manifesto," 20.

14.   References to Nadeau in this book are to the English translation.

15.   A notable exception to this generalization is Franklin Rosemont, ed., *Surrealism and Its Popular Accomplices* (San Francisco: City Lights Books, 1980; orig. special double-issue of *Cultural Correspondence* no. 10/11, Fall 1979). The selections in Rosemont focus nearly exclusively on American sources of popular culture, although the issue contains a number of good snippets of French surrealist criticism in English translation. The intersection of surrealism and motion pictures has received substantial treatment in Ado Kyrou, *Le Surréalisme au cinéma*, rev. ed. (Paris: Le Terrain Vague, 1963); J. H. Matthews, *Surrealism and Film* (Ann Arbor: University of Michigan Press, 1971); Linda Williams, *Figures of Desire: A Theory and Analysis of Surrealist Film* (Urbana: University of Illinois Press, 1984); and

Rudolf E. Keunzli, ed., *Dada and Surrealist Film* (New York: Willis Locker and Owens, 1987). For introductions to early popular French cinema, see Richard Abel, *The Ciné Goes to Town: French Cinema, 1896–1914* (Berkeley and Los Angeles: University of California Press, 1994), and *French Cinema: The First Wave, 1915–1929* (Princeton: Princeton University Press, 1984).

16.   Lucien Febvre and Henri-Jean Martin, *The Coming of the Book*, trans. David Gerard (London: Verso Press, 1984); Robert Mandrou, *An Introduction to Modern France, 1500–1650*, trans. R. E. Hallmark (New York: Holmes and Meir, 1976); Jean Delumeau, *La Mort des pays de Cocagne* (Paris: Université de Paris, 1976); and Robert Muchembled, *Culture populaire et culture des élites dans la France moderne* (Paris: Flammarion, 1977).

17.   Peter Burke, *Popular Culture in Early Modern Europe* (New York: Harper Touchstone, 1978).

18.   For France, see Eugen Weber, *Peasants Into Frenchmen: The Modernization of Modern France, 1870–1914* (Stanford: Stanford University Press, 1976) and *France, Fin-de-Siècle* (Cambridge, Mass.: Harvard University Press, Belknap Press, 1986); and Rosalind Williams, *Dream Worlds: Mass Consumption in Late Nineteenth-Century France* (Berkeley and Los Angeles: University of California Press, 1982).

19.   Henri Lefebvre, *Everyday Life in the Modern World*, trans. Sacha Rabinovitch (New York: Harper and Row, 1971); Max Horkheimer and Theodor Adorno, *The Dialectic of Enlightenment*, trans. John Cumming (New York: Continuum, 1972); and T. J. Jackson Lears, "The Concept of Cultural Hegemony: Problems and Possibilities," *American Historical Review*, vol. 90, no. 3, 1985, 567–93.

20.   For a recent summation of debates among American historians over the relationship of mass to popular culture, see "AHR Forum on Popular Culture," *American Historical Review*, vol. 97, no. 5 (1992), 1369–1430. The seminal works of French cultural and social history that effectively challenged the mass-versus-popular distinction were Natalie Zemon Davis, *Society and Culture in Early Modern France* (Stanford: Stanford University Press, 1975); and Roger Chartier, *The Cultural Uses of Print in Early Modern France*, trans. Lydia G. Cochrane (Princeton: Princeton University Press, 1987). The recent advent of cultural studies as an academic discipline has quickly produced a plethora of theoretical perspectives that call into question the presumed homogeneous ideological effects of mass culture: cf. Simon During, ed., *The Cultural Studies Reader* (London: Routledge, 1993). Some works that have generally informed my thinking about these issues include Michel de Certeau, *The Practice of Everday Life*, trans. Steven Rendall (Berkeley and Los Angeles: University of California Press, 1984); Jim Collins, *Uncommon Cultures: Popular Culture and Postmodernism* (New York: Routledge, 1989); Andreas Huyssen, *After the Great Divide: Modernism, Mass Culture, Postmodernism* (Bloomington: Indiana University Press, 1986); Alice Yeager Kaplan, *Reproductions of Banality: Fascism, Literature, and French Intellectual Life* (Minneapolis: Uni-

versity of Minnesota Press, 1986); William W. Stowe, "Popular Fiction as Liberal Art," *College English*, vol. 48, no. 7, 1986, 646–63; and Slavoj Zizek, *Looking Awry: An Introduction to Jacques Lacan through Popular Culture* (Cambridge, Mass.: M. I. T. Press, 1991), and *Enjoy Your Symptom! Jacques Lacan in Hollywood and Out* (New York: Routledge, 1992).

21.   I borrow the term "secret history" from Greil Marcus, *Lipstick Traces: A Secret History of the Twentieth Century* (Cambridge, Mass.: Harvard University Press, 1989).

22.   I have formulated these principles from general guidelines provided in Stuart Hall, "Notes on Deconstructing 'The Popular'," in Raphael Sammuel, ed., *People's History and Socialist Theory* (London: Routledge and Kegan Paul, 1981), 227–40.

23.   Sidra Stich, *Anxious Visions: Surrealist Art*, with essays by James Clifford, Tyler Stovall, and Steven Kovács (New York: Abbeville Press, 1990); Kirk Varnedoe and Adam Gopnik, *High & Low: Modern Art and Popular Culture* (New York: Museum of Modern Art, 1991); and Jeffrey Weiss, *The Popular Culture of Modern Art: Picasso, Duchamp, and Avant-Gardism* (New Haven: Yale University Press, 1994). See also the "High/Low" special issue of *October*, no. 56 (Spring 1991).

24.   Francis Lacassin, "Préface," in Pierre Souvestre and Marcel Allain, *Fantômas*, vol. 1, series «Bouquins» (Paris: Robert Laffont, 1987), 12.

25.   Matthews, *Surrealism and Film*, 15.

CHAPTER 1. THE BAEDEKER OF HIVES

1.   Louis Aragon, "Le Paysan de Paris," *La Revue Européenne*, Part I, nos. 16–19 (June–September, 1924), and Part II, nos. 25–28 (March–June, 1925).

2.   Louis Aragon, *Le Paysan de Paris* (Paris: Livre de poche, 1966), 106–7.

3.   Aragon, *Le Paysan de Paris*, 107.

4.   Aragon, *Le Paysan de Paris*, 111.

5.   Bernard Delvaille, *Passages et galeries du 19e siècle*, photographs by Robert Doisneau (Paris: A. C. E. Éditeur, 1981), 32–35; Johann Friedrich Geist, *Arcades: The History of a Building Type*, trans. Jane O. Newman and John H. Smith (Cambridge, Mass.: M. I. T. Press, 1983), 480–88; and Patrice de Moncan and Christian Mahout, *Le Guide des passages de Paris* (Paris: Seesam-R. C. I., 1990). As a point of practical consideration, Margaret Cohen points out that the temptation to treat Aragon's novel as a documentary source stems from a general lack of easily found sources of information about the Opera Passageway, in *Profane Illumination: Walter Benjamin and the Paris of Surrealist Revolution* (Berkeley and Los Angeles: University of California Press, 1993), 95.

6.   Adolphe Joanne, *Paris illustré: Nouveau guide de l'étranger et du parisien*, 2nd ed. (Paris: Librarie de L. Hachette et Cie., 1863; 1st ed. 1855), 187.

7.   Bertrand Lemoine, "Index chronologique," *Les Passages couverts en France* (Paris: Délégation à l'Action Artistique de la Ville de Paris, 1989), 246–47.

8.   Amédée Kermel, *Le Livre des Cent et Un* (1831), quoted in Moncan and Mahout, *Le Guide des passages*, 44.

9.   Susan Buck-Morss, *The Dialectics of Seeing: Walter Benjamin and the Arcades Project* (Cambridge, Mass.: M. I. T. Press, 1989); Hal Foster, *Compulsive Beauty* (Cambridge, Mass.: M. I. T. Press, 1993); and Cohen, *Profane Illumination*. See also Josef Fürnkas, *Surrealismus als Erkenntnis: Walter Benjamin, Weimarer Einbahnstraße und Pariser Passagen* (Stuttgart: J. B. Metzeler, 1988).

10.   Walter Benjamin, "Paris, capitale du XIXe siècle" in *Paris, capitale du XIXe siècle: Le Livre des passages*, trans. Jean Lacoste (Paris: Les Éditions du Cerf, 1989), 35–59. English translation, Walter Benjamin, "Paris: Capital of the Nineteenth Century," in *Reflections: Essays, Aphorisms, Autobiographical Writings*, trans. Edmund Jephcott (New York: Schocken Books, 1986), 146–62.

11.   "Chaque époque rêve la suivante." Michelet, *Avenir! Avenir!*, quoted in Benjamin, "Paris, capitale," 36.

12.   Walter Benjamin, "The Work of Art in the Age of Mechanical Reproduction" and "Theses on the Philosophy of History," in *Illuminations: Essays and Reflections*, trans. Harry Zohn (New York: Schocken Books, 1969), 217–64.

13.   See Buck-Morss, *Dialectics of Seeing*, 287–330; and Cohen, *Profane Illumination*, 17–55.

14.   Benjamin, "Surrealism, The Last Snapshot of the European Intelligentsia," in *Reflections*, trans. Jephcott, 177–92.

15.   See Buck-Morss, *Dialectics of Seeing*, esp. 217–21.

16.   Breton, "Introduction to the Discourse on the Paucity of Reality," in *What is Surrealism?*, trans. Rosement, 17.

17.   Breton, "Introduction to the Discourse," 19.

18.   Georges Hugnet, "Dada in Paris," in Robert Motherwell, ed., *The Dada Painters and Poets: An Anthology*, 2nd ed. (Cambridge, Mass.: Harvard University Press, Belknap Press, 1981), 165–96; and Nadeau, *History of Surrealism*, 59–68.

19.   Michael Beaujour, "From Text to Performance," in Denis Hollier, ed., *A New History of French Literature* (Cambridge, Mass.: Harvard University Press, 1989), 866–71.

20.   Foster, "Outmoded Spaces," in *Convulsive Beauty*, 157 f.

21.   The favorable assessments of the Opera Passageway seem to be drawn primarily from Richard, *Le Véritable conducteur parisien* (1828); Amédée Kermel, *Les Passages de Paris*, in *Paris, ou le Livre des Cent et Un* (1831–34); and Edouard Kolloff, *Schilderungen aus Paris*, 2 vols. (1839), frequently cited in Geist, *Arcades*, and in Moncan and Mahout, *Le Guide des passages*. Some of the unfavorable assessments are treated in the body of my discussion.

22.   Frances Trollope, *Paris and the Parisians in 1835* (New York: Harper and Brothers, 1836), 357.

23.   *Le Guide des acheteurs, ou Almanach des Passages de l'Opéra* (Paris: Imprimerie de David, 1828). See also Geist, *Arcades*, 485. The term *bimbeloterie* was not used in the *Guide* but was recorded in city of Paris *cadastre* and *patentes* of the arcade's shops.

24.   Galerie de l'Horloge, nos. 10/12 MM. Baruch and Cerf Weil (porcelaines), no. 15 M. J. F. Veyrat (orfèverie plaquée d'or et d'argent), nos. 19/21 M. Bourguignon (perles artificielles), in *Le Guide des Acheteurs*, 28–31.

25.   Amédée Achard, "Rue de la Chaussée d'Antin," in Louis Lurine, ed., *Les Rues de Paris* (Paris: G. Kugelmann, Éditeur, 1844), 39–48; Brazier, Gabriel, and Dumersan, *Les Passages et les rues, ou la guerre déclarée*, Vaudeville en un acte (Paris: Chez Duvernois, Librairie, 1827).

26.   Archives de Paris, DQ18 331, Cadastre 1809–51 [–1870], 2me Arrondissement, Quartier de la Chaussée d'Antin. Registration of commercial establishments in the Opera Passageway was spotty from the Restoration through the Second Empire. Still, high turnover may be inferred from the lack of coincidence between the more than fifty businesses registered in the *cadastre* and the owners of establishments listed in the *Guide des Acheteurs*.

27.   "Boulevard des Italiens," in Bernard de Montgolfier, ed., *Les Grandes Boulevards* (Paris: Paris-Musées, 1985), 38.

28.   The separation of the arcade from the Opéra was inevitable, with or without the incineration of the Royal Academy of Music; Garnier's new opera house was slated for opening in 1875.

29.   Georges Cain, "Le Passage de l'Opéra," in *À travers Paris* (Paris: Ernest Flammarion, n.d. [1907]), 336.

30.   Moncan and Mahout, *Le Guide des passages*, 49–52.

31.   Commission Municipale du Vieux Paris, "Séance du samedi 9 décembre 1916," Item no. 32, "Les passages couverts," *Procès-verbaux, année 1916* (Paris: Imprimerie Municipale, 1918), 270–73.

32.   Moncan and Mahout, *Le Guide des passages*, 54–65.

33.   *Calignani's New Paris Guide* (Paris: A. and W. Calignani and Co., 1844), 124. The English translation is from the guide.

34.   *Calignani's New Paris Guide for 1873* (Paris: A. and W. Calignani and Co., 1873), 32.

35.   Moncan and Mahout, *Le Guide des passages*, 61.

36.   Edmond Beaurepaire, *La Chronique des rues*, series "Paris d'Hier et d'Aujourd'hui" (Paris: P. Sevin et E. Rey, Libraries, 1900), 64.

37.   Commission Municipale du Vieux Paris, "Séance du samedi 9 décembre 1916," 271.

38.   Archives de Paris, DP4 1876, Cadastre, Passage de l'Opéra (1876), D9 P2 420, Faubourg-Montmartre Patentes (1905), D9 P2 530, Faubourg-Montmartre Patentes (1910).

39.   Arrigoni's restaurant moved to the Passage des Princes, cf. Sommerville Story, *Dining in Paris* (New York: Robert M. McBride and Co., 1927), 115. The Certa café moved to the rue d'Isly, cf. Aragon, *Le Paysan de Paris*, 101.

40.   The answers the these questions were later provided by Gilbert Joassart, owner of the Certa café. A Dada is a layered cocktail of port, sherry, and Madeira, invented by Aragon, Breton, and Soupault in 1919. The *dame au mouchoirs* was imprisoned in her shop by Aragon and Breton, who blocked her door with the heavy potted palm plants used to decorate the gallery. She remained trapped until a passerby moved the planters out of the way. Cf. Marie-Louise Coudert, "Au temps du «Certa»," *Europe*, nos. 454/455 (1967), 231-37.

41.   Molly Nesbit, *Atget's Seven Albums* (New Haven: Yale University Press, 1992), 198.

42.   Commission Municipale du Vieux Paris, "Séance du samedi 9 décembre 1916," 270.

43.   Beaurepaire, *La Chronique des rues*, 67.

44.   Aragon, *Le Paysan de Paris*, 62-63; and Benjamin, "Surrealism," 190-91.

45.   As shown, for example, in the works of François Victor Fournel: *Enigmes des rues de Paris* (Paris: E. Dentu, 1860); *Tableau de vieux Paris: Les Spectacles et les artistes de rues* (Paris: E. Dentu, 1863); *Chroniques et legendes des rues de Paris* (Paris: E. Dentu, 1864); and *Les Rues de vieux Paris: Galerie populaire et pittoresque*, 2nd ed. (Paris: Firmin-Didot, 1881).

46.   P. L. Jacob, *Curiosités de l'histoire du vieux Paris* (Paris: Adolphe Delahays, libraire-éditeur, 1858; orig. published 1834), 6.

47.   The Commission Municipale du Vieux Paris was established by the Paris Préfecture in two meetings of the municipal council, 15 November 1897 and 17 December 1897; cf. Commission Municipale du Vieux Paris, Séance du vendredi 28 janvier 1898, *Procès-verbaux, année 1898* (Paris: Imprimerie Municipale, 1899), 1.

48.   Commission Municipale du Vieux Paris, 1897-1900, *Guide à l'Exposition Universelle* (Paris: Ville de Paris, 1900).

49.   Commission, *Guide*, 12.

50.   See Nesbit, "Ombres Portées," in *Atget's Seven Albums*, 154-211.

51.   A representative slice of André Warnod's books about *Vieux Paris* during the period include *Le Vieux Montmartre* (Paris: Eugene Figuière, 1912); *Bals, cafés et cabarets* (Paris: E. Figuière, 1913); *La Brocante et les petits marchés de Paris* (Paris: E. Figuière et cie., 1916); *Les Bals de Paris* (Paris: G. Crès, 1922), *Lily, modèle* (Paris: L'Édition française illustrée, 1919); *Les Plaisirs de la rue* (Paris: Éditions française illustrée, 1920); *Les Berceaux de la jeune peinture: Montmartre, Montparnasse . . .*

(Paris: A. Michel, n.d. [1925]); *Les Peintres de Montmartre: Gavarni, Toulouse-Lautrec, Utrillo* (Paris: La Renaissance du livre, 1928); *Les Artistes du livre: Dignimont*, lettre-préface de Colette (Paris: Henry Babou, 1929); *Visages de Paris* (Paris: Firmin-Didot et Cie. [1930]); and *Ancien Théâtre Montparnasse* (Paris: Coutan-Lambert, 1937). After the World War II, Warnod wrote reminiscences of his years in Montmartre, as well as an embellished biography of Henri Murger, whom Warnod regarded as a bohemian brother, in *La Vraie bohème de Henri Murger* (Paris: Editions Paul Dupont, 1947).

52.   Robert Bonfils, *Les Cent vues de Paris* (Paris: Librarie Larousse, 1924).

53.   I.e., Restif de La Bretonne, *Le Paysan perverti* (1775), and *La Paysanne pervertie* (1784), published together as *Le Paysan et la Paysanne pervertis, ou les Dangers de la ville* (1787). The surrealists considered Restif a spiritual ancestor.

54.   Aragon, *Le Paysan de Paris*, 34–38.

55.   Georges Montorgueil, "Feu le passage de l'Opéra," *Le Temps*, 3 February 1925, 4.

56.   "Haussmann-Les Italiens. Au confluent de deux boulevards, deux époques sont aux prises," *Le Matin*, 5 February 1925, 1.

57.   Ibid.

58.   Clément Vautel, "Mon Film," *Le Journal*, 13 October 1924, 1.

59.   In French, a play of words on *livre*: "La livre aura chassé le livre!"

60.   Emile Darsy, "Un boulevard chasse l'autre. Hier, le 'Pousset' a fermé," *Le Figaro*, 4 February 1925, 1. Aragon, Breton, and Soupault also frequented *Le Pousset*.

61.   Montorgueil, "Feu le passage de l'Opéra," *Le Temps*, 3 February 1925, 4. According to Paris *cadastre* records, the barbershop had been in business since 1889, or for thirty-five years.

62.   "Bientôt le passage de l'Opéra ne sera plus qu'un souvenir," *Le Journal*, 6 February 1925, 1. The quote plays on the double-meaning of *passage*—a passageway and as a passage in time: "Tout passe, même les passages."

63.   Ibid.

64.   "Circuler," *L'Intransigeant*, 27 October 1924, 1.

65.   "Anniversaire d'un coup de pioche," *L'Intransigeant*, 15 February 1924, 1. See also "Le Boulevard en perce," 19 January 1924, 1; "Vieux Refrains. Contrusions . . . Contrusions . . . C'est la pioche du démolisseur qui répond," 6 August 1924, 1; "Paris qui se transforme," 17 January 1925, 1; "Les rues qui marchent," 28 January 1925, 1.

66.   "Le Paris qui s'en ira," *L'Intransigeant*, 8 August 1924, 1.

67.   "Place au boulevard Haussmann!" *L'Intransigeant*, 9 January 1925, 1.

68.   "La Lumière qui s'étient," *L'Intransigeant*, 24 February 1925, 1.

69.   Lucien Descaves, "Paris qui s'en va: Le Passé d'un passage," *L'Intransigeant*, 21 September 1924, 1.

70.   Aragon, *Le Paysan de Paris*, 23–24.

71.   Philippe Soupault, "Théâtre Moderne: *Fleur-de-Péché*," *Littérature*, no. 14 (June 1920); and André Breton, *Nadja* (Paris: Gallimard, 1964), 43–44.

72.   Rose M. Avila, "The Function of Surrealist Myths in Louis Aragon's *Paysan de Paris*," *French Forum*, vol. 3, no. 3 (1978), 232–39.

73.   Marquis de Rochegude and Maurice Dumolin, *Guide pratique à travers le Vieux Paris*, nouvelle édition (Paris: Librairie ancienne Édouard Champion, éditeur, 1923).

74.   Rochegude and Dumolin, *Guide pratique*, 271–89. The quotations and summaries that follow are all taken from this source.

75.   Rochegude and Dumolin, *Guide pratique*, 276.

76.   Benjamin, "Surrealism," in *Reflections*, 179.

77.   *Guide des Plaisirs à Paris*, nouvelle édition (Paris: Édition Photographique, n.d. [1900]).

78.   Basil Woon, *The Paris That's Not in the Guidebooks* (New York: Bretano's Publishers, 1926); Bruce Reynolds, *Paris With the Lid Lifted* (New York: George Sully and Co., 1927), and *A Cocktail Continentale* (New York: George Sully and Co., 1926).

79.   Aragon, *Le Paysan de Paris*, 44.

80.   André Breton, *Les vases communicants* (Paris: Gallimard, 1955), 53.

81.   Avila, "The Function of Surrealist Myths," 232–39.

82.   Foster, "Outmoded Spaces," 159 f.

83.   Cohen, *Profane Illumination*, 34.

84.   Peter Collier, "Surrealist City Narrative: Breton and Aragon," in Eduard Timms and David Kelley, eds., *Unreal City: Urban Experience in Modern European Literature and Arts* (London: Manchester University Press, 1985), 220.

85.   "L'Arrivée à Paris," in *Guide de Poche 1900*, 1–12.

86.   Karl Baedeker, *Paris and Its Environs. Handbook for Travellers*, 19th ed. (Leipzig: Karl Baedeker, pub., 1924), v.

87.   Baedeker's guides were published continuously from 1865 on. Hachette's earlier *Guides Joanne* (1855) were replaced by the *Guides Bleus* in 1921. The summary that follows is based on a random collection of Baedeker and Hachette guides published between 1884 and 1924.

88.   This argument was first developed in Roland Barthes, "The *Blue Guide*," in *Mythologies*, trans. Annette Lavers (New York: Hill and Wang, 1972), 74–77. See also Cohen, "Ghosts of Paris," in *Profane Illumination*, 77 f.

89.   Sidra Stich, ed., *Anxious Visions: Surrealist Art*, with essays by James Clifford, Tyler Stovall, and Steven Kovács (New York, Abbeville Press 1990).

90.   The phrase is taken from a collection of poems by Paul Éluard, *Capitale de la douleur* (Paris: Éditions Gallimard, 1926).

91.   Soupault, *Last Nights*, trans. William Carlos Williams, 133–34.

92.   Collier, "Surrealist City Narrative," 214.

93. Charles Baudelaire, "The Painter of Modern Life" in *The Painter of Modern Life and Other Essays,* trans. Jonathan Mayne (London: Phaidon Press, 1995), 1–42.

94. Aragon, *Le Paysan de Paris,* 233 f.

95. Fernand Léger, "Images Mobiles. Spectacle." *L'Intransigeant,* 29 May 1924, 1.

96. Pierre Mac Orlan, "Le Fantastique de la nuit," *L'Intransigeant,* 2 July 1924, 1. His series "Petits Films de Paris" ran on the front page of *L'Intransigeant,* 12 June to 29 August 1924.

97. André Salmon, "Poètes sans le savoir," *L'Intransigeant,* 28 June 1924, 1.

98. Philippe Soupault, "L'Autre pain quotidien. «Mon journal»." *L'Intransigeant,* 14 June 1924, 1.

CHAPTER 2. THE LAMENT OF FANTÔMAS

1. Robert Desnos, "La Complainte de Fantômas," in *Fortunes* (Paris: Gallimard, 1945), 101–109.

2. John Ashbery, introduction to Marcel Allain and Pierre Souvestre, *Fantômas* (New York: William Morrow and Co., 1986), 1–9; Francis Lacassin, "Fantômas, ou L'Énéide des temps modernes" in *Fantômas,* series "Bouquins" (Paris: Robert Laffont, 1987), 7–30; and "Fantômas, ou L'Opéra à treize sous" in *A la recherche de l'empire caché* (Paris: Julliard, 1991), 99–143.

3. Louis Chavance, "La Morale de Fantômas," and Jean-Pierre Bouyxou, "Dégénérescence d'un mythe," *Europe, revue littéraire mensuelle* nos. 590–591, special "Fantômas" issue, June-July 1978, 64–72; Fred Bourguignon, "Bon à bruler," *La Tour de feu* no. 88, special issue "Fantômas? . . . c'est Marcel Allain," December 1965, 8–10.

4. Advertisement in Émile Gaboriau, *Le Dossier No 113* (Paris: Arthème Fayard, éditeur, [1905]).

5. Léo Malet, *La Vache enragée* (Paris: Éditions Hoëbeke, 1988), 21–22.

6. Alfu, Patrice Caillot, and François Ducos, *Gino Starace, l'illustrateur de "Fantômas"* (Paris: Encrage, 1988), 62.

7. Juliette Rabbe and Francis Lacassin, *La Bibliothèque idéale des littératures d'évasion* (Paris: Éditions universitaires, 1969), 79.

8. *Larousse du XXe siècle* (Paris: Librarie Larousse, 1930), s.v. "Rocambolesque."

9. See Louis Chevalier, *Laboring Classes and Dangerous Classes in Paris during the First Half of the Nineteenth Century,* trans. Frank Jellinek (New York: Howard Fertig, 1973).

10. Jean-Claude Vareille, *L'Homme masqué, le justicier et le détective* (Lyon: Presses Universitaires de Lyon, 1989), 32–33. See also Mikhail Bakhtin. *Rabelais and His World.* trans. Hélène Iswolsky (Cambridge, Mass.: Harvard University Press, 1968), and *The Dialogic Imagination,* trans. Michel Holquist and Caryl Emerson (Austin: University of Texas Press, 1981).

11.   Peter Brooks, *The Melodramatic Imagination: Balzac, Henry James, Melodrama, and the Mode of Excess* (New Haven: Yale University Press, 1976), 10.

12.   Brooks, *The Melodramatic Imagination*, 36.

13.   Vareille, *L'Homme masqué*, 32, Brooks, *The Melodramatic Imagination*, 20.

14.   Marc Angenot, *Le Roman populaire: Recherches en paralittérature* (Montréal: Presses l'Université du Québec, 1975), 103–104.

15.   Pierre Souvestre and Marcel Allain, *Le Pendu de Londres* (Paris: Robert Laffont, 1962), 294.

16.   The other two series of previously unpublished novels in *Le livre populaire* were Aristide Bruand's *Les Bas-Fonds de Paris* (1910–11) and Gaston Leroux's *Chéri Bibi* (1913–25).

17.   Pierre Scize "49.280.000 lignes, c'est à quoi se monte la production d'un des auteurs de *Fantômas*," *Paris-Journal*, 20 June 1924, 1.

18.   After Souvestre's untimely death from Spanish influenza in 1914, Marcel Allain resumed the production of Fantômas adventures from the 1920s to the 1950s in various formats, including weekly magazines (fascicules), newspaper installments (feuilletons), and comic books (bandes dessinnées). See "Bibliographie de Fantômas," Europe, nos. 590/591, June/July 1978, 141–61.

19.   Other detective weeklies, ranging in price from 10 to 25 centimes, appearing in the decade before the Great War included *Lord Lister, le grand inconnu*, 30 issues (Eichler, 1908); *Marc Jordan, exploits surprenants du plus grand détective français*, 51 issues (J. Férenczi, 1910s); *Souvenirs de Monsieur de Paris, par un de ses aides*, 16 issues (La Nouvelle Populaire, 1908–9); Jean Petithuguenin, *Ethel King, le Nick Carter féminin*, 83 issues (Eichler, 1912–13); and *Tip Walter, le prince des détectives*, 55 issues (J. Férenczi, 1912). Source: Jacques Bisceglia, *Trésors du roman policier* (Paris: Les éditions de l'amateur, 1986).

20.   Other detective weeklies appeared in France throughout the 1920s, and ranged in price from 30 centimes to 1F, 50. With the exception of *Harry Dickson*, they failed to obtain the longevity of either *Nick Carter* or *Nat Pinkerton*. These included *Lord Lister, le mystérieux inconnu*, 83 issues (Hachette); "The Captain Browning" (pseudonym of Jacques Ribières and jurist Jean-Charles Lagaillarde), *Dick Cartter, le roi des détectives*, 21 issues (Prima); Marcel Allain, *Les Nouvelles aventures inédites de Fantômas*, 34 issues (Société parisienne d'édition, 1926); Gaston Le Rouge, *Les Aventures de Todd Marvel, détective milliardaire*, 20 issues; P. Yrondy, *Marius Pegomas, détective Marseillais*, 36 issues (Baudinière); A. Galopin, *Le Petit Détective*, 83 issues (Albin-Michel, 1934–35); and Jean Ray, *Harry Dickson, le Sherlock Holmes américain*, 178 bi-monthly issues (Société Anonyme Roman-Boek en Kunsthandel, 1929–38). Source: Bisceglia, *Trésors du roman policier*.

21.   Lacassin, "Préface," 22–23; Géo Vadieu, "Fantômin et Lupinas," *Europe* 590/591, 108–11.

22.   "Observation présentée par M. Philippe Soupault (auteur en collaboration

avec M. André Breton des «Champs Magnetiques»)," *La Révolution Surréaliste,* no. 4, 15 July 1925, 8.

23.   *Histoire de la Librairie Arthème Fayard* (Paris: Fayard, 1961), 10–11.

24.   Louis Feuillade, dir., *Fantômas, Juve contre Fantômas, Le mort qui tue, Fantômas contre Fantômas,* and *Le faux magistrat* (Gaumont, 1913–14).

25.   Guillaume Apollinaire, "Fantômas," *Mercure de France,* 16 July 1914, 422–23.

26.   For typical mystery plot devices, see Dennis Porter, *The Pursuit of Crime: Art and Ideology in Detective Fiction* (New Haven: Yale University Press, 1981).

27.   Uri Eisenzweig, *Le Récit impossible* (Paris: Christian Bourgeois Éditeur, 1986). Eisenzweig argues that the detective novel is foremost a *récit impossible* of "factual indecision"—paradoxes, detours, and displaced identities—and only secondarily about the coherent elucidation of an enigma, which is, after all, merely the invention of the author, not any true "solution."

28.   Vareille, *L'Homme masqué,* 47.

29.   Vareille, *L'Homme masqué,* 144.

30.   Linda Williams, *Figures of Desire: A Theory and Analysis of Surrealist Film* (Ann Arbor: University of Michigan Press, 1971), 214.

31.   Pierre Souvestre and Marcel Allain, *Fantômas se venge* [*Le Mort qui tue*] (Paris: Livre de poche, 1961), 313–14.

32.   Roger Connah, *Writing Architecture: Fantômas, Fragments, Fictions: An Architectural Journal through the Twentieth Century* (Cambridge, Mass.: M. I. T. Press, 1989). "Fantômas" or the "swerve" was one of the basic design principles of Finnish architect Reima Pietila. As a schoolboy, Pietila was a *Fantômas* fan.

33.   Louis Aragon, *Le Paysan de Paris* (Paris: Live de poche, 1966), 85–86; André Breton, *Nadja* (Paris: Gallimard, 1964).

34.   J.-B. Pontalis, "Between Dream as Object and the Dream-Text," in *Frontiers in Psychoanalysis: Between the Dream and Psychic Pain,* trans. Catherine Cullen and Philip Cullen (London: Hogarth Press, 1981), 49–55.

35.   Pierre Souvestre and Marcel Allain, *Le Pendu de Londres* (Laffont, 1962), 326.

36.   Georges Sadoul, "Souvenirs d'un témoin," *Surréalisme et Cinéma (1),* special issue of *Études Cinématographiques,* nos. 38–39, 1965, 12.

37.   In the "Documents" portion at the end of the first two volumes of the *Fantômas* «Bouquins» series published by Laffont (1987, 1988), Francis Lacassin has gathered a collection of "Fantômas vu par les poètes," including poems by Robert Desnos, Jean Cocteau, Max Jacob, Pablo Neruda, Ernest Moerman, Claude Veillot, Michel Boujut, Aimé Patri, Paul Gilson, Frédéric de Towarnicki, André Malraux, and Alexandre Vialatte. Fantômas-inspired poems are also included in the "Fantômas? c'est Marcel Allain" issue of *La Tour de feu.*

38.   Ernest Moerman, dir., "Mr. Fantômas, 280.000e chapitre" (Belgium, 1936, silent, 20 min). On Resnais, see Daniel Toscan du Plantier, "Feuillade, mon prédécesseur," *L'Avant Scène* nos. 271/272, 1/15 July 1981, 25.

39.   Patrick Waldberg, *René Magritte*, trans. Austryn Wainhouse (Brussels: André de Riche, Pub., 1965). According to Waldberg, Fantômas was a surrealist aesthetic principle for Magritte: "Only substitute *poetry* or *mystery* for the word *crime* . . . " (p. 28).

40.   *Littérature, nouvelle série*, nos. 11/12, 1921, 24–25.

41.   "Comme il fait beau!" *Littérature*, nouvelle série no. 9, 1923, 6.

42.   Pierre Prevert, dir., *Paris la belle* (France, 1959). The black-and-white compilation film clips were shot during the interwar era.

43.   "Projet d'histoire littéraire contemporaine," *Littérature*, nouvelle série, no. 4, 1 September 1922, 3.

44.   Philippe Soupault, *Mort de Nick Carter* (Paris: Lachenal et Ritter, 1986; orig. 1926).

45.   Guillaume Apollinaire, "Fantômas," *Mercure de France*, 16 July 1914, 422–23.

46.   Roger Caillois, *Le Roman policier* (Buenos Aires: Éditions des lettres françaises, 1941), 72–73.

CHAPTER 3. MURDER, MIRTH, AND MISOGYNY

1.   *Littérature*, no. 18 (March 1921), 1–7, 24.

2.   André Breton, *Anthologie de l'humour noir* (Paris: Jean-Jacques Pauvert, 1972), English translation, "Anthology of Black Humor (Excerpts)" in *What is Surrealism? Selected Writings*, ed. and trans. Franklin Rosemont (New York: Monad, 1978), 190.

3.   Quoted in Henri Béraud, Emmanuel Bourcier, and André Salmon, *L'Affaire Landru* (Paris: Albin Michel, éditeur, 1924), 7–8.

4.   Quoted in Béraud, Bourcier, and Salmon, *L'Affaire Landru*, 13.

5.   "Un nouveau Barbe-Bleue?" *Le Matin*, 14 April 1919, 3.

6.   "Landru a-t-il tué ses quatres maîtresses?" *Le Journal*, 14 April 1919, 3.

7.   See Louis Chevalier, *Montmartre du plaisir et du crime* (Paris: Éditions Robert Laffont, 1980).

8.   Georges Bataille, *The Trial of Gilles de Rais*, trans. Richard Robinson (Los Angeles: Amok Books, 1991), 13–15. Bataille argues that in popular memory, Gilles de Rais and the folktale figure of Bluebeard have been conflated into the same, legendary monster. It is also notable that the most exhaustive studies of Gilles de Rais were produced during the general period of the Landru Affair: Abbot A. Bourdeaut, *Chantocé, Gilles de Rays et les Ducs de Bretagne*, 8 vols. (Rennes, 1924); Emile Gabory, *La Vie et la Mort de Gilles de Raiz, dit à tort Barbe-Bleue* (Paris, 1926); and Lodovico Hernandez, *Le Procès inquisitorial de Gilles de Rais, Maréchal de France*, 8 vols. (Paris, 1922).

9.   "Nouveau chapitre au roman de Landru," *Le Figaro*, 17 April 1919, 2. In May 1919, *Le Matin* covered Landru's case under the headline, "Le Roman des fiancées."

10.   "Le mystère des fiancées disparues," *Le Matin*, 18 April 1919, 3.

11.   "L'affaire Landru. Retrouvra-t-on Ketty l'amie de la belle Mithèse?" *Le Petit Parisian*, 18 April 1919, 2.

12.   "Quelles sont ces fillettes?" *Le Journal*, 20 April 1919, 3.

13.   "Landru ne dupait pas que de faibles femmes. Il était passé maître en escroqueries. Chez une rescapée," *Le Petit Parisian*, 27 April 1919, 2; "La dernière fiancée de Landru. Une idylle dans le métro," *Le Journal*, 27 April 1919, 3.

14.   "Nouvelles Divers. L'affaire Landru," *Le Figaro*, 18 June 1919, 2; "Faits Divers. L'affaire Landru," *Le Temps*, 19 June 1919, 4.

15.   "Les Souvenirs d'une rescapée, par Fernande Segret," *Le Journal*, 31 October—6 November, 1921.

16.   "Landru est écroué à la Santé," *Le Journal*, 28 April 1919, 1.

17.   "Notre enquête à Gambais," *Le Matin*, 24 April 1919, 3; "L'affaire Landru. Chez la nièce d'Anette Pascal (de notre correspondant particulier)," *Le Petit Parisien* 25 April 1919, 3.

18.   "La tombe des fiancées," *Le Journal*, 27 April 1919, 3.

19.   "Les victimes de Landru. On découvre des os calcinés et des taches de sang. Les fouilles continuent aujourd'hui à Gambais," *Le Journal*, 30 April 1919, 1; "Landru dit «Barbe-Bleue» à la villa de Gambais," *Le Figaro*, 30 April 1919, 2; "Dans la cuisine de Landru. Le Secret de la villa de Gambais," *Le Matin*, 30 April 1919, 1; "Dans la villa de Gambais. On trouve à Gambais des ossessments humains et des taches de sang," *Le Petit Parisien*, 30 April 1919, 1; "Find Burned Bones in Landru's Stable. Gruesome Discovery on Premises of Parisian Suspected of Killing Ten Fiancees," *New York Times*, 30 April 1919, 11.

20.   "Ce qu'on découvre à Gambais," *Le Matin*, 3 May 1919, 1.

21.   " La leçon que la police tire de l'affaire Landru. A l'habilité croissante des criminelles doit opposer des méthodes plus scientifiques," *Le Journal*, 20 May 1919, 1. A police laboratory team was called in from Lyon to examine the villa at Vernouillet, but it produced no results.

22.   "Try French 'Bluebeard'," *New York Times*, 22 October 1920, 15; "To Deport 'Bluebeard'," *New York Times*, 29 October 1920, 17.

23.   "Entrevue avec Maître de Moro-Giaferri," *Littérature, nouvelle série*, no. 1 (March 1922), 23–24.

24.   "Landru," *Le Temps*, 7 November 1921, 1.

25.   Victor Snell, "Philosophie de l'affaire Landru," *L'Humanité*, 27 April 1919, 2.

26.   "Landru devant ses juges," *Le Figaro*, 11 November 1921, 1. *Filandru* is a play on words combining the adjectives *filandreux*, meaning tough and intertwined, and *dru*, meaning strong, vigorous, and ribald.

27.   "Landru qu'on accuse d'avoir quatre femmes, avait quatre noms et quatre domiciles," *Le Journal*, 15 April 1919, 1. A similar series of connections appeared in *Le Matin* the same day: "Deux garages, deux villas, 35.000 francs," 15 April 1919, 2.

28. "Landru, l'escamoteur de femmes, a été amené hier au Palais de Justice," *Le Matin.* 28 April 1919, 1.

29. See Émile Laurent, *L'Anthropologie Criminelle, et les nouvelles théories du crime,* dieuxième édition (Paris: Société d'Éditions scientifiques, 1893), and *Le Criminel aux points de vue anthropologique. psychologique et social,* préface de M. le Professeur Lacassagne (Paris: Vigot Frères, éditeurs, 1908).

30. Emile Laurent, *Les Habitués des Prisons de Paris, étude d'anthropologie et de psychologie criminelle* (Paris: G. Masson, 1890).

31. Ruth Harris, *Murders and Madness: Medicine, Law, and Society in the Fin de Siècle* (Oxford: Clarendon Press, 1989); and Edward Berenson, *The Trial of Madame Caillaux* (Berkeley and Los Angeles: University of California Press, 1992).

32. Laurent, *Le Criminel,* 236.

33. Louis Proal, *Passion and Criminality: A Legal and Literary Study,* trans. A. R. Allinson (Paris: Charles Carrington, 1901), 649.

34. For a concise summary of Bertillon's anthropometric system, see Dr. Edmond Locard, *Manuel de Technique policière (enquête criminelle)* (Paris: Payot, 1923).

35. Marcel Coulon, "L'Affaire Landru," *Mercure de France,* no. 144, 1920, 222–25.

36. "L'homme aux fiancées. Landru l'irrésistible. Une curieuse étude sur sa physionomie," *Le Journal,* 24 May 1919, 1, translated and reprinted as "Physiognomy and Crime: An Analysis of Landru's Character," in *London Times,* 27 May 1919, 11.

37. *Le Journal,* 15 April 1919, 1.

38. *Le Matin,* 25 February 1922, 1; *L'Humanité,* 22 February 1922, 1.

39. Photos and sketches of Landru in *Le Matin* during the 1921 trial emphasized this ratlike and crazed Landru.

40. "Comment le préférez-vous?" *Le Matin,* 6 November 1921, 4.

41. Edmond Locard, *Policiers de roman et policiers de laboratoire* (Paris: Payot, 1924).

42. Edmond Locard, *L'Enquête criminelle et les méthodes scientifiques* (Paris: Ernest Flammarion, éditeur, 1920), 17 f.

43. During Landru's interrogatory trial undertaken by the Sûreté, the police attempted unsuccessfully to decode the numbers to correspond with the missing women. A fictional account of the Landru Affair using the *carnet* number codes is found in René Masson, *Les Roses de Gambais* (Paris: Presses de la Cité, 1963), English trans., *Number One: A Story of Landru,* trans. Gillian Tindall (London: Hutchinson and Co., Ltd., 1964). In Masson's novel, "Number One" refers to Landru, "two" to his wife, "three" through "six" to his children, and "seven" to Fernande Segret. Such simplification remains a fictional device, however.

44. Most recently, French historian Pierre Darmon has undertaken a detailed analysis of the *carnet,* the dossiers, and the massive amount of circumstantial evidence collected by the state. Cf. Pierre Darmon, *Landru* (Paris: Plon, 1994), and

"Landru: Les archives d'un criminel," *L'Histoire*, no. 176, April 1994, 24–29. Still, the "impossible how" of murder remains a mystery. In Darmon's view, "*Il semble établi que* [emphasis added] l'assassin, après avoir dépecé le cadavre (il a acheté plus de soixante-dix scies à métaux en quatre ans), a fait incinérer les têtes, les mains et les pieds dans sa légendaire cuisinière, les autres tronçons étant dispersés dans la nature" ("Landru," 29). Yet the circumstantial evidence in the Landru Affair did not necessarily suggest this particular murder scenario; there are many problems with the scenario, which Darmon, like all its proponents, avoids. Even in Darmon's account, the murderous fantasies of the Bluebeard of Gambais continue to exceed the bounds of the "realistic" reconstruction of the crime.

45.   Benjamin F. Martin, *Crime and Criminal Justice Under the Third Republic: The Shame of Marianne* (Baton Rouge: Louisiana State University Press, 1990), 11–31.

46.   Georges Claretie, "Nouvelles Diverses. Landru est-il fou?" *Le Figaro,* 22 August 1919, 3.

47.   "Je ne suis pas fou, donc je suis innocent, déclare Landru," *Le Journal,* 23 November 1921, 1–2.

48.   *Le Figaro,* 21 November 1921, 1. For similar remarks, see also *Le Figaro,* 14 November 1921, 2; *Le Temps,* 7 November 1921, 1; *Le Journal,* 4 May 1919, 1.

49.   "Landru a-t-il tué ses quatres maîtresses?" *Le Journal,* 14 April 1919, 3. The association with Dumolard was also recounted in *Le Temps,* 7 November 1921, 1.

50.   "'Mon film' par Clément Vautel," *Le Journal,* 4 May 1919, 1.

51.   "Les précurseurs de Landru. Le crime d'Euphrasie Mercier ou le mystère de Villemomble." *Le Journal,* 14 November 1921, 1.

52.   "Les Ossements trouvés à Gambais appartenaient à trois cadavres. L'hypothèse du crime sans traces." *Le Journal,* 25 November 1921, 1.

53.   Georges Claretie, "La vie au Palais. Un précurseur de Landru," *Le Figaro,* 7 November 1921, 2. See also Henry B. Irving, *Studies of French Criminals of the Nineteenth Century* (London: William Heinemann, 1901), 225–83.

54.   The theme of the banality of the heinous criminal as "everyman," with Landru as one of the examples, is developed in some detail in Carolyn Dean, *The Self and Its Pleasures: Bataille, Lacan, and the History of the Decentered Subject* (Ithaca: Cornell University Press, 1992), 207–13.

55.   Edgar Troimaux, "Landru: The Comic Side of Murder," *The Living Age,* vol. 311, no. 4041, 17 December 1921, 716.

56.   Béraud, Bourcier, and Salmon, *L'Affaire Landru,* 34.

57.   "La Vie au Palais. La Preuve," *Le Figaro,* 14 November 1921, 2. See also Locard, *L'Enquête criminelle,* 10–12.

58.   Emile Vuillermoz, "L'affaire Landru, après le verdict," *L'Illustration,* 10 December 1921, 580.

59.   *Le Journal,* 2 December 1921, 1.

60.   Breton, *Anthologie,* 14–15, "Anthology," 188.

61.   Breton, *Anthologie*, 16, "Anthology," 189. Breton took the example from Freud in *Jokes and Their Relation to the Unconscious*.

62.   John D. Erickson, "Surrealist Black Humor as Oppositional Discourse," *Symposium* 17:3 (1988), 198–215.

63.   Mireille Rosello, *L'Humour noir selon André Breton* (Paris: Librairie José Corti, 1987), 9.

64.   Breton, *Anthologie*, 177, "Anthology," 194–95.

65.   "Les promiscuités de la cour d'assisses," *La Croix*, 2 December 1921, 1.

66.   *Le Journal*, 19 November 1921, 1.

67.   Robert Dieudonné, "Au jour le jour. Après le Verdict," *Le Figaro*, 2 December 1921, 1.

68.   See Sigmund Freud, "Instincts and Their Vicissitudes (1915)," in John Rickman, ed., *A General Selection from the Works of Sigmund Freud* (Garden City: Doubleday Anchor Books, 1957), 70–86.

69.   Camille Mauclair, "Le Mythe de la curiosité feminine," *Le Figaro*, 21 November 1921, 1.

70.   "Physiognomy and Crime: An Analysis of Landru's Character," *London Times*, 27 May 1919, 11. (Translation of "L'homme aux fiancées," *Le Journal*, 24 May 1919, 1).

71.   *Le Journal*, 17 April 1919, 1.

72.   The "opposite" or "complementary" gender qualities of French men and women, central to bourgeois social reproduction, are discussed in Robert Nye, "Sex Differences and the 'Separate Spheres'," in *Masculinity and Male Codes of Honor in Modern France* (New York: Oxford University Press, 1993), 47–71. My specific line of interpretation concerning the gender of the *fait-divers* reader is indebted to Carol Clover's discussion of the "slasher" film viewer in *Men, Women and Chain Saws: Gender in the Modern Horror Film* (Princeton: Princeton University Press, 1992).

73.   "Landru," *Le Libertaire*, 2nd series, no. 147, 11 November 1921, 3.

74.   Doctoresse Pelletier, "Landru et le féminisme," *Le Libertaire*, 2nd series, no. 143, 18 November 1921, 3.

75.   *Le Temps*, 18 April 1919, 4.

76.   "L'affaire Landru. Une mystification," *Le Figaro*, 30 May 1919, 2.

77.   "Nouvelles Diverses. L'affaire Landru," *Le Figaro*, 7 August 1919, 3. Such witticisms abound in secondary accounts of Landru.

78.   *Le Journal*, 5 November 1921, 1.

79.   *Le Journal*, 7 November 1921, 1.

80.   *Le Journal*, 8 November 1921, 1.

81.   *Le Journal*, 13 November 1921, 1.

82.   *Le Journal*, 26 November 1921, 1.

83.   "La Véridique histoire de Barbe-Bleue (complainte)," *Le Matin*, 13 No-

vember 1921, 4; "La Véridique histoire de Barbe-Bleue," *Le Journal,* 14 November 1921, 4.

84.   *Le Journal,* 1 November 1921, 5.

85.   *Le Journal,* 15 November 1921, 3.

86.   Dieudonné, "Après le Verdict," *Le Figaro,* 2 December 1921, 1.

87.   "L'autre Barbe-bleue en feuilleton," *La Croix,* 3 December 1921, 1.

88.   "L'avant-dernière toilette," *Le Matin,* 25 February 1922, 1.

89.   "L'exécution de Landru," *Le Figaro,* 25 February 1922, 2.

90.   Paul Bringuier, "Avouez-Donc, Landru!" *Détective* no. 110, 4 December 1930, 9. These jokes about Landru not drinking or smoking are frequently found in secondary sources, although none I have found thus far predate Bringuier's article. Still, since the rest of Bringuier's article is derivative of newspaper accounts, I consider it possible that the jokes were in circulation before 1930.

91.   "All the Old Forms Preserved," *New York Times,* 27 February 1922, 12.

92.   André Salmon, "Landru a été éxécuté hier matin à Versailles," *Le Matin,* 26 February 1922, 1. Salmon's coverage is reprinted as the final section of Béraud, Bourcier, and Salmon, *L'affaire Landru.*

93.   Pierre Mac Orlan, "Les assassins de Paris," *Mercure de France,* no. 173 (1924), 811–14.

94.   Aragon, *Nightwalker (Le Paysan de Paris),* trans. Frederick Brown (Englewood Cliffs: Prentice-Hall, Inc., 1970), 35.

95.   Archives de Paris, D9 P2 1382, *Faubourg-Montmartre Patentes,* 1920.

CHAPTER 4. IS SUICIDE A SOLUTION?

1.   *La Révolution Surréaliste* no. 1, 1 December 1924, 2.

2.   *Reims, la ville martyre, 1914–1918,* Guides Diamant (Paris: Librairie Hachette et Cie., 1919); *Lille avant et pendant la guerre,* Guides illustrés Michelin des champs de bataille (1914–1918) (Clermont-Ferrand: Michelin et Cie., 1919).

3.   *La Révolution surréaliste,* no. 2, 15 January 1925, 8.

4.   Maurice Nadeau, *The History of Surrealism,* trans. Richard Howard (Cambridge, Mass.: Harvard University Press, Belknap Press, 1989), 43–58. See also Robert Wohl, *The Generation of 1914* (Cambridge, Mass.: Harvard University Press, 1979).

5.   Georges Auclair, *Le Mana quotidien: Structure et fonctions de la rubrique des faits divers* (Paris: Anthropos, 1970); Maurice Merleau-Ponty, "On News Items," in *Signs,* trans. Richard C. McCleary (Evanston: Northwestern University Press, 1964), 311–13; and Jules Gritti, "Le Fait Divers," in Fred Forest, *Bourse de l'imaginaire: Bourse du fait divers. Expérience de presse* (Paris: Éditions du Territoire, 1982), 26–33.

6.   Michael M. Davis, Jr., "The Scope and Limits of Imitation" and "Imitation

and Suggestion in Society," in *Psychological Interpretations of Society* (New York: AMS Press, 1968; facsimile reprint of 1909 ed.), 143–90.

7.   A wonderfully melodramatic example is Olympe Audouard, "Suicide ou Infamie! Drame de la vie réelle," in *Les Roses Sanglantes* (Paris: E. Dentu, éditeur, 1880).

8.   Dr. [Paul] Moreau de Tours, *Suicides et crimes étranges* (Paris: Société d'Éditions Scientifiques, 1899), 1.

9.   The suicide categories and details that follow are taken from Moreau de Tours, *Suicides*, 9–40.

10.   Moreau de Tours, *Suicides*, 44.

11.   Moreau de Tours, *Suicides*, 138–40.

12.   Emile Laurent, *L'Anthropologie criminelle, et les nouvelles théories du crime*, 2nd ed. (Paris: Société d'Éditions Scientifiques, 1893), 139–48.

13.   Henry Morselli, *Suicide: An Essay on Comparative Moral Statistics* (New York: D. Appleton and Co., 1882), 145.

14.   Laurent, *L'Anthropologie criminelle*, 145.

15.   The English phrase "struggle for life" was often employed in these French texts. E.g., "ses individus mal armés pour le combat de la vie, pour le *struggle for life* . . . ", in Laurent, *Les Habitués des prisons*, 605.

16.   Laurent, *L'Anthropologie criminelle*, 187.

17.   Paul Aubry, *La Contagion du meurtre: Étude d'anthropologie criminelle*, with a preface by Dr. A. Corre (Paris: Félix Alcan, 1896).

18.   On Tarde's concept of "social somnambulism," see Susanna Barrows, *Distorting Mirrors: Visions of the Crowd in Late Nineteenth-Century France* (New Haven: Yale University Press, 1981), 139 f.

19.   Aubry, *La Contagion du meurtre*, 180–83.

20.   Séverin Icard, "De la contagion du crime et du suicide par la presse," *Nouvelle Revue* (15 April 1902) (reprint Paris: Editions de *La Nouvelle Revue*, 1902).

21.   Icard, *De la contagion*, 9.

22.   Icard, *De la contagion*, 5. The phrase is italicized in the original French.

23.   Dr. Lorthiois, *De l'automutilation, mutilations et suicides étranges* (Paris: Vigot Frères, 1909).

24.   Lorthiois, *De l'automutilation*, 12.

25.   While French criminal anthropologists generally criticized the biological determinism of Lombroso, they seemed less adverse to using it in the case of women and children. See Laurent, "La femme criminelle," in *L'Anthropologie criminelle*, 125–32.

26.   It is worth noting that the case-study evidence in these works of medical research and criminal anthropology was derived both from professional journals and the daily press. Lorthiois's cases, for example, are drawn from over thirty

medical and psychiatric studies but also from accounts of automutilation and suicide published in a number of newspapers, including *La Démocratie Pacific, La Dépêche (Lille), Le Droit, L'Écho du Nord, Le Matin, Le Moniteur du Puy-de-Dôme, Le Monde, Le Nouveau Précurseur (d'Anvers), Le Progrès du Nord,* and *L'Univers.*

27.   De Guerry, *Statistique morale de la France* (1835); Tissot, *De la manie du suicide et de l'esprit de révolte* (1841); and Etoc-Demazy, *Recherches statistiques sur le suicide* (1844), cited in Emile Durkheim, *Le Suicide: Étude de sociologie,* nouvelle édition (Paris: Librairie Félix Alcan, 1930), 17.

28.   Durkheim, "Tableau III," in *Le Suicide,* 14. Suicide rates in France continued to rise in the decade before the Great War, dropping during the war, and then stabilizing in the 1920s. See also Charles Candiotti et al., "Tableau A," *Considérations statistiques sur le suicide en France et à l'Étranger: Ses répercussions socials,* Institut National d'Hygiène (Paris: J.-B. Baillière et fils, 1948), 4.

29.   Durkheim, *Le Suicide,* 15.

30.   Durkheim, *Le Suicide,* 107−38.

31.   Durkheim, *Le Suicide,* 134.

32.   See Dominick LaCapra, *Emile Durkheim: Sociologist and Philosopher* (Chicago: University of Chicago Press, 1972).

33.   In favor of the psychological perspective, see Emmanuel Alphy, *De la répression du suicide* (Paris: Arthur Rousseau, 1910); Charles Blondel, *La Conscience morbide, essai de psychopathologie générale,* 2nd ed. (Paris: Librarie Félix Alcan, 1928), *The Troubled Conscience and the Insane Mind,* intro. F. G. Crookshank, Psyche Miniatures Medical Series, no. 10 (London: Kegal Paul, Trench, Trubner and Co., 1928), and *Le Suicide* (Strasbourg: Librarie Universitaire d'Alsace, 1933); and F. Achille-Delmas, *Psychologie pathologique du suicide* (Paris: Librarie Félix Alcan, 1932). In favor of the sociological perspective, see Maurice Halbwachs, *Les Causes du suicide* (Paris: Librarie Félix Alcan, 1930), English edition: *The Causes of Suicide,* trans. Harold Goldblatt (London: Routledge and Kegan Paul, 1978); and Bel-El-Mouffok Abderrahman, *Du Suicide émotif et du suicide non pathologique* (Paris: Librarie L. Rodstein, 1933).

34.   Albert Bayet, *Le Suicide et la morale* (Paris: Librarie Félix Alcan, 1922), 57−70.

35.   See Alain Monestier, *Le Fait divers* (Paris: Éditions de la Réunion des musées nationaux, 1982); and Roger Chartier, *Figures de la gueuserie,* series "Bibliothèque bleue" (Paris: Montalba, 1982).

36.   See Jean-Pierre Seguin, *Les Canards illustrés du 19e siècle: Fascination du fait divers* (Paris: Musée-Galerie de la Seita, 1982).

37.   Claude Bellanger et al., *Histoire générale de la presse française,* III: *De 1871 à 1940* (Paris: Presses Universitaires de France, 1972), 140−41.

38.   On the *quatre grands* and press circulation figures, see Bellanger et al., *Histoire générale de la presse française,* 3:294−316. For a good introduction in English

to the development of the *quatre grands* and *faits divers*, see Edward Berenson, *The Trial of Madame Caillaux* (Berkeley and Los Angeles: University of California Press, 1992), 209–20 and 226–235.

39.   Bellanger et al., *Histoire générale de la presse française*, 3:7–21.

40.   Over the course of the interwar period, all four newspapers moved to the extreme political right, openly supporting French and Italian fascism, as well as German Nazism, by the end of the 1930s. See Philippe Bernard and Henri Dubief, *The Decline of the Third Republic, 1914–1938*, trans. Anthony Forster (Cambridge: Cambridge University Press and Paris: Éditions de la maison des sciences de l'homme, 1988), 262–65.

41.   Monestier, "Crime, suicide, folie," 72–73.

42.   In addition to its regular *Fait-divers* column, *Le Matin* would intersperse *Faits divers en trois lignes* announcements throughout the newspaper.

43.   Paul Bringuier, "Un fait divers," *Détective* no. 117, 22 January 1931, 3–5.

44.   Emily Apter, "Allegories of Reading / Allegories of Justice: The Gidean Fait Divers," *Romantic Review*, no. 80, 1989, 564.

45.   Emily Apter, "*Stigma indelebile*: Gide's Parodies of Zola and the Displacement of Realism," *MLN* 101 (1986), 857.

46.   The banality of suicide methods runs against conventional wisdom, which tends to focus upon bizarre or unusual suicides—certainly so in *faits divers*. See Christian Baudelot and Roger Establet, "Fait divers et fait social," in *Durkheim et le suicide* (Paris: Presses Universitaires de France, 1984), 76–88; and Monestier, "Crime, suicide, folie," 72–73. I do not challenge this general assessment. Rather, I suspect that the discrepancy between the extraordinary and the banal may lie in the difference between a *grand fait divers* and a *fait divers en trois lignes;* that is, extended and condensed texts may well function according to different narrative strategies.

47.   My 1924 newspaper sample of suicide motives accords well with a similar comparison done in Bayet, *Le Suicide et la morale*, 68. In Bayet's random sampling of *Le Petit Journal* (1863, 1873, 1883, 1893) and *Le Petit Parisien* (1883, 1893, 1903), the known/unknown ratio of motives ran 2:1 and 3:1. The major difference in our samples is that, in Bayet, *misère* and *chagrin d'amour* constitute the dominant categories of known motives. By 1924, *neurasthénie* was the most frequently cited motive category (absent from Bayet). While *chagrin d'amour* was still important in 1924, *misère* was rarely mentioned.

48.   Sidra Stich, *Anxious Visions: Surrealist Art*, with essays by James Clifford, Tyler Stovall, and Steven Kovács (New York: Abbeville Press, 1990), 26.

49.   Bayet, *Le Suicide et la morale*, 69.

50.   Subsequent examples, quotes, and phrases in response to the suicide inquiry are all taken from *La Révolution Surréaliste* no. 2, 15 January 1925, 8–15.

51.   Roger Conover, Terry Hale, and Paul Lenti, eds., *Four Dada Suicides: Selected*

Texts of Arthur Cravan, Jacques Rigaut, Julien Torma and Jacques Vaché, trans. Terry Hale et al. (London: Atlas Press, 1995).

52.   "Jacques Rigaut," *La Révolution Surréaliste*, no. 12, 15 December 1929, 56.

53.   The events of June 1935 and Crevel's suicide are recounted in detail in Helena Lewis, *The Politics of Surrealism* (New York: Paragon House Publishers, 1988), 129–31; and Herbert Lottman, *The Left Bank Writers: Artists and Politics from the Popular Front to the Cold War* (Boston: Houghton Mifflin Co., 1982), 1–4.

54.   There is some confusion as to this person's name. Each time he wrote to *La Révolution Surréaliste*, he used a slightly different name: E. Gegenbach, Abbé E. Gegenbach, Jean Genbach. Jean Genbach was the name used in the index of the final issue of *La Révolution Surréaliste*, (no. 12, 15 December 1929, 78). Genbach is also the name used in Henri Béhar, *André Breton: Le grand indésirable* (Paris: Calmann-Lévy, 1990), 200.

55.   E. Gegenbach, "Une Lettre," *La Révolution Surréaliste*, no. 5, 15 October 1925, 1.

56.   Abbé E. Gegenbach, "Correspondance," *La Révolution Surréaliste*, no. 8, 1 December 1926, 28–30; and Jean Genbach, "Correspondance," *La Révolution Surréaliste*, no. 11, 15 March 1928, 29–32.

57.   Gegenbach, "Une Lettre," 2.

CONCLUSION

1.   Louis Aragon, *Traité du Style* (Paris, Gallimard, 1928), 18.

2.   Aragon, *Traité du Style*, 187–92.

3.   Elyette Benassaya, "Le Surréalisme face à la presse," *Mélusine*, Cahiers du Centre de Recherche sur le Surréalisme (Paris III), no. 1 (Lausanne: L'Age d'Homme, 1979), 131–50.

4.   Benassaya, "Le Surréalisme," 144–45.

5.   André Breton, "Second Manifeste du Surréalisme," *La Révolution Surréaliste*, no. 12, 15 December 1929, 3.

6.   Quoted in Jean Starobinski, "Face diurne et face nocturne," in Charles Goerg, ed., *Regards sur* Minotaure, *la revue à tête de bête* (Geneva: Musée d'art et d'histoire, 1987), 31.

7.   Quoted in José Pierre, "André Breton et/ou «Minotaure»," in Goerg, ed., *Regards sur* Minotaure, 100.

8.   Kenneth E. Silver, *Esprit de Corps: The Art of the Parisian Avant-Garde and the First World War, 1914–1925* (Princeton: Princeton University Press, 1989), 304–14 and 390–97.

9.   Jacques Prévert, quoted in Maurice Nadeau, *The History of Surrealism*, trans. Richard Howard (Cambridge, Mass: Harvard University Press, Belknap Press, 1989), 276.

10.   Helena Lewis, *The Politics of Surrealism* (New York: Paragon House Publishers, 1988), 129–31; Herbert Lottman, *The Left Bank Writers: Artists and Politics from the Popular Front to the Cold War* (Boston: Houghton Mifflin Co. 1982), 1–4; and Nadeau, *History of Surrealism*, 191–98.

11.   Breton, "Second Manifeste," 3.

12.   Louis Aragon, "Introduction à 1930," *La Révolution Surréaliste*, no. 12, 15 December 1929, 64.

13.   Georges Sadoul, "Bonne Année! Bonne Santé!," *La Révolution Surréaliste*, no. 12, 15 December 1929, 45–47.

14.   This discussion of *Détective*'s format is based on the magazine's format between 1930 and 1931.

15.   Sadoul, "Bonne Année!" 46.

16.   A related and more extensive analysis of *Détective* magazine along these lines is made in Adrian Rifkin, *Street Noises: Parisian Pleasures, 1900–1940* (Manchester: Manchester University Press, 1993).

17.   Maxime du Camp, *Paris, ses organes, ses fonctions et sa vie dans la seconde moitié du XIXe siècle*, 6 vols., 7th ed. (Paris: Librairie Hachette, 1883).

18.   Du Camp, *Paris*, 3:50.

19.   Xavier de Hauteclocque, *Pègre et Police Internationales*, collection «La vie d'aujourd'hui» (Paris: Nouvelle Revue Critique, 1934), 7–8.

20.   Hauteclocque, *Pègre et Police*, 9.

21.   Alfred Morain, *The Underworld of Paris: Secrets of the Sûreté* (New York: E. P. Dutton, 1931), 46.

22.   See Dominique Kalifa, *L'Encre et le sang: Récits de crimes et société à la Belle Époque* (Paris: Fayard, 1995). See also Alain Monestier, "Un univers de signes," in *Le Fait Divers* (Paris: Éditions de la réunion des musées nationaux, 1982), 99–101.

23.   Entirely new series of crime fiction published in Paris during the interwar period in France included "A ne pas lire la nuit" (Les Éditions de France), "L'arc-en-ciel" (Maison de la Bonne Presse/B. Arthaud), "L'Aventure" (Fayard), "Aventures" (Plon), "Aventures Policières" (Rouff), "Les bas-fonds" (Ferenczi et fils), "Bibliothèque Jaune" (Dupuis, fils et Cie.), "Collection Blanche/Les Livres du Jour" (Nouvelle Revue Française), "Edward Brooker" (Les Publications Georges Ventillard), "Les Chefs-d'oeuvre du Roman d'Aventures" (Gallimard), "La Clé" (Rouff), "Collection du lecteur" (Les Éditions Cosmopolites), "Crime et Police" (Ferenczi/Livre Moderne), "Crimes et Chatiments" (Livre National/Jules Tallendier), "Crimes et Criminels" (Calmann-Lévy), "Criminels et Policiers" (Livre National/Jules Tallendier), "Détective" (Gallimard), "Le Disque Rouge" (La Renaissance du Livre), "Dix Heures d'Angoise" (Ferenczi et fils), "Les Documents du Siècle" (Nouvelle Librairie Française), "Le Domino Noir" (Alexis Reiderk), "Les Dossiers Secrets de la Police" (Ferenczi et fils), "L'Empreinte" (Nouvelle

Revue Critique), "Enigma" (Librarie Bernardin-Béchet), "Fantômas" (Société Parisienne d'Édition), "Fatala" (Ferenczi), "Galerie Criminelle" (Tallandier), "Collection Gaston Leroux" (Jeanne Gaston-Leroux), "Le Livre d'Aujourd'hui" (Les Éditions de France), "Le Livre de l'Aventure" (Ferenczi et fils), "Le Livre Épatant" (Ferenczi et fils), "Collection du Livre National/Bibliothèque des Grandes Aventures/Collection Bleue/Collection Rouge" (Tallandier), "Le Livre Populaire" (Fayard), "Loisirs-Police" (Éditions des Loisirs), "Le Lynx" (Tallandier), "Les Enquêtes du Commissaire Maigret" (Fayard), "Les Maîtres du Roman Populaire" (Fayard), "Mystère-Aventure-Police" (Le Livre de l'avenir), "Le Masque" (Librarie des Champs-Elysées), "Les Meilleurs Romans Etrangères" (Hachette), "Les Meilleurs Romans Policiers" (Éditions Baudinière), "Miss-Teria" (Ferenczi), "Mon Livre Favori" (Ferenczi et fils), "Mr. Allou, Juge d'Instruction" (Gallimard), "Mystères l'X" (Excelsior), "Les Oeuvres Libres" (Fayard), "Le Petit Livre/Le Petit Roman/Le Petit Roman Policier" (Ferenczi et fils), "La P. J." (La Technique du livre), "Le Point d'Interrogation" (Lafitte), "Police et Mystère" (Ferenczi et fils), "Police-Roman/Police-Film" (Offenstadt), "Police-Secours" (R. Simon), "Police Sélection" (Librarie des Champs-Elysées), "Les Rapaces" (Librarie des Champs-Elysées), "Le Roman Policer" (Ferenczi et fils), "Les Romans d'Aventures" (Ferenczi et fils), "Les Romans Mysterieux" (Tallandier), "Les Romans Policiers" (Baudinière), "Romans pour la Jeunesse" (Rouff), "Le Scarabée d'Or" (Gallimard), "Série Emeraude" (Librarie des Champs-Elysées), "Sur la Piste" (Baudinière), "La Tache de Sang" (Baudinière), "Tigris" (Ferenczi et fils), "Voyages et Aventures" (Ferenczi et fils). Source: Jacques Bisceglia, *Trésors du Roman Policier*, 2nd ed. (Paris: Les Éditions de l'Amateur, 1984).

24.   Emily Apter, "Allegories of Reading/Allegories of Justice: The Gidean Fait Divers," *Romantic Review*, no. 89, 1980, 857–70.

25.   Advertisements for "*La Séquestrée de Poitiers*, documents réunis par André Gide (nrf)," in *Détective*, no. 89, 10 July 1930, 15, and no. 91, 24 July 1930, 6.

26.   See Carolyn Dean, *The Self and Its Pleasures: Bataille, Lacan, and the History of the Decentered Subject* (Ithaca: Cornell University Press, 1992).

27.   André Breton et al., *Violette Nozières: Poèmes, dessins, correspondance, documents* (Bruxelles: Éditions Nicolas Flamel, 1933, reprint Paris: Terrain Vague, 1991); and Alain Grosrichard, "Dr Lacan, «Minotaure», surréalistes rencontres," in Goerg, ed., *Regards sur Minotaure*, 159–73.

28.   Blaise Cendrars, *Panorama de la Pègre* (Grenoble: B. Arthaud, 1935), 11–12. Cendrars employed the invented English word, *gangsland*, in his French text.

29.   See Noël Arnaud, Francis Lacassin, and Jean Tortel, *Entrentiens sur la paralittérature* (Paris: Plon, 1970). This work is a collection of papers, discussions and interviews from the landmark conference held at Cerisy-la-Salle, 1–10 September 1967, on "para-literature"—e.g., melodrama, popular novels, photo-

novels, *bandes-dessinées*. Today, there is a branch in Limoges of the Centre National de la Recherche Scientifique (CNRS) dedicated to the study of popular literature. American researchers of French mass culture are recommended to begin their investigations with Pierre L. Horn, ed., *Handbook of French Popular Culture* (New York: Greenwood Press, 1991).

30.   See Brian Rigby, *Popular Culture in Modern France: A Study of Cultural Discourse* (New York: Routledge, 1991).

31.   Michel Lebrun and J.-P. Schweighaeuser, *Le Guide du polar: Histoire du roman policier français* (Paris: Syros, 1987), 7.

32.   Pierre Enckell, "Le groupe surréaliste," in Olivier Barrot and Pascal Ory, eds., *L'Entre-deux-guerres: La Création française, 1919–1939* (Paris: Éditions François Bourin, 1990), 38–39.

Bibliography

PRIMARY SOURCES

Passages de l'Opéra and Paris Guides

Archives de la Ville de Paris
DQ 18 331. Deuxième Arrondissment, Quartier de la Chaussée d'Antin.
Cadastre, 1809–51.
DP 4 1876. Quartier—Faubourg Montmartre. Cadastre, 1876.
D9 P2. Faubourg Montmartre Patentes, 1900–20.
D2 P4. Contributions des Patentes, Annexe.
Newpapers. Paris, 1924–25.
L'Intransigeant
Le Journal
Le Matin
Le Temps

Baedeker, Karl, pub. *Paris and Its Environs: Handbook for Travelers.* Leipzig: Karl
Baedeker, pub., 1884–1924.

Beaurepaire, Edmond. *La Chronique des rues*. Paris: P. Sevrin et E. Rey, 1900.

Bonfils, Robert. *Les Cent vues de Paris*. Paris: Librairie Larousse, 1924.

Brazier, Gabriel, and Dumersan. *Les Passages et les rue, ou la guerre déclarée*. Vaudeville en un acte. Paris: Chez Duvernois, 1827.

Cain, Georges. *À travers Paris*. Paris: Ernest Flammarion, n.d. [1907].

Calignani's New Paris Guide. Paris: A. and W. Calignani and Co., 1844 and 1873.

Cheronnet, Louis. *A Paris . . . vers 1900*. Paris: Éditions des Chroniques du jour, 1932.

Commission Municipale du Vieux Paris. *Procès-Verbaux*, 1898–1930.

——. *Guide à l'Exposition Universelle*. Paris: Ville de Paris, 1900.

Du Camp, Maxime. *Paris*. 6 Vols. 7th ed. Paris: Librairie Hachette, 1883.

Fournel, François Victor. *Chroniques et légendes des rues de Paris*. Paris: E. Dentu, 1864.

——. *Enigmes des rues de Paris*. Paris: E. Dentu, 1860.

——. *Les rues de vieux Paris: Galerie populaire et pittoresque*. 2nd ed. Paris: Firmin-Didot, 1881.

——. *Tableau de vieux Paris: Les spectacles et les artistes de rues*. Paris: E. Dentu, 1863.

Guide de l'étranger dans Paris et ses environs. Paris: Grand Hotel, 1876.

Guide de poche 1900. Paris: S. Schwartz Éditeur, n.d. [1900].

Guide des Acheteurs, ou almanach des Passages de l'Opéra. Paris: Imprimerie de David, 1828.

Guide des Plaisirs à Paris. Nouvelle édition. Paris: Édition Photographique, n.d. [1900].

Muirhead, Findlay, ed. *Paris and Its Environs*. 3rd ed. "The Blue Guides." Paris: Hachette, 1924.

Jacob, P. L. *Curiosités de l'histoire du vieux Paris*. Paris: Adolphe Delahays, 1858.

Joanne, Adolphe. *Paris Illustré: Nouveau guide de l'étranger et du parisien*. 2nd ed. Paris: L. Hachette et Cie., 1863.

Lurine, Louis. *Les Rues de Paris*. Paris: G. Kugelmann, 1844.

Pugin, Augustus. *Paris and Its Environs*. 2 vols. London: Jennings and Chaplin, 1831.

Reynolds, Bruce. *A Cocktail Continentale*. New York: George Sully and Co., 1926.

——. *Paris with the Lid Lifted*. New York: George Sully and Co., 1927.

Rochegude, Marque de, and Maurice Dumolin. *Guide pratique à travers le Vieux Paris*. Nouvelle édition. Paris: Librairie ancienne Édouard Champion, 1923.

Story, Sommerville. *Dining in Paris*. New York: Robert M. McBridge and Co., 1927.

Trollope, Frances. *Paris and the Parisians in 1835*. New York: Harper and Brothers, 1836.

Warnod, André. *Bals, cafés et cabarets.* Paris: E. Figuière, 1913.

Woon, Basil. *The Paris That's Not in the Guidebooks.* New York: Brentano's Publishers, 1926.

Fantômas

The Fantômas Novels (in chronological order)

Souvestre, Pierre, and Marcel Allain. *Fantômas.* Series "Le Livre Populaire."
32 Vols. Paris: Arthème Fayard, 1911–13. 1. *Fantômas.* 2. *Juve contre Fantômas.*
3. *Le Mort qui tue.* 4. *L'Agent secret.* 5. *Un Roi prisonnier de Fantômas.* 6. *Le
Policier apache.* 7. *Le Pendu de Londres.* 8. *La Fille de Fantômas.* 9. *Le Fiacre de
nuit.* 10. *La Main coupée.* 11. *L'Arrestation de Fantômas.* 12. *Le Magistrat cambrioleur.* 13. *La Livrée du crime.* 14. *La Mort de Juve.* 15. *L'Évadée de Saint-Lazare.*
16. *La Disparition de Fandor.* 17. *Le Marriage de Fantômas.* 18. *L'Assassin de Lady
Beltham.* 19. *La Guêpe rouge.* 20. *Les Souliers du mort.* 21. *Le Train perdu.* 22. *Les
Amours d'un prince.* 23. *Le Bouquet tragique.* 24. *Le Jockey masqué.* 25. *Le Cercueil
vide.* 26. *Le Faiseur de reines.* 27. *Le Cadavre géant.* 28. *Le Voleur d'or.* 29. *La Série
rouge.* 30. *L'Hôtel du crime.* 31. *La Cravate de chanvre.* 32. *La Fin de Fantômas.*
————. *Fantômas.* 12 Vols. Paris: Robert Laffont, 1961–65.
————. *Fantômas.* Series "Bouquins." 3 Vols. Paris: Robert Laffont, 1986–89.
Allain, Marcel. *Fantômas.* Series "Nouvelles aventures inédites." 34 weekly magazine installments (*fascicules*). Paris: Société Parisienne d'Éditions, April–
December 1925. Reissued in 5 novels. Paris: Arthème Fayard 1934–35.
1. *Fantômas est-il ressuscité?* 2. *Fantômas roi des recéleurs.* 3. *Fantômas en danger.*
4. *Fantômas prend sa revanche.* 5. *Fantômas attaque Fandor.*

Fantômas in English Translation

Souvestre, Pierre, and Marcel Allain. *Fantômas.* Trans. Cranstoun Metcalfe. Lon-
don: Stanley Paul/New York: Brentano's, 1915. Reissued as *Fantômas.* Intro.
John Ashbery. New York: William Morrow, 1986.
————. *The Exploits of Juve* (*Juve contre Fantômas*). London: Stanley Paul/New
York: Brentano's, 1917. Reissued as *The Silent Executioner.* Intro. Edward
Gorey. New York: William Morrow, 1987.
————. *Messengers of Evil* (*Le Mort qui tue*). London: Stanley Paul/New York:
Brentano's, 1917.
————. *A Nest of Spies* (*L'Agent secret*). London: Stanley Paul/New York:
Brentano's, 1917.
————. *A Royal Prisoner* (*Un Roi prisonnier de Fantômas*). London: Stanley
Paul/New York: Brentano's, 1918.

————. *The Long Arm of Fantômas* (*Le Policier apache*). Trans. A. R. Allinson. New York: The Macauley Co., 1924.

————. *Slippery as Sin* (*Le Pendu de Londres*). Trans. B. J. London: Stanley Paul, 1920.

Allain, Marcel. *The Lord of Terror (Fantômas est-il ressuscité?)*. Trans. A. R. Allinson. Philadelphia: David McKay, 1924.

————. *Juve in the Dock (Fantômas roi de recéleurs)*. Trans. A. R. Allinson. Philadelphia: David McKay, 1926.

————. *Fantômas Captured. (Fantômas en danger)*. Trans. A. R. Allinson. Philadelphia: David McKay, 1926.

————. *The Revenge of Fantômas (Fantômas prend sa revanche)*. Trans. A. R. Allinson. Philadelphia: David McKay, 1927.

Contemporary Imprints on Fantômas

Apollinaire, Guillaume. "Fantômas." *Mercure de France*. 16 July 1914, 422–23.

Desnos, Robert. "La Complainte de Fantômas." In *Fortunes*. Paris: Gallimard, 1945.

Scize, Pierre. "49.280.000 lignes, c'est à quoi se monte la production d'un auteurs de *Fantômas*." *Paris Journal*. 20 June 1924, 1.

Landru

Newpapers. Paris, 1914, 1921–22.
  La Croix
  Le Figaro
  L'Humanité
  L'Intransigeant
  Le Journal
  Le Libertaire
  Le Matin
  Le Petit Journal
  Le Temps
Newpapers. English Language, 1914, 1921–22.
  London Times
  New York Times

Béraud, Henri. Emmanuel Bourcier, and André Salmon. *L'Affaire Landru*. Paris: Albin Michel, 1924.

Coulon, Marcel. "L'Affaire Landru." *Mercure de France*. 1 April 1920, 222–25.

Laurent, Emile. *L'Anthropologie Criminelle, et les nouvelles théories du crime*. 2nd ed. Paris: Société d'Éditions Scientifiques, 1893.

————. *Le Criminel aux points de vue anthropologique, psychologie et sociale.* Paris: Vigot Frères, 1908.

————. *Les Habitués de prisons de Paris: Étude d'anthropologie et de psychologie criminelle.* Paris: G. Masson, 1890.

Locard, Edmond. *L'Enquête criminelle et les méthodes scientifiques.* Paris: Ernest Flammarion, 1920.

————. *Manuel de Technique policière (enquête criminelle).* Paris: Payot, 1923.

————. *Policiers de roman et policiers de laboratoire.* Paris: Payot, 1924.

Mac Orlan, Pierre. "Les Assassins de Paris." *Mercure de France.* 1 August 1924, 811–14.

Proal, Louis. *Passion and Criminality: A Legal and Literary Study.* Trans. A. R. Allinson. Paris: Charles Carrington, 1901.

Troimaux, Edgar. "Landru: The Comic Side of Murder." *The Living Age.* Vol. 311, no. 4041. 17 December 1921, 716.

Vuillermoz, Emile. "L'Affaire Landru, après le verdict." *L'Illustration.* 10 December 1921, 447–580.

Suicide and Faits Divers

Newpapers. October and November, 1924.
   Le Figaro
   L'Intransigeant
   Le Journal
   Le Matin

Abderrahman, Bel-El-Mouffok. *Du Suicide émotif et du suicide non pathologique.* Paris: L. Rodstein, 1933.

Achille-Delmas, F. *Psychologie pathologique du suicide.* Paris: Félix Alcan, 1932.

Alphy, Emmanuel. *De la répression du suicide.* Paris: Arthur Rousseau, 1910.

Aubry, Paul. *La Contagion du meurtre.* Paris: Félix Alcan, 1896.

Audouard, Olympe. "Suicide ou Infanie! Drame de la vie réelle." In *Les Roses Sanglantes.* Paris: E. Dentu, 1880.

Bayet, Albert. *Le Suicide et la morale.* Paris: Félix Alcan, 1922.

Blondel, Charles. *La Conscience morbide.* Paris: Félix Alcan, 1928.

————. *Le Suicide.* Strasbourg: Librarie Universitaire d'Alsace, 1933.

————. *The Troubled Conscience and the Insane Mind.* Intro. F. G. Crookshank. Psyche Miniatures Medical Series, no. 10. London: Kegan Paul, Trench, Trubner and Co., 1928.

Davis, Michael M., Jr. *Psychological Interpretations of Society.* New York: AMS Press, 1968; facsimile reprint of 1909 edition.

Durkheim, Emile. *Le Suicide*. Nouvelle édition. Paris: Félix Alcan, 1930; orig. edition 1897.

Halbwachs, Maurice. *Les Causes du suicide*. Paris: Félix Alcan, 1930.

————*The Causes of Suicide*. Trans. Harold Goldblatt. London: Routledge and Kegan Paul, 1978.

Icard, Séverin. "De la contagion du crime et du suicide par la presse." *Nouvelle Revue*, 15 April 1902; pamphlet reprint Paris: Editions de la *Nouvelle Revue*, 1902.

Lorthiois, Dr. *De l'automutilation, mutilations et suicides étranges*. Paris: Vigot Frères, 1909.

Moreau de Tours, Dr. [Paul]. *Suicides et crimes étranges*. Paris: Société d'Éditions Scientifiques, 1899.

Morselli, Henry. *Suicide: An Essay on Comparative Moral Statistics*. New York: D. Appleton and Co., 1882.

General Sources (English translations follow French editions)

Aragon, Louis. "Introduction à 1930," *La Révolution Surréaliste*, no. 12, 15 December 1929.

————. "Le Paysan de Paris." *La Revue Européenne*. Part I, nos. 16–19, June–September 1924; Part II, nos. 25–28, March–June 1925.

————. *Le Paysan de Paris*. Paris: Livre de poche, 1966; orig. 1926.

————. *Nightwalker (Le Paysan de Paris)*. Trans. Frederick Brown. Englewood Cliffs: Prentice-Hall, Inc., 1970.

————. *Paris Peasant*. Trans. Simon Watson Taylor. Boston: Exact Change, 1994.

————. *Traité du style*. Paris: Gallimard, 1928.

————. *Treatise on Style*. Trans. and intro. Alyson Walters. Lincoln: University of Nebraska Press, 1991.

Baudelaire, Charles. *The Painter of Modern Life and Other Essays*. Trans. Jonathan Mayne. London: Phaidon Press, 1995.

Benjamin, Walter. *Illuminations*. Trans. Harry Zohn. New York: Schocken Books, 1978.

————. *Paris, Capitale du XIXe siècle: Le Livre des Passages*. Trans. Jean Lacoste. Paris: Les Éditions du Cerf, 1989.

————. *Reflections: Essays, Aphorisms, Autobiographical Writings*. Trans. Edmund Jephcott. New York: Harcourt Brace Jovanovich, 1979.

Breton, André. *Anthologie de l'humour noir*. Paris: Jean-Jacques Pauvert, 1972; orig. 1941.

————. *Manifestoes of Surrealism*. Trans. Richard Seaver and Helen Lane. Ann Arbor: University of Michigan Press, 1969.

————. *Nadja*. Paris: Gallimard, 1964; orig. 1928.

————. *Nadja*. Trans. Richard Howard. New York: Grove Press, 1960.

————. *What is Surrealism? Selected Writings*. Ed. and trans. Franklin Rosemont. New York: Monad, 1975.

Breton, André, et al. *Violette Nozières: Poèmes, dessins, correspondance, documents*. Brussels: Éditions Nicolas Flamel, 1933.

Cendrars, Blaise. *Panorama de la pègre*. Grenoble: B. Arthaud, 1935.

Détective, le grand hebdomadaire des faits-divers. Paris, 1930–31.

Hauteclocque, Xavier de. *Pègre et police internationales*. Paris: Nouvelle Revue Critique, 1934.

Larbaud, Valery. "Élémir Bourges." *La Revue Européenne*. No. 25, 1 March 1925, 1–13.

Lille avant et pendant la guerre. Guides illustrés Michelin des champs de bataille (1914–1918). Clermont-Ferrand: Michelin et Cie., 1919.

Littérature. Paris, 1919–21.

Littérature, nouvelle série. Paris, 1922–24.

Man Ray, dir. *Étoile de mer*. France, 1928.

Prévert, Jacques, dir. *Paris la belle*. France, 1959.

Reims, la ville martyre. Guides Diamant. Paris: Librairie Hachette et Cie., 1919.

La Révolution Surréaliste. Paris, 1924–25.

Soupault, Philippe. *Les Dernières Nuits de Paris*. Paris: Gallimard, 1928.

————. *The Last Nights of Paris*. Trans. William Carlos Williams. Cambridge, Mass.: Exact Change, 1992; orig. 1928.

————. *Mort de Nick Carter*. Paris: Lachenal et Ritter, 1986; orig. 1926.

Le Surréalisme au service de la Révolution. Paris, 1930–33.

Vedres, Nicole, dir. *Paris 1900*. France, 1946–47.

SECONDARY SOURCES

Abel, Richard. *The Ciné Goes to Town: French Cinema, 1896–1914*. Berkeley and Los Angeles: University of California Press, 1994.

————. *French Cinema: The First Wave, 1915–1929*. Princeton: Princeton University Press, 1984.

"AHR Forum on Popular Culture." *American Historical Review*. Vol. 97, no. 5. 1992, 1369–1430.

Alfu. *L'Encyclopédie de Fantômas: Étude sur un classique*. Paris: Autoédition, 1981.

Alfu, Patrice Caillot, and François Ducos. *Gino Starace, l'illustrateur de "Fantômas"*. Paris: Encrage, 1988.

Angenot, Marc. *Le Roman populaire: Recherches en paralittérature*. Montréal: Presses de l'Université du Québec, 1975.

Apter, Emily. "Allegories of Reading/Allegories of Justice: The Gidean Fait Divers." *Romantic Review*. No. 80, 1980, 560–70.

_____. "*Stigma indelible*: Gide's Parodies of Zola and the Displacement of Realism." *MLN*. No. 101. 1986, 857–70.

Arnaud, Noel, Francis Lacassin, and Jean Tortel. *Entretiens sur la para littérature.* Paris: Plon, 1970.

Auclair, Georges. *Le Mana quotidien: Structures et fonctions de la rubrique des faits divers.* Paris: Anthropos, 1970.

Avila, Rose M. "The Function of Surrealist Myths in Louis Aragon's *Paysan de Paris*." *French Forum*. Vol. 3, no. 3, 1978, 232–39.

Bakhtin, Mikhail. *Rabelais and His World.* Trans. Hélène Iswolsky. Cambridge, Mass.: Harvard University Press, 1968.

Bakis, Henry. "Formation et developpement du réseau téléphonique française." *Information Historique.* Vol. 49, no. 1, 1987, 31–43.

Balakian, Anna. *André Breton: The Magus of Surrealism.* New York: Oxford University Press, 1971.

Balakian, Anna, and Rudolf E. Kuenzli, eds. *André Breton Today.* New York: Willis Locker and Owens, 1989.

Bardens, Dennis. *The Ladykiller: The Life of Landru, the French Bluebeard.* London: Peter Davies, 1972.

Barrot, Olivier, and Pascal Ory, eds. *Entre-deux-guerres: La création française, 1919–1939.* Paris: Éditions François Bourin, 1990.

Barrows, Susanna. *Distorting Mirrors: Visions of the Crowd in Late Nineteenth-Century France.* New Haven: Yale University Press, 1981.

Barthes, Roland. *Mythologies.* Trans. Annette Lavers. New York: Hill and Wang, 1972.

Batailles, Georges. *The Trial of Gilles de Rais.* Trans. Richard Robinson. Los Angeles: Amok Books, 1991.

Baudelot, Christian, and Roger Establet. *Durkheim et le suicide.* Paris: Presses Universitaires de France, 1984.

Béhar, Henri. *André Breton: Le grand indésirable.* Paris: Calmann-Lévy, 1990.

Béhar, Henri, and Michel Carassou, eds. *Le Surréalisme.* Paris: Librairie Générale Française, 1984.

Belin, Jean. *Secrets of the Sûreté: The Memoirs of Commissioner Jean Belin.* New York: G. P. Putnam, 1950.

Bellanger, Claude, et al. *Histoire Générale de la presse française. III, De 1871 à 1940.* Paris: Presses Universitaires de France, 1972.

Beltrain, Alain. "De luxe au coeur du système. Électricité et société dans la région parisienne, 1880–1939." *Annales ESC.* Vol. 44, no. 5. 1989, 1113–36.

Benassaya, Elyette. "Le Surréalisme face à la presse." *Mélusine.* No. 1. Lausanne: L'Age d'Homme, 1979.

Berenson, Edward. *The Trial of Madame Caillaux.* Berkeley and Los Angeles: University of California Press, 1992.

Bernard, Philippe, and Henri Dubief. *The Decline of the Third Republic, 1914–1938*. Trans. Anthony Forster. Cambridge: Cambridge University Press/ Paris: Éditions de la Maison des Sciences de l'Homme, 1988.

Birchall, Ian. "'Des Marteaux Matérials': The Relation between Art and Politics." *French Studies*. Vol. 44, no. 3, 1990, 300–318.

Bisceglia, Jacques. *Trésors du roman policier*. Paris: Les éditions de l'amateur, 1986.

Bozo, Dominique. *André Breton: La Beauté convulsive*. Paris: Éditions du Centre Pompidou, 1991.

Brooks, Peter. *The Melodramatic Imagination*. New Haven: Yale University Press, 1976.

Buck-Morss, Susan. *The Dialectics of Seeing: Walter Benjamin and the Arcades Project*. Cambridge, Mass.: M. I. T. Press, 1989.

Burke, Peter. *Popular Culture in Early Modern Europe*. New York: Harper Touchstone, 1978.

Caillois, Roger. *Le Roman policier*. Buenos Aires: Éditions des lettres françaises, 1941.

Candiotti, Charles, et al. *Considérations statistiques sur le suicide en France et à l'Étranger: Ses répercussions sociales*. Institut National d'Hygiène. Paris: J.-B. Ballière et fils, 1948.

Carré, Patrice. "Le réseau téléphonique entre Paris et banlieue, 1880–1939," *Cahiers de l'Institute d'Histoire du Temps Présent*. No. 12, 1989, 63–70.

Caws, Mary Ann. *André Breton*. New York: Twayne Publishers, Inc., 1971.

Caws, Mary Ann, Rudolf E. Kuenzli, and Gwen Raaberg, eds. *Women and Surrealism*. Cambridge, Mass.: M. I. T. Press, 1991.

Certeau, Michel de. *The Practice of Everyday Life*. Trans. Steven Rendall. Berkeley and Los Angeles: University of California Press, 1984.

Chabrol, Claude, dir. *Landru*. Screenplay by Françoise Sagan. France, 1965.

Chadwick, Whitney. *Women Artists and the Surrealist Movement*. New York: New York Graphic Society, 1985.

Chartier, Roger. *Figures de la guerseurie*. Series "Bibliothèque bleue." Paris: Montalba, 1982.

————. *The Cultural Uses of Print in Early Modern France*. Trans. Lydia G. Cochrane. Princeton: Princeton University Press, 1987.

Chevalier, Louis. *Laboring Classes and Dangerous Classes in Paris*. Trans. Frank Jellinek. New York: Howard Fertig, 1973.

————. *Montmartre du plaisir et du crime*. Paris: Robert Laffont, 1980.

Clover, Carol. *Men, Women and Chain Saws: Gender in the Modern Horror Film*. Princeton: Princeton University Press, 1992.

Cohen, Margaret. *Profane Illumination: Walter Benjamin and the Paris of Surrealist Revolution*. Berkeley and Los Angeles: University of California Press, 1993.

Collins, Jim. *Uncommon Cultures: Popular Culture and Post-Modernism*. New York: Routledge, 1989.

Connah, Roger. *Writing Architecture: Fantômas. Fragments, Fictions: An Architectural Journal through the Twentieth Century*. Cambridge, Mass.: M. I. T. Press, 1989.

Conover, Roger, Terry Hale and Paul Lenti, eds. *Four Dada Suicides: Selected Texts of Arthur Cravan, Jacques Rigaut, Julien Torma and Jacques Vaché*. Trans. Terry Hale et al. London: Atlas Press, 1995.

Cortazar, Julio. *Fantomas contra los vampiros multinacionales: Una utopia realizable*. Mexico City: Excélsior, 1975.

Coudert, Marie-Louise. "Au temps du «Certa»." *Europe*. Nos. 454/455, 1967, 231–237.

Darmon, Pierre. "Landru: Les archives d'un criminel." *L'Histoire*. No. 176, April 1994, 24–29.

——. *Landru*. Paris: Plon, 1994.

Davis, Natalie Zemon. *Society and Culture in Early Modern France*. Stanford: Stanford University Press, 1975.

Dean, Carolyn. *The Self and Its Pleasures: Bataille, Lacan, and the History of the Decentered Subject*. Ithaca: Cornell University Press, 1992.

Delumeau, Jean. *La Mort des pays de Cocagne*. Paris: Université de Paris, 1976.

Delvaille, Bernard. *Passages et Galeries du 19e siècle*. Paris: A. C. E. Éditeur, 1981.

During, Simon, ed. *The Cultural Studies Reader*. London: Routledge, 1993.

Eisenzweig, Eri. *Le Récit impossible*. Paris: Christian Bourgeois, Éditeur, 1986.

Eksteins, Modris. *Rites of Spring: The Great War and the Birth of the Modern Age*. New York: Doubleday, 1989.

Erickson, John D. "Surrealist Black Humor as Oppositional Discourse." *Symposium*. Vol. 17, no. 3, 1988, 198–215.

"Fantômas." Special Issue of *Europe*. Nos. 590/591, 1978.

"Fantômas? . . . c'est Marcel Allain." Special Issue of *La Tour de feu*. No. 88, 1965.

Febvre, Lucien, and Henri-Jean Martin. *The Coming of the Book*. Trans. David Gerard. London: Verso Press, 1984.

"Feuillade Fantômas." Special Issue of *L'Avant-Scène*. Nos. 271–72, 1 July 1981.

Fleuriant-French. *Le Secret de Landru: Il n'a pas brûlé ses fiancées!* Paris: Librairie Bernardin-Béchet, 1930.

Forest, Fred. *Bourse de l'imaginaire. Bourse de fait divers. Experience de presse*. Paris: Éditions du Territoire, 1982.

Foster, Hal. *Compulsive Beauty*. Cambridge, Mass.: M. I. T. Press, 1993.

Freud, Sigmund. *A General Selection from the Works of Sigmund Freud*. Ed. John Rickman. Garden City: Doubleday Anchor Books, 1957.

Fricker, Bernard. *Scènes de la vie parisienne et études philosophiques, poé-montage réalisé par Fantômas en collaboration avec Maldoror, et imprimé au dépens de*

Bernard Fricker, qui vous présente ses meilleurs voeux pour 1967. Vanves (Hauts-de-Seine): Presses de Kapp, 1966.

Fussell, Paul. *The Great War and Modern Memory*. Oxford: Oxford University Press, 1975.

Fürnkäs, Josef. *Surrealismus als Erkenntnis: Walter Benjamin, Weimarer Einbanstraße und Pariser Passagen*. Stuttgart: J. B. Metzeler, 1988.

Geist, Johann Friedrich. *Arcades: The History of a Building Type*. Trans. Jane O. Newman and John H. Smith. Cambridge, Mass.: M. I. T. Press, 1983.

Gerould, Daniel. *The Guillotine: Its Legacy and Lore*. New York: Blast Books, 1992.

Goerg, Charles, ed. *Regards sur Minotaure, la revue à tête de bête*. Geneva: Musée d'art et d'histoire, 1987.

Hall, Stuart. "Notes on Deconstructing 'The Popular'." In Raphael Sammuel, ed. *People's History and Socialist Theory*. London: Routledge and Kegan Paul, 1981, 227–40.

Hamon, Philippe. *Expositions: Literature and Architecture in Nineteenth-Century France*. Trans. Katia Sainson-Frank and Lisa Maguire. Berkeley and Los Angeles: University of California Press, 1992.

Harris, Ruth. *Murders and Madness: Medicine, Law, and Society in the Fin de Siècle*. Oxford: Clarendon Press, 1989.

Histoire de la Librairie Arthème Fayard. Paris: Fayard, 1961.

Hollier, Denis, ed. *A New History of French Literature*. Cambridge, Mass.: Harvard University Press, 1989.

Horkheimer, Max, and Theodor Adorno. *The Dialectic of Enlightenment*. Trans. John Cumming. New York: Continuum, 1972.

Horn, Pierre L., ed. *Handbook of French Popular Culture*. New York: Greenwood Press, 1991.

Huyssen, Andreas. *After the Great Divide: Modernism, Mass Culture, Postmodernism*. Bloomington: Indiana University Press, 1986.

Irving, Henry. *Studies of French Criminals of the Nineteenth Century*. London: William Heinemann, 1901.

Jauss, Hans Robert. *Toward an Aesthetic of Reception*. Trans. Timothy Bahti. Minneapolis: University of Minnesota Press, 1982.

Jay, Martin. *Downcast Eyes: The Denigration of Vision in Twentieth-Century French Thought*. Berkeley and Los Angeles: University of California Press, 1993.

Jean, Marcel, ed. *The Autobiography of Surrealism*. New York: Viking Press, 1980.

Jouffroy, *La Vie réinventée: L'explosion des années 20 à Paris*. Paris: Robert Laffont, 1982.

Kalifa, Dominique. *L'Encre et le sang: Récits de crimes et société à la Belle Époque*. Paris: Fayard, 1995.

Kaplan, Alice Yeager. *Reproductions of Banality: Fascism, Literature, and French Intellectual Life*. Minneapolis: University of Minnesota Press, 1986.

Kern, Steven. *The Culture of Time and Space, 1880–1918.* Cambridge, Mass.: Harvard University Press, 1983.

Kuenzli, Rudolf E., ed. *Dada and Surrealist Film.* New York: Willis Locker and Owens, 1987.

Kraus, Rosalind, ed. "High/Low." Special Issue of *October.* No. 56, 1991.

Kyrou, Ado. *Le Surréalisme au cinéma.* Rev. ed. Paris: Le Terrain Vague, 1963.

LaCapra, Dominick. *Emile Durkheim: Sociologist and Philosopher.* Ithaca: Cornell University Press, 1972.

Lacassin, Francis. *Mythologie du roman policier.* Rev. ed. Paris: Union Générale d'Éditions, 1987.

———. *A la recherche de l'empire caché.* Paris: Julliard, 1991.

Lanoux, Armand. *Paris 1925.* Paris: Robert Delpire, 1957.

Larroque, Dominique. "L'Expansion des tramways urbains en France avant la première guerre mondiale." *Histoire, Économie et Société.* Vol. 9, no. 1, 1990, 135–68.

———. "Transporte urbaine et transformations de l'espace parisien." *Cahiers de l'Institute d'Histoire du Temps Présent.* No. 12, 1989, 41–56.

Lears, T. J. Jackson. "The Concept of Cultural Hegemony: Problems and Possibilities." *American Historical Review.* Vol. 90, no. 3, 1985, 567–93.

Lebrun, Michel, and J.-P. Schweighaeuser. *Le Guide du polar: Histoire du roman policier français.* Paris: Syros, 1987.

Lefebvre, Henri. *Everyday Life in the Modern World.* Trans. Sacha Rabinovitch. New York: Harper and Row, 1971.

Le Queux, William. *Landru: His Secret Love Affairs.* London: Stanley Paul and Co., 1922.

Ledos, Jean-Jacques. "Les Débuts de la radio en France: Des 'Merveilles de la science' à la confiscation." *Gavroche.* No. 56, 1991, 10–15.

Leed, Eric J. *No Man's Land: Combat and Identity in World War I.* Cambridge: Cambridge University Press, 1979.

Lemoine, Bertrand. *Les Passages couverts en France.* Paris: Délégation à l'Action Artistique de la Ville de Paris, 1989.

Lewis, Helena. *The Politics of Surrealism.* New York: Paragon House Publishers, 1988.

Lottman, Herbert. *The Left Bank Writers: Artists and Politics from the Popular Front to the Cold War.* Boston: Houghton Mifflin Co., 1982.

Lowe, Donald M. *The History of Bourgeois Perception.* Chicago: University of Chicago Press, 1982.

Mackenzie, F. A. *Landru.* New York: Charles Scribners' Sons, 1928.

Malet, Leo. *La Vache enragée.* Paris: Éditions Hoëbeke, 1988.

Mandrou, Robert. *An Introduction to Modern France, 1500–1650.* Trans. R. E. Hallmark. New York: Holmes and Meier, 1976.

Marcus, Greil. *Lipstick Traces: A Secret History of the Twentieth Century.* Cambridge, Mass.: Harvard University Press, 1989.

Martin, Benjamin F. *Crime and Criminal Justice Under the Third Republic: The Shame of Marianne.* Baton Rouge: Louisiana State University Press, 1990.

Marville, Charles. *Charles Marville: Photographs of Paris at the Time of the Second Empire.* New York: Alliance Française, 1981.

Masson, René. *Les Roses de Gambais.* Paris: Presses de la Cité, 1963.

———. *Number One: A Story of Landru.* Trans. Gillian Tindall. London: Hutchinson and Co., 1964.

Matthews, J. H. *An Introduction to Surrealism.* University Park: Pennsylvania State University Press, 1965.

———. *Surrealism and Film.* Ann Arbor: University of Michigan Press, 1971.

Mayeur, Jean-Marie. *The Third Republic from Its Origins to the Great War, 1871–1914.* Trans. J. R. Foster. Cambridge: Cambridge University Press/Paris: Éditions de la Maison des Sciences et de l'Homme, 1987.

Mehlman, Jeffrey. "The 'Floating Signifier': From Lévi-Struass to Lacan." *Yale French Studies.* No. 48, 1972, 10–37.

Melly, George. *Paris and the Surrealists.* New York: Thames and Hudson, 1991.

Merleau-Ponty, Maurice. *Signs.* Trans. Richard C. McCleary. Evanston: Northwestern University Press, 1964.

Monestier, Alain. *Le Fait divers.* Paris: Éditions de la Réunion des Musées Nationaux, 1982.

Monhan, Patrice de, and Christian Mahout. *Le Guide des Passages de Paris.* Preface by Annabel Buffet. Paris: Seesam-R. C. I., 1990.

Montgolfier, Bernard de. *Les Grands Boulevards.* Paris: Paris-Musées, 1985.

Morain, Alfred. *The Underworld of Paris: Secrets of the Sûreté.* New York: E. P. Dutton, 1931.

Motherwell, Robert, ed. *The Dada Painters and Poets: An Anthology.* 2nd Edition. Cambridge, Mass.: Harvard University Press, Belknap Press, 1981.

Muchembled, Robert. *Culture populaire et culture des élites dans la France moderne.* Paris: Flammarion, 1977.

Nadeau, Maurice. *L'Histoire du Surréalisme.* 2 vols. Paris: Éditions du Seuil, 1944–48.

———. *The History of Surrealism.* Trans. Richard Howard. Cambridge, Mass.: Harvard University Press, Belknap Press, 1989.

Nesbit, Molly. *Atget's Seven Albums.* New Haven: Yale University Press, 1992.

Novi, Marc. *Landru.* Grenoble: Glénat, 1981.

Nye, Robert. *Crime, Madness and Politics in Modern France: The Medical Concept of National Decline.* Princeton: Princeton University Press, 1984.

———. *Masculinity and Male Codes of Honor in France.* New York: Oxford University Press, 1993.

Perrot, Michelle. "Fait divers et histoires du XIXe siècle (Note critique)." *Annales ESC.* Vol. 38, no. 4, 1983, 911–19.

Polizzotti, Mark. *Revolution of the Mind: The Life of André Breton.* New York: Farrar, Straus and Giroux, 1995.

Pontalis, J.-B. *Frontiers in Psychoanalysis: Between the Dream and Psychic Pain.* Trans. Catherine Cullen and Philip Cullen. London: The Hogarth Press, 1981.

Porter, Dennis. *The Pursuit of Crime: Art and Ideology in Detective Fiction.* New Haven: Yale University Press, 1981.

Prendergast, Christopher. *Paris and the Nineteenth Century.* Oxford: Blackwell, 1992.

Rabbe, Juliette, and Francis Lacassin. *La Bibliothèque idéale des littératures d'évasion.* Paris: Éditions Universitaires, 1969.

Regards sur Minotaure, *la revue à tête de bête.* Geneva: Musée d'art et d'histoire, 1987.

Rifkin, Adrian. *Street Noises: Parisian Pleasure, 1900–1940.* Manchester: Manchester University Press, 1993.

Rigby, Brian. *Popular Culture in Modern France: A Study of Cultural Discourse.* New York: Routledge, 1991.

Rosello, Mireille. *L'Humour noir selon André Breton.* Paris: Librairie José Corti, 1987.

Rosemont, Franklin. *Surrealism and Its Popular Accomplices.* San Francisco: City Lights Books, 1980.

Rubin, William S. *Dada and Surrealist Art.* New York: Harry S. Abrams, 1968.

Seguin, Jean-Pierre. *Les Canards illustrés du 19e siècle: Fascination du fait divers.* Paris: Musée-Galerie de la Seita, 1982.

Seigel, Jerrold, *Bohemian Paris: Culture, Politics, and the Boundaries of Bourgeois Life, 1830–1930.* New York: Penguin Books, 1986.

Shattuck, Roger. *The Banquet Years: The Origins of the Avant Garde in France, 1885 to World War One.* Rev. ed. New York: Vintage Books, 1968.

Short, Robert. *Dada and Surrealism.* London: Octopus Books, 1980.

Silver, Kenneth. *Esprit de Corps: The Art of the Parisian Avant-garde and the First World War, 1914–1925.* Princeton: Princeton University Press, 1989.

Stich, Sidra. *Anxious Visions: Surrealist Art.* With essays by James Clifford, Tyler Stovall, and Steven Kovács. New York: Abbeville Press, 1990.

Stowe, William. "Popular Fiction as Liberal Art." *College English.* Vol. 48, no. 7, 1986, 646–663.

Surréalisme et Cinéma (1). Special Issue of *Études Cinématographiques.* Nos. 38–39, 1965.

Sylvester, David, ed. *René Magritte: Catalogue raisonné.* 2 Vols. London: The Menil Foundation / Philip Wilson, 1993.

Thiesse, Anne-Marie. "Mutations et permanences de la culture populaire: La lecture à la Belle Époque." *Annales ESC*. Vol. 39, no. 1, 1984, 71–91.

————. *Le Roman du quotidien: Lecteurs et lectures populaire à la Belle Époque*. Paris: Chemin Vert, 1984.

Timms, Eduard, and David Kelly, eds. *Unreal City: Urban Experience in Modern European Literature and Arts*. London: Manchester University Press, 1985.

Vareille, Jean-Claude. *L'Homme masqué: Le Justicier et le détective*. Lyon: Presses Universitaries de Lyon, 1989.

Varnedoe, Kirk, and Adam Gopnik. *High & Low: Modern Art and Popular Culture*. New York: Museum of Modern Art, 1991.

Waldberg, Patrick. *René Magritte*. Trans. Austryn Wainhouse. Brussels: André de Riche, Pub., 1965.

Weber, Eugen. *Peasants into Frenchmen: The Modernization of France, 1870–1914*. Stanford: Stanford University Press, 1976.

————. *France, Fin-de-Siècle*. Cambridge, Mass.: Harvard University Press, Belknap Press, 1986.

Weiss, Jeffrey. *The Popular Culture of Modern Art: Picasso, Duchamp, and Avant-Gardism*. New Haven: Yale University Press, 1994.

Willet, John. *Art and Politics in the Weimar Period: The New Sobriety, 1917–1933*. New York: Pantheon Books, 1978.

Williams, Linda. *Figures of Desire: A Theory and Analysis of Surrealist Film*. Urbana: University of Illinois Press, 1984.

Williams, Rosalind. *Dream Words: Mass Consumption in Late Nineteenth-Century France*. Berkeley and Los Angeles: University of California Press, 1982.

————. "When the Eiffel Tower was New." *Technology and Culture*. Vol. 32, no. 1, 1991, 102–5.

Williot, J.-P. "Naissance d'un réseau gazier à Paris au XIXme siècle: Distribution gazière et éclairage." *Histoire, Économie et Société*. Vol. 8, no. 4, 1989, 569–91.

Wiser, William. *The Crazy Years: Paris in the Twenties*. New York: Thames and Hudson, 1983.

Wohl, Robert. *The Generation of 1914*. Cambridge, Mass.: Harvard University Press, 1979.

Zizek, Slavoj. *Enjoy Your Symptom! Jacques Lacan in Hollywood and Out*. New York: Routledge, 1992.

————. *Looking Awry: An Introduction to Jacques Lacan through Popular Culture*. Cambridge, Mass.: M. I. T. Press, 1991.

Index

Page numbers appearing in italics refer to illustrations.